SHIFTING PARADIGMS
IN STUDENT AFFAIRS

*To Arthur Chickering,
with great appreciation
for all that you
have contributed to
my professional practice
& the student affairs
profession*

Jan Fried

4/2003

SHIFTING PARADIGMS IN STUDENT AFFAIRS

Culture, Context, Teaching, and Learning

Jane Fried & Associates

American College Personnel Association

Copyright © 1995 by
the American College Personnel Association

University Press of America,® Inc.
4720 Boston Way
Lanham, Maryland 20706

3 Henrietta Street
London, WC2E 8LU England

Library of Congress Cataloging-in-Publication Data

Fried, Jane
Shifting paradigms in student affairs : culture, context, teaching,
and learning / Jane Fried and associates.
p.cm.
Includes bibliographical references.
1. Student affairs services—Social aspects—United States. 2. Universities
and colleges—United States—Sociological aspects. 3. Pluralism (Social
sciences)—United States. I. American College Personnel Association. II.
Title.
LB2342.9.F75 1995 378.1'94—dc20 95-22394 CIP
ISBN 1-883485-07-X (cloth: alk. paper)
ISBN 1-883485-08-8 (paper: alk. paper)

Dedication

To the Smith family who, through the countless details of daily life,
taught me about diversity, acceptance, and love;

and

To Burns Ballantyne Crookston, my wise teacher,
who remains a continuing inspiration

Contents

Foreword

Once science believed in the determinateness of the values of all physical properties in the universe. This belief held that the universe is predictable. An all-powerful intelligence or computational scheme predicated on complete information of initial conditions and a complete set of physical laws could predict with almost complete accuracy subsequent events. This belief system or paradigm has sometimes been called "scientific determinism."

But now we know better. The universe is not totally predictable; nor is this piece of the universe on which we live. Even a system, which is characterized by point values that evolve along a unique trajectory according to clearly stated differential equations will be unpredictable if differences in initial conditions occur. Small differences which occur in initial conditions lead to widely separated trajectories. All open systems generate small differences so the likelihood of completely accurate predictions in these systems is almost nil. College campuses today are very open systems and can be compared metaphorically to unpredictable systems which must respond to constantly changing conditions and inputs. Carrying the metaphor further, one student from a distant land where a revolution has suddenly sprung into the open, can change life for many people on a campus in the United States if he or she is concerned enough about events at home.

Nevertheless, the scientific study of unpredictable systems can have significant predictive power. This is a paradox, an irreconcilable state of affairs in which two seemingly different circumstances co-exist simultaneously. This paradox can be seen most easily, perhaps, in the statistical study of physical, biological and social systems. Certain large-scale or long-term patterns appear in behavior that are reasonably constant, even though some details which constitute the pattern may be unpredictable. In biology organisms do not merely evolve, but co-evolve with other organisms and with a changing environment. Flowers and insects have co-evolved. The flower evolves to attract insects which act to pollinate flowers. Insects evolve to obtain food from flowers. These interacting processes demonstrate that adaptation by one kind of organism alters both the fitness of the organism and the fitness of the landscape in which both organisms exist. All species or systems continue to change and interact with each other in comparable ways to form patterns of behavior that are generally predictable on a large scale, moderately predictable on an intermediate scale and almost unpredictable at the level of specific detail. In large scale situations, students from Arab countries will probably have significant differences and conflicts with students from Israel. At the specific level of friendship, it is impossible to predict with great accuracy who will become friends with whom.

Conditions in the world change and bring about new issues and new problems. New problems require new knowledge and new vision that leads to solutions. Solutions require change, changes in the way we see and do things, changes in our behavior and changes in the way we affect each other and the environment as we continue to adapt and grow. Jane Fried and associates present ideas in college student affairs which are designed to challenge the reader to think and act in new ways. Their purpose is to reemphasize the educational functions of student affairs and to situate student development education within the mission of U.S. colleges and universities. They propose to do this through the examination of the diversity issues troubling many campuses today.

Diverse interacting individuals and groups that are a part of each other's environment expend energy continuously to adjust their boundaries and internal processes to one another. In some instances, some groups may seem to pose a threat to other groups' existence. It is not so much a simple dislike for something different as it is at some level, a threat to a way of life that members of a group believe is either desirable or even sacred. Throughout history people have learned to tolerate and even seek out differences between themselves and people from other countries, cultures and ethnic background. These differences may be considered interesting or curious, easily tolerated until they reach a critical mass. At this moment the differences begin to compete with a person's preferred way of life, even threatening to dilute or take over the world a person claims as his or her own.

> This world is my world. It gives me my identity and holds deep meaning that may be signified as patriotic, sacred or our way of doing things. It may even more importantly be an economic threat. You may come into my house and I will in some reasonable way attempt to honor your customs and beliefs. But, you are not expected to stay too long, and when you leave, I expect that everything will return to 'normal', the way it was before your entered.

On the other hand, every group wishes to expand and strengthen its role in the larger system. This behavior may not be consciously performed at the expense of other group's existence, but the similarly unconscious response may be as if it does. A major question now to be addressed is whether systems which have evolved to meet cultural and biological needs and values should be overridden to achieve more harmonious interactions among diverse groups, creating a larger, symbiotic and mutually supportive system.

Social psychology teaches that human beings organize the world perceptually in order to know what to expect and how to interact in it. We are first taught by others—parents, relatives, friends, teachers, clergy and other members of our group—how to see the world so that we will respond in expected ways by the people with whom we live and identify. In the process deep meanings are developed for these perceptual frameworks. To change or remove the perceptual guidelines can result in a sense of loss, abandonment and chaos. This process can be painful and strongly resisted until a new order with some sense of security is developed.

The authors of this work have written with the intention of impacting our thinking about diversity in society and particularly in higher education in the United States. They describe a paradigm or "lens" through which the majority culture views the world and some of the results this world view produces. They discuss the role of the college student affairs professional working with campus environments that are rich in cultural diversity.

Student affairs professionals are asked to undertake an enormous task which will require conscious and intentional effort guided by knowledge, wisdom and great patience. This book should be of assistance to those who choose to take up this task.

Richard Caple
University of Missouri

Preface

This book is addressed to all student affairs professionals whose primary professional concern is student learning. It will be understood and used differently by faculty members in preparation programs, by senior administrators and by student development educators who work in residence halls, student unions or career counseling offices. Nevertheless, it has a common purpose for all readers. The purpose of the book is to reemphasize the educational functions of student affairs and services and to situate student development education solidly within the mission of colleges and universities in the United States. The means to accomplish this goal is through examination of some of the diversity issues which are troubling so many campuses in the United States. Diversity is broadly construed to include differences related to race, ethnicity, sexual orientation, gender, and disability status as well as differences in perspective generated by professional roles and philosophy.

This book presents a new paradigm for the profession of student affairs and the practice of student development education. The new paradigm incorporates insights from anthropology, physics, history, philosophy, religion, and cultural psychology. The paradigm is an expression of a larger body of work generally called systems or bootstrap theory (Capra, 1989) in which no element of the system is considered fundamental, and all the elements are interconnected. In this paradigm teaching, learning, cultural difference and the creation of a common language to enhance mutual understanding are considered interactive and interrelated processes. An understanding of culture forms the basis for the paradigm. The definition of culture is very broad, describing all groups who share significant life experience and generate common perspectives on the world and methods for living in it. Culture is treated as a dynamic, constantly changing experience in which all people participate, whether they realize it or not. People participate in many cultures simultaneously. These cultures shape both interpersonal communication and internal monologues, or self-talk. Student affairs professionals, students and campus colleagues are members of many cultures simultaneously. In any particular situation, different cultures become salient for the people involved.

Shifting Paradigms in Student Affairs takes advantage of our current national preoccupation with cultural diversity to rethink some professional assumptions about higher education and the educational role of student affairs. Culture is discussed both as a literal set of experiences which varies by group and as a metaphor for the processes by which people shape their understanding of the world. Understanding culture as process and metaphor encourages understanding of and respect for differences of all sorts, creating the possibility of multicultural empathy.

> Toleration is the greatest gift of the mind;
> It requires that same effort of the brain that it takes to balance oneself on a bicycle.
> > Helen Keller
> > (Anderson [Ed], 1990, p. 55)

Insight into difference can shape respectful problem-solving strategies in which differences of perception and opinion achieve visibility and legitimacy. Acknowledgment of different perspectives encourages discussion of decision-making processes and provokes learning among participants regardless of the setting. Thus learning about culture and experiencing one's own culture in comparison to others becomes part of one's educational experience, regardless of the setting in which it occurs.

The inspiration for this book came as I was thinking about the problems of cultural coexistence in the United States and the various approaches to "diversity training" I had used with college students, student affairs staff members and faculty. Suddenly I imagined that the United States might never become a truly diverse country for one critical reason—people in the United States who perceive and interpret their world through the dominant belief system don't believe in diversity. Many Americans don't think that diversity, beyond certain narrow limits, is a good idea. Acceptance of the broad scope of human diversity has implications which create a great deal of discomfort for many Americans, particularly those who are white, Christian, of AngloEuropean ancestry, able bodied, heterosexual, and consider themselves self-reliant and independent. Not all members of this group devalue diversity and not all members of groups with other characteristics value diversity. On the whole, however, it seems that people who look, believe and act like stereotypic Americans consider diversity a temporary stage in our national progress toward some sort of uniformity. This concept of national unity is generally described as a melting pot. Laws and institutional policies have changed public behavior in the past half-century, but intergroup conflict and the continuing presence of racism, sexism, homophobia haunt our personal lives and relationships, escalating fear, mistrust and general feelings of exclusion among people who differ in some significant way from Americans of the dominant culture. There seems to be a profound element of resistance to diversity which is part of our national psyche (Minow, 1991).

I started to think about the conditions which have provoked our current concern with diversity: rapidly shifting, transnational economics; instability in domestic employment and the perceived closing of opportunities; ethnic warfare, increasingly desperate refugee problems, the increased speed of communication which leaves little time for thinking before reacting to problems and a general sense of being overwhelmed by the global stew. There is no hiding from world events and very little time in which to become informed about them. The constant collision among nationalism, politics, economics, ethnicity, religion and cultural rules about acceptable behavior is bubbling into many of our institutions: elementary and secondary schools, colleges and universities, religious institutions, the media, the health care system and even the neighborhood grocery store. We are facing a rising tide of multi-cultural interactions which threaten to overwhelm us. Americans are coping with so much new information about different cultures that we often don't know what to do or how to act. There are so many areas of historical prejudice and ignorance that the elimination of one often uncovers another. We may not understand how our students, our colleagues, our grocers or our health care providers think. We need to communicate and are desperately trying to keep track of the right words to use, words to avoid, whether or not to shake hands, make direct eye contact, ask about families, get down to business, arrive on time or take fifteen minutes to get to the point of our meeting. The problems are serious, interconnected and changing with unprecedented speed.

Further thought about this apparently intractable problem suggested another insight. I believe that we are interpreting the problems brought about by increasing diversity through a lens that is designed to emphasize unity and conformity while de-emphasizing and devaluing difference. This lens is a product of American history and culture and originated around the time that the first European settlers arrived in the "new world". The origins and implications of this way of seeing the world will be discussed at length later in this book. The lens has also been called a paradigm, a frame of reference which shapes our view of the world and governs our values, our beliefs and our behavior. A paradigm, in this sense, is a belief system so widely shared that people are unaware of it. Rather than appearing as "the way we see things," it appears as "the way things are" or "common sense". One aspect of the American paradigm has been a belief in assimilation, the essential similarity of all people and the ability and willingness of all immigrants to substitute American beliefs, values and behaviors for those of their native land. Another aspect of our paradigm is the conviction that reality exists externally, independent of our beliefs about it. We tend to believe that people discover reality and play no part in creating or shaping it. These two aspects of our American cultural paradigm constitute a significant part of the problem we are experiencing as we try to cope with diversity.

PROFESSIONAL CONTEXTS AND CULTURES

In addition to examining ethnic cultures, this book also discusses some of the cultures in higher education, particularly academic affairs and student affairs (Kuh, 1993). The student affairs profession shares certain values and beliefs with non-dominant cultures in the United States. These include an emphasis on relationships rather than things, an appreciation of subjective experience and personal meaning, an emphasis on experiential learning and interpersonal collaboration and a belief that the community and context in which education occurs are as important as the information acquired. The profession of student affairs tends to believe that "education serve(s) the whole person solving real problems within the 'broad context of culture'" (Schetlin, 1968, p. 12). This contrasts with an impersonal academic approach in which students learn information defined by discipline and tested in laboratories which are isolated from the rest of life. Respect for individual perspective and cultural experience often makes student affairs professionals willing to tolerate ambiguity and realize that there may be more than one right answer in a given situation. Members of the student affairs profession are accustomed to handling student problems in which there is no way to determine what "really" happened, as distinct from each student's perspective and experience. We have also learned about the numerous student subcultures within each of the major "official" cultural categories which significantly alter students' perception and meaning attribution in specific situations. We have learned to use subcultures within ethnic groups to help students learn from their own experience how to empathize and build coalitions in pursuit of common goals.

The chronic sense of second-class citizenship which so many members of the student affairs profession so often complain about may actually be a reflection of a much larger social phenomenon, the process of viewing diversity through a lens which privileges a single and dominant perspective and calls that perspective "truth". Just as cultural difference is either ignored or denigrated in many parts of American society, the educational contributions of the student affairs profession are often denigrated, ignored or misperceived on campus by the academic, financial and administrative segments of the university. The lens through which academicians view education, i.e. theoretical assertions and hypotheses augmented by empirical research, does not focus on alternative ways to teach and learn. Learning from context and experience while addressing real life problems is an approach that the student affairs profession typically uses but which tends to be absent from the traditional classroom.

PRECEDENTS FOR PARADIGM SHIFTS

Previous eras of societal transformation have yielded similar efforts to rethink the role of higher education and student affairs. In the early twentieth century the United States underwent a significant transition when the country absorbed enormous numbers of immigrants and integrated them into its social and economic fabric. The schools were expected to educate the immigrants for citizenship and give them the personal skills to earn a living in their new country, generally in urban environments. John Dewey addressed many of these problems in *Democracy and Education* (1916). During the 1930s and 1940s a major war and the subsequent political and economic disruption, brought thousands of refugees to the United States seeking sanctuary and a better life. Returning veterans also had to be reintegrated into the economic and social life of the country. The American Council on Education issued two editions of the *Student Personnel Point of View* during this period (1937, 1949) which specified the approach colleges should take to attending to their students' individual needs for character development and "social competence" (1940). Subsequently Esther Lloyd-Jones issued her call to consider student personnel work as "deeper teaching" (1954), seeing the role of the student affairs profession as helping students integrate what they were learning in all aspects of their college experience into their sense of self, their values and their behavior. Lloyd-Jones was concerned about the emphasis on intellectual education to the exclusion of character development and on helping students learn the skills of democratic citizenship along with thinking and career skills. During the Vietnam era of the 1960s and 1970s, the student affairs profession once again called attention to the role of colleges and universities in teaching students life skills and integrating academic and personal learning. Some of the documents in this era included *THE Phase II* (1975), an acronym for "Tomorrow's Higher Education", "Education for Human Development" (Crookston, 1973), *The Future of Student Affairs* (Miller & Prince, 1976) and *Freedom to Learn* (Rogers, 1969).

The time has come again to examine the educational role which student affairs plays in the academy and the paradigm which shapes our professional practice. The United States is once again dealing with massive immigration, this time from Latin America, Asia and Africa. International economic turbulence, regional wars, changing demographics among college students, domestic unemployment and economic disruption and the increased speed of global communication all combine to complicate and destabilize the management of our colleges and universities. International students are an important presence on many campuses. These students bring their own cultural perspectives to American higher education and their perspectives often challenge the assumptions that many student affairs professionals use in their work. Problems have become more complex and the time to find solutions has decreased. Pressure on our colleges and universities to educate students for economic, interpersonal and civic competence has increased as financial resources have decreased.

Today's college students need to learn academic skills, technical skills, interpersonal skills and multicultural skills. In the current global economy, a engineer who can't work in groups or communicate with engineers from Europe or Asia simply is not as effective as one who can. A health care provider who doesn't understand that Saudis have different ideas about touching and male/female relations than Americans do is going to make some very upsetting mistakes on the job. A student who has read the works of Shakespeare, Goethe, Austin, Arnold and Eliot, but is unaware of Mishima, Singer, Baldwin, Morrison or Allende has a very limited understanding of the range of human literary expression. Students who make friends only with members of their own groups, however they define the groups, have a limited range of interpersonal skill which will impede their professional success as well as their personal growth. And finally, student affairs members and academic faculty who believe that all significant learning takes place in the library, the classroom and the laboratory will devalue their own contributions, fail to appreciate their colleagues and impoverish their students by the narrowness of their vision.

Why are we having so much difficulty with diversity? Why is the profession of student affairs not perceived as central to the educational mission of our colleges and universities? Why are we often willing to permit one way of seeing or defining reality to devalue, exclude or silence other paradigms or ways of viewing and interpreting experience? *Shifting Paradigms* is an attempt to shed some light on these questions. If the tendency to permit domination were replaced by a belief in interdependence or dynamic balance, our view of the world would be richer, our relationships less conflicted and our ideas about change quite different. Diversity would become less of a problem and more of a resource. In addition to race, culture and gender, the notion of diversity would also apply to different approaches to teaching, learning, valuing and making meaning. Diversity is a term often associated with richness or wealth, as in "biodiversity"—and all wealth brings us face to face with choice. How shall we value this asset? How shall we use it? How shall we choose among possibilities? How can we move forward together?

If we continue to construe diversity as a problem, I believe that student affairs and many of the traditional approaches to teaching and learning will become obsolete in higher education. In this age of diminishing financial resources for colleges and universities, only work that is directly related to the educational goals of our institutions and the learning needs of our students will continue to receive funding. Diversity among students, diversity of approaches to teaching and learning and diversity of perspectives are all assets if we define them as assets. How will we choose? Where will we be if we don't see the choices? It is imperative that we realize how much of our problem with diversity is directly related to the way we think about diversity, how we organize our ideas and data and what frame of reference we use to interpret them. This book is an effort to help student affairs professionals examine the paradigms we use to make sense of our world, to look *at* our frames of reference rather than *through* them, and to move toward new, more complex and holistic ways of thinking about teaching, learning and diversity of culture and experience.

CHAPTER DESCRIPTIONS

Shifting Paradigms in Student Affairs is divided into two sections. The first section is theoretical and conceptual. It contains discussions of American history, philosophy, science and religious belief. It presents some of the historical roots which have shaped our current understanding of diversity as a social, cultural and educational issue. This section explores the notions of culture, paradigm, teaching and learning and the various ways these phenomena interact in higher education. Chapter 1 explains the historical origins of current American beliefs about diversity and the reasons why so many Americans from the dominant cultural group have so much difficulty with the concept and the experience. Chapter 2 defines the terms paradigm, culture and frame of reference. It explains how individuals construct their own interpretations of reality by using different frames of reference, or lenses, under different sets of circumstances. This chapter introduces questions for readers to think about as they begin to become aware of their own lenses, paradigms and cultural points of view. Chapter 3 presents the principal components of the American cultural paradigm in detail, so that readers can begin to realize the source of many of their

American beliefs which may have been invisible or taken for granted until this point. Chapter 4 describes the borders between some of the many cultures which co-exist in American life. It describes borders between people and borders which often exist within people because of their own complex cultural perspectives. Finally, the chapter describes the fears which often exist on both sides of a border and some effective methods initiating successful crossings. Chapter 5 uses the notion of border crossing to explore traditional American ideas about teaching and learning to suggest the changes which might occur if pragmatist, Afrocentric and feminist perspectives began to reshape those ideas. These perspective changes would also reshape our notions of the student affairs role in higher education.

The second section of the book describes the practical implications of the ideas presented in the first section. In Chapter 6, Dawn Person describes the processes by which students shape their own cultures, including variations of the dominant American culture and variations among ethnic student cultures. She discusses the limits of the racial lens in working with diverse student cultures and explores some of the methods by which knowledge of student cultures can be used to improve student services. In Chapter 7, Amy Reynolds focuses on redefining counseling and advising in student affairs to include skills which are relevant to working with non-dominant groups and to focus on the educational processes involved in counseling and advising. In Chapter 8, Jane Fried describes collaboration between student affairs professionals and academic faculty for the creation of educational programs. These programs bridge the gap between academic and student affairs, taking academic and student affairs cultures as well as student cultures into account. In Chapter 9, Ann Galligan describes experiential and service learning, presenting both theory and practice. She describes the strong connections which exist between student affairs approaches to learning and this type of education. Service/experiential learning is an excellent model for the evolving paradigm shifts in higher education. Chapter 10, also written by Fried, describes several approaches to transforming student affairs preparation programs so that graduates will be skilled in educating multicultural populations and communicating with colleagues of all cultural backgrounds. Chapter 11, written by Raechele Pope, provides a framework for multicultural organization development. In order to achieve many of the changes described in the previous chapters, student affairs professionals must be skilled in recognizing cultural bias and in helping organizations welcome different cultures and comprehend different world views. The final chapter suggests continuing approaches to the development of a multicultural paradigm for student affairs in our evolving era of bootstrapping, intentional worlds and continuing change. It recognizes that few people in higher education know with certainty what the future will look like and that our best hope is to continue our dialogue, despite the inevitable differences, in the hope of shaping a vision which will serve us all.

REFERENCES

American Council on Education, Committee on Student Personnel Work (1949) *The student personnel point of view. (rev. ed) Series 6. No. 13.* Washington, DC: American Council on Education.

American Council on Education. (1937) *The student personnel point of view. Series 1. Vol. 1. No. 3.* Washington, DC: American Council on Education.

Anderson, P. (Ed.) (1990) *Great quotes from great leaders.* Lombard, IL: Celebrating Excellence.

Capra, F. (1989) *Uncommon wisdom: Conversations with remarkable people.* New York: Bantam Books.

Crookston, B. (1973) Education for human development. In C. Warnath. *New directions for college counselors.* (pp. 47-65). San Francisco: Jossey-Bass.

Dewey, J. (1916) *Democracy and education.* New York: Macmillan.

Kuh, G. (Ed.) (1993) *Cultural perspectives in student affairs work.* Washington, DC: American College Personnel Association.

Lloyd-Jones, E. & Smith, R. (Eds.) (1954) *Student personnel work as deeper teaching.* New York: Harper and Brothers.

Lloyd-Jones, E., (1940). *Social competence and college students. Series VI, #3.* Washington, DC: American Council on Education.

Minow, M. (1991) *Making all the difference: Inclusion, exclusion and American law.* Ithaca, NY: Cornell University Press.

Rogers, C. (1969) *Freedom to learn.* Columbus, OH: Charles Merrill.

Schetlin, E. (1968) Guidance and student personnel work as reflected by Esther Lloyd-Jones from 1929 to 1966. *Journal of the National Association of Women Deans and Counselors. 31.* (3) 97-102.

T.H.E. Phase II Model Building Conference. A student development model for student affairs in tomorrow's higher education. (1975) *Journal of College Student Personnel. 16.* 334-341.

1

Searching for Clarity

The time is out of joint.
O cursed spite that ever I was born to set it right!

Hamlet, Act I, 189-190

A butterfly is not just a caterpillar who grows wings.
Becoming a butterfly requires a total transformation,
dissolving and reforming.

Anonymous

Every society ever known rests on some set of largely tacit basic
assumptions about *who we are, what kind of universe we are in, and
what is ultimately important to us.* [These assumptions] are typically not formulated or taught because they don't need to be—they
are absorbed by each person born into the society as though by
osmosis.

(Harman, 1988, p. 10)

In order to create a truly multicultural organization we must start
from scratch: organizations that already exist must be disbanded.
There is no way to add people of color after the fact and still create a multicultural organization.

(Angela Davis, April, 1989)

SCENES FROM A CAMPUS

Scene 1

It was the end of the semester. The course was "Introduction
to Theories of Student Development." The professor had presented the major theories of cognitive, moral and psycho-social de-

1

velopment and discussed identity formation theories which describe African Americans, women, gay and lesbian individuals and other minorities. She had "covered the material," and believed she had conveyed the complexity of the topic to these first year students. In the final evaluation discussion, an African American student who had attended predominantly white schools for her entire academic career asked a question she had been pondering for some time. "These theories are all very interesting, but which one is right?"

Scene 2
  Euro-American RA speaking to supervisor: I don't know what to do about Sujata. She's really upset. Her parents came here from India in the 1960s, but she's an American like us. She's premed and hates it. So she's thinking of committing suicide. Why can't she just talk to her parents about it like normal people do? They may freak out but they'll get over it.

Scene 3
  One student activities advisor to another: I'm having trouble keeping the African American students from fighting with the Latino students in the music lounge of the union. They don't like the same kind of music and each group always thinks the other is getting too much time. So far nothing serious has happened but I want to get them cooled off. I asked a labor negotiation professor to come over and help me run a conflict management session, but he says he doesn't have time till next quarter. What's the matter with the faculty? Don't they care about real problems or students' lives?

Scene 4
  White graduate student to advisor: I need to do some reading really fast. I've been working with white students but now I've got a job on a campus where all the students are minorities. Professor: Then that makes you a minority. Student: silence.

Scene 5
  The Director of Admissions is presenting enrollment data to the faculty senate. He describes admission and retention of students who fall into two categories: regular students and minorities. Nobody raises any questions. The senators accept these categories as givens.

E PLURIBUS UNUM? E UNIBUS PLURUM?
E PLURIBUS WHAT?

Why do we, as student affairs professionals, need to understand cultural diversity? Initially, this seems like an elementary question with an obvious answer. Our campus demographics have changed dramatically in the past 25 years (Garland, 1985; Almanac Issue, 1993). Elements of civility which campus professionals had taken for granted seem to have disappeared (Boyer, 1990). If we are to meet student needs, we must understand those needs as both the students and the institution perceive them. This level of understanding reflects both the pragmatist orientation of the student affairs profession and our historic concern for helping to educate the whole student (American Council on Education, 1937; ACE, 1949; NASPA, 1987). Changes in demographics have also been reflected in changes in teaching and learning styles (Schroeder, 1993), curricula (Gamson, 1993), student development (Astin, 1993) and organizational patterns (Scott and Awbrey, 1993).

On a more basic level, we need to understand both the *roots* and the *consequences* of the current American preoccupation with cultural diversity. The United States is in the midst of a profound transformation which is shifting our fundamental view of reality. This paradigm shift affects our "basic ways of perceiving, thinking valuing and doing" (Harman, 1988, p. 10). The last comparable change occurred in Europe during the Age of Enlightenment, when notions of fundamental reality shifted from faith to reason. Truth came to be identified with corroboration through empirical data rather than wisdom or revelation (Harman, 1988; West, 1993). Science came to dominate religion as the perspective which shaped credible understandings of life and world events. Medieval science, with its goal of understanding meaning and significance, was transformed into modern science with its goal of prediction and control (Capra, 1982). The change took at least 300 years to become pervasive, beginning in the Renaissance (mid-16th century) and becoming dominant during the Industrial Revolution (late 19th century).

Because the scientific way of perceiving and understanding the world has become so totally pervasive in American culture, we are generally not aware of the ways in which it shapes our view of events. Science tends to assume that there is an absolute separation between the observer and the observed. The observer examines data in order to discover patterns inherent in it which then can serve as categories upon which future analyses are conducted and future events predicted. The process of creating categories involves sorting out complex phenomena into relatively discrete groups. All reliable data are empirical, that is able to be observed and measured with regard to their physical characteristics or behavior. Since categories are assumed to be discovered "in" the data rather than created by the observer, the role of human perception, assumptions or values in this process is minimized or denied.

In our day to day lives, we create categories all the time. This is an essential skill for children to learn early in life (Minow, 1990). It helps them understand culturally and situationally appropriate behavior. For example children learn that any object one sits on can be called a chair. These objects are distinct from other objects that we recline on called beds or objects we stand on called stools. These classifications seem natural and universal. Beyond simple categories of utilization, some types of beds, stools or chairs are also considered better, fancier or more worth having than others. The determination of what seems better is not an objective process, but rather one based on cultural values and/or personal preferences. Categories are defined by people who use various lenses, either physical or metaphorical, to enhance certain similarities and differences and ignore others. What is the "significant" difference between a low table and a stool? Who determines the categories of stool vs. table? People can also be sorted into categories. People who have lots of nice chairs in their houses may be considered more worth associating with than people who don't. The infinite number of categories by which we make sense of our complex life experiences are created by processes which combine observation of empirical data and value judgments about the data. Many categories through which Americans structure their lives appear "natural" and "objective" to us and yet might appear quite bizarre or distorted to people from another culture. Our commitment to the separation of Church and State is one such set of categories. Many countries in the Arab world are governed by Islamic law under which this distinction or the separation of God's will from human behavior is inconceivable and deplorable. Category construction is governed by psychological and sociological learning processes which are governed by the variability of cultural difference, not by the uniformity of scientific principles (Ziman, 1978).

The social sciences have historically "discovered" their analytic categories by using conceptual approaches which are similar to those used in the physical and biological sciences. However, social scientists have had more difficulty discovering sharp, clear categories which are relevant and significant for the issues they study than have their colleagues in the natural sciences. Scientific observation methods assume that all human beings can be considered interchangeable observers and that one person's accurate observation is synonymous with the existence of that data as objective "fact" (Ziman, 1978). Therefore, categories and factual descriptions should be uniform across observers. This assumption tends to break down when describing social phenomena in field sites rather than physical phenomena in laboratories. "One comes away from accounts of such research somewhat skeptical of its ultimate value as a source of deep understanding of human behavior" (Ziman, 1978, p. 167).

Although values may be more or less excluded from the creation of categories used to understand atomic or chemical phenomena, they are much more likely to intrude in category creation used to describe social phenomena. This is problematic when conducting research which uses precise methodology. It becomes much more problematic in daily life when no such precise analysis is expected.

> [T]he map of natural science becomes itself a paradigm apparently covering a much broader domain of reality than has been strictly surveyed. This paradigm has transformed our individual pictures of social reality, giving them spurious coherence and simplicity (Ziman, 1978, p. 183).

For example, gender definitions create important categories in the United States. One might ask if it is really "natural" for women to marry, stay home, bear the major responsibility for childrearing and become extremely preoccupied with their physical attractiveness to men, or is this set of behaviors illustrative of the category "feminine" as constructed by the heads of various television networks, publications and advertising agencies (Faludi, 1991)? Is it natural for husbands to dominate their wives, or it this relationship a category constructed within a Judeo-Christian culture which defines its preferred values as natural?

Race is an important category in the United States. Race is

defined as including skin color and a range of other physical, particularly facial, features. When we say race is a problem, we don't generally examine how we define race or why it is a problem. Race is an accepted category of analysis. Once we accept the category, we lose sight of the social process by which the category was created. Later in this volume, the construction of race in the United States and the means by which it has been used to elevate the value of light-skinned people and denigrate the value of dark-skinned people is discussed at length. We act as if we discovered this phenomenon, observed it without lenses and made no judgments about it. "It" is simply out there and we have to cope with it. A society could conceivably exist in which skin color/race was not a significant category, but social class and economic status served as important categories for sorting people into groups. Biologically, race is an illusion. Sociologically it is a pervasive phenomenon.

In the same fashion, many faculty members believe that their ideas about education are the correct ideas, or the only valid ideas, and that people who play different roles with students are not part of the educational process. This is not to suggest that the non-educational status ascribed to the student affairs profession is as severe a problem on our campuses as racism. However, the difference in power and influence between student affairs professionals and academicians flows from a similar element of the American paradigm, the belief that categories exist *a priori*, and that people fit data into them rather than vice-versa. Knowledge gleaned from books and laboratory experiments is considered more valuable and legitimate on American campuses than knowledge gleaned from holding a leadership role and talking about what one has learned with an advisor or group of peers. The classic question which curriculum committees put to student affairs professionals when they seek acknowledgment of their educational work with students is "Why should we award academic credit for this ?" It is a question which often strikes articulate people dumb (Barr & Fried, 1981). The category of "academic credit" in relation to learning is so well defined in our minds that even we, the members of a profession which constantly helps students learn, often can't answer it. We have not perceived academic credit/learning as a constructed category which could be reconstructed in a different way.

The scientific paradigm which has dominated American thinking is characterized by rationality, materialism, objectivity and belief in linear cause/effect change. The emerging paradigm emphasizes dynamic, complex interrelationships between people and events, mutual shaping, context and an awareness of spirituality as an important aspect of human life (Capra, 1982; Kuh, Whitt & Shedd, 1987; Myers, 1993). The shift has been provoked, for the most part, by increasing intercultural communication and the rapid rate of technological change which has speeded up communication in all aspects of business, politics and education. In the earlier paradigm, the change process might be compared to a game of billiards in which one action provokes another in a fairly predictable linear progression. In the second paradigm, one event can cause any number of consequences which then set other events in motion in apparently random order, often with unpredictable consequences. This type of change has been compared to shaking a web. Events in one part of the web may cause minor disturbances nearby, but may be amplified throughout the system and have major consequences in unanticipated locations. Because of the rapidity of the current change as well as transformations in global communication we are, as a society, extremely aware of the shift in progress. Our awareness leads to greater visibility of the assumptions which shaped the old paradigm if only because many are so uncomfortable with the loss of certainty which this change and the emerging paradigm often provokes. On campus, many paradigms operate simultaneously because students, faculty and staff come from so many different cultures, life experiences and academic disciplines. The non-dominant paradigms are often invisible or difficult to perceive because the Anglo-American scientific paradigm dominates most discussions and official interpretations of events. Nevertheless, clashes between dominant and non-dominant perspectives on problematic events continue to create tension.

PARADIGMS SHAPE OUR VISION

A societal or dominant paradigm can be compared to a lens or set of lenses. Anyone who has ever received a prescription for a new set of glasses or contact lenses is familiar with the experience of adjusting to new vision. Prior to receiving the new prescription, vision becomes a bit blurry in one's familiar world. One can perceive well enough, get around because of familiarity with the terrain and manage by making compensations and guesses based on past experience. New lenses bring new clarity, changing focus, a new sense of perspective and awareness of new elements in the environment which had previously been blurred. One is most acutely aware of the role which lenses play in shaping vision at the time of changing lenses. We are now changing lenses. We can still get along with the old ones, but they distort, confuse and mislead under certain circumstances. However, they also provide a sense of comfort because of their familiarity. All the scenes at the beginning of this introduction can be viewed as presentations of the problems caused by changing lenses. The student who wanted to know which theory was right is used to having right answers. She has been conditioned by all her schooling as well as her participation in American, scientifically-oriented culture to look for the single right answer which best accounts for the most data. Theories aren't as reliable as facts for her. Sujata, the Indian American isn't acting normal in the eyes of the RA. The American RA can only see the American Sujata. The Indian elements of her personality and culture, which involve family loyalty and obedience, are invisible or relatively insignificant to the Anglo-American RA. The white graduate student can't comprehend being defined as a minority. His construction of minority is based on race, or skin color. He assumes that light skin color, white, Euro-American ancestry makes him a member of the majority group no matter what the context. The ability of these students to "see" events in their complexity is profoundly limited by their American cultural lens. This lens often has a narrow focus and those who use it to perceive the world are often unaware of its effects. If we don't see clearly or more completely, how can we act effectively now or in the future, on campus or in the larger world?

In order to understand how our American lens shapes our view of the world, it is helpful to know how and under what circumstances the lens was created. A brief review of the historical, intellectual and spiritual roots which gave rise to the creation of the original thirteen English colonies can provide some insight into our current perspective.

Roots

American culture uses a "pattern of opposed dualities" (Merelman, 1984, p. 22) in establishing acceptable beliefs and behaviors, determining who's "in" and who's "out". This pattern is the social equivalent of two valued logic used in science. Who hasn't seen the "America—Love it or Leave It" bumper sticker? The message behind "love it" can easily be interpreted to mean, "act like the dominant group," or "blend into the melting pot." American culture has been nominally assimilationist since its founding but successful assimilation has been compared to committing cultural suicide for those whose home culture is significantly different from their adopted culture (Phelan, Davidson & Hanh, 1993). Ideologically, everybody was welcome in America, but pragmatically those most welcome were those most like the original English immigrants (Gleason, 1992). America developed a cultural system with its own cultural codes by which Americans made and continue to make sense out of their world. This culture is loosely bounded, depends on a pattern of opposed dualities and helps Americans tell who is "one of us," and who is not (Merelman, 1984). Being loosely bounded means that people can enter the culture provided that they conform to its expectations. Anyone really can become an American if she or he adopts the right attitudes, beliefs and behaviors.

The least permeable boundary of Americanism remains that of skin color, which is considered synonymous with race in this country. Many people of color believe that it is impossible for one of them to become a fully accepted American simply because of their skin color, regardless of their conformity to the behavioral code. When Arsenio Hall's popular talk show was canceled, one of his friends commented, "For a brief minute, he felt he would be allowed to play ball with the white boys and get his fair chance at bat. The Leno-Letterman situation let him know real quick he was just another ball boy . . . He tried to please The Man and The Man still jacked him in the end so now he knows" (Hamilton & Samuels, 1994, June 6, p. 45). The phenomenon is more extensively documented in such works as *Faces at the Bottom of the Well* (Bell, 1992) and *The Rage of a Privileged Class* (Cose, 1993).

Beyond certain boundaries, diversity is construed as messy, disorderly, ignorant or intimidating. Conformity to American cultural codes are the means by which immigrants assimilate. For example, African American teenagers are often considered extremely noisy, and white people express fear or discomfort in the presence of these young people. The noise level acceptable to white people sets the standard. Men who come to the United

States from Mediterranean countries quickly learn not to embrace or kiss each other on the street, behavior which makes many acculturated Americans extremely uncomfortable and causes the other men to be categorized as gay. People who come from cultures which encourage large families, early marriage and emphasis on loyalty do not fit easily into the current American norm of small families, later marriage and "doing your own thing." Many American living units do not provide sufficient room for these "extended families." Attempts to squeeze a family of five siblings, two parents, an uncle and a grandmother into an affordable apartment are considered evidence of squalid living and irresponsibility in family and economic planning.

Norms and Values:
The American Cultural Code

What are the major norms and values which traditionally have governed American behavior and belief? The dominant culture generally manifests the following characteristics: It places 1) high value on emotional control, individual autonomy and achievement; 2) the written over the spoken word; 3) youth over age; 4) an emphasis on the future rather than the past or present (Ivey, Ivey & Simek-Morgan, 1993). It also believes in 5) the right of humans to dominate nature (Ibrahim, 1991) and 6) monotheistic, rather intolerant religions (Armstrong, 1993). The culture assumes that values are hierarchical. Moving up the ladder of success is an important metaphor for Americans.

Our founding fathers were white, Christian or Deistic Europeans for the most part and their vision of what an American looked like and believed in has shaped ours (Takaki, 1993). Their values were rooted in Enlightenment Christianity. The ability of their Anglo-European frame of reference to dominate evolving American culture was enhanced by the geographic isolation of the North American continent. Interaction between the masses of Americans and people from other parts of the world was quite limited during the first 200 years of our national existence and didn't really begin to break down until World War I. The dominance of a singular cultural perspective has tended to disadvantage members of non-dominant groups including native people and those who trace their roots to other parts of the world (Minow, 1990).

Reason and Intellect

Our intellectual inheritance is also derived from the European Enlightenment. This period was characterized by an increasing faith in man's [sic] ability to understand how the universe worked. Mystery became less important than logic and data (Todorov, 1984). Galileo, whose work preceded the Enlightenment and made subsequent development possible, believed that truth could be expressed mathematically and that the entire physical universe could be described in quantifiable terms (Capra, 1982). Pascal, an Enlightenment philosopher, tried to find God through the use of reason and failed in despair. The new system of making meaning which swept Europe did not permit him to maintain a faith-centered personal universe. Other thinkers adapted the empirical scientific method to investigate both the material world and the world of faith. Descartes compared God's laws to the laws of geometry and asserted that any God who could produce perfect geometric laws could also be assumed to produce perfect laws to govern the rest of the world. These mechanical laws, once established, did not require any Divine intervention. People were seen as self-governing, thinking beings who could survive independently and understand the world by use of reason, logic and experimentation. Isaac Newton compared God to a mechanic. Newton's self-chosen task was to discover (God's) physical laws so that people could more accurately understand, predict and control the physical world.

Enlightenment thinkers downplayed the role of emotions in human behavior and the value of differences between people. In their search for universal principles, they considered differences anomalies which were confusing, misleading or temporary. Anomalies were expected to disappear when a sufficiently general explanation for a phenomenon was discovered. These thinkers functioned in a relatively homogeneous intellectual environment with minimal exposure to Semitic, Asian or African ideas. They extended the search for scientific truth to other aspects of human experience, assuming that this application of science was viable and accurate. In early psychological studies of human development, for example, women were considered anomalies whenever their attributes seemed to differ from those of men. Carol Gilligan (1982) was among the first to point out that patterns of women's development might be generally different from patterns of men's development and that two sets of

explanatory principles might be in operation. The same processes have unfolded recently in studies of identity formation among
African American students (McEwan, Roper, Bryant & Langen,
1990), gay men (D'Augelli, 1991) and biracial individuals (Poston, 1990). Researchers now assert that different patterns of development seem to operate among different groups of people, as
identified by race, culture, gender and other factors and that no
single pattern can explain development or identity formation in
all groups. Enlightenment thinking considers diversity to be
messy, inconclusive and temporary.*

Faith

Our attitude toward religion is relatively tolerant of variations
in monotheism, but not of other traditions and practices. The
Constitution prevents the state from establishing an official religion and many immigrant groups came to the United States for
religious freedom. As a people, we have learned to live with a
range of Christian and Jewish approaches to religion even
though there is much intolerance of Judaism in Christian scholarship and lay attitudes and much intolerance of Christian thinking among Jewish scholars and laity. Jews and Christians achieve
the highest level of mutual toleration when they focus on their
common belief in one God. Both religions reject the beliefs of
non-theistic faiths like Buddhism, polytheistic faiths like Hindu-
ism and pantheistic faiths which characterize native people all
over the world. Americans are now struggling to understand
how to relate to Islam which shares the Judeo-Christian monotheistic perspective, but has not been widely practiced in this
country until very recently (Armstrong, 1993). The *Bible* of Christians and Jews instructs people to subdue the earth and have
dominion over it (Gen. 1: 28), not to live in harmony with all
forms of life and to respect them. This belief has shaped American behavior throughout our national history as we have dominated indigenous cultures within our borders, assimilated
members of other immigrant ethnic groups and Americanized
countries which we have occupied for economic or security rea-

---

*For a more extensive discussion of the effects of Enlightenment science
on modern thought see *The Turning Point* by Frijtof Capra. Complete
reference follows.

sons or both (Takaki, 1993). Our reliance on a belief in One God amplifies the Enlightenment belief that the best explanation for anything is the one that explains the most details in a single theoretical framework.

Democracy and Individualism

Liberal democracy shapes American government and provides the next overlay in our cultural value system. Liberal democracies emphasize self-expression and self-development as the primary goals of government. The goal of government is to maximize opportunities for the individual while maintaining some type of social contract in which the needs of the group are also acknowledged (Margolis, 1979, p. 26). This form of democracy enhances our beliefs in autonomy, achievement, emphasis on the future and the virtues of youth as a source of energy and ideas. These democracies tend to focus on enhancing the freedom of individuals to do what they wish and to focus on meeting the needs of communities only when forced to do so. Liberal democracies have been considered very effective at preserving the rights of free speech, fairness in legal and judicial processes, tolerating difference and guaranteeing that no group will be totally excluded from the system (Merelman, 1984). However, they are considered less effective in building trust between members of groups which have different values and behavior patterns or in establishing consensus under any but the most serious of circumstances such as in time of war (Merelman, 1984). This problem appears constantly in the form of conflicts between conservationists and developers, supporters of strong social welfare systems and supporters of free enterprise and rugged individualism, people who believe in affirmative action and people who believe in equal treatment for all regardless of circumstances. Conflicts over first amendment rights also fall into this category, particularly free speech vs. hate speech. Because of the emphasis on individuality and autonomy, citizens of liberal democracies are often unaware of the social contexts and cultural values that shape individuals (Merelman, 1984). This makes it difficult for Americans to differentiate between cultural and personal differences. Cultural differences may be bothersome, but are unlikely to change. Personal differences are much more susceptible to adjustment and compromise.

The emphasis on individualism in American culture is considered extreme by many social critics (Bellah, Madsen, Sullivan, Swidler & Tipton, 1985; Lasch, 1979; Merelman, 1984). Our historical concern with the rights of the individual over the welfare of the community has been exacerbated by the recent flood of immigration, particularly from the non-European parts of the globe (Reimers, 1992) which are shaped by different values, behaviors and beliefs. Given the historical emphasis on individualism, the cultural preoccupation with finding unifying principles and singular explanations, and the social fragmentation which has both plagued and energized this country since the 1960s, most Americans do not have a mental map to help them make their way in this very confusing society. Our national identity has historically been based on the belief in a unified American culture as described earlier. Yet, "By 2056 most American will trace their descent to Africa, Asia, the Hispanic world, the Pacific Islands, Arabia—almost anywhere but white Europe" (Takaki, 1993, p. 2). The national identity and sense of self described in our history books is inaccurate and misleading. It is currently impeding our ability to function as a multicultural internally cohesive society because the metaphor and myth excludes and ignores members of many non-dominant groups, most obviously those who trace their roots to places other than Europe.

Consequences for Higher Education and Student Affairs

Why do we as student affairs professionals need to study cultural diversity? The vast majority of student affairs professionals are cultural or acculturated Americans. Therefore we see and interpret the world through the lens just described. This lens provides us with our most comfortable, familiar view and interpretation of the world. Ours is a fairly narrow lens, almost a monocle or a short range telescope. It focuses on a future, narrowly defined, but does see or comfortably tolerate a wide range of human experiences, particularly those shaped by cultures other than our own. An Irish student recently repeated a joke she had heard while traveling through Europe. "A person who speaks three languages is trilingual. A person who speaks two languages is bilingual. A person who speaks one language is an American." Americans have trouble seeing or understanding culture because we generally lack a point of comparison and have not crossed any borders into other cultures from which our own might be viewed as an artifact or human creation. We experience our own culture as reality because it is the only reality we see on a day to day basis.

Those of us who exemplify the dominant culture most completely, that is Anglo- or Euro-American, white, male, able-bodied, heterosexual and Christian, are generally the ones facing the greatest challenge to learn to see with new lenses. Our world is constantly interpreted to us and for us through the American monocle. The world through this lens appears to be synonymous with reality, not one perspective on reality. We rarely see or hear contrasting perspectives unless we read the foreign press or listen to international radio or television. Those of us who lack one or more aspects of the dominant heritage have probably been forced into an awareness of lenses sometime during our lives. Jews know about Christians because they cannot avoid the contrast, particularly during the Christmas and Easter seasons. It is relatively easy in most parts of the country for Christians to remain unaware of Jewish holidays. Americans of color know about Anglo-Americans because they dominate the media and all of the major institutions in the country and outnumber them in the population. Until the past 20 years or so, one could not tell from reading advertisements that people of color in the United States brushed their teeth, smoked, washed their clothes or ate at fast food restaurants. People in the ads were white and the ads were in English. The exceptions occurred in the African American and Spanish presses of the nation whose circulation was generally limited to their own communities. People of color cannot avoid seeing the contrasts between themselves and members of the dominant culture because they cross the border between cultures daily. During this same period gays, lesbians and people with disabilities were also invisible in the media. Gays and lesbians learned to hide or pass. People with disabilities were hidden away. Successful people from all these non-dominant groups learned to pass, to act like members of the dominant culture. Choosing to achieve success in the dominant culture was directly connected to choosing to hide one's differences. Those who choose to hide their differences are acutely aware of boundaries.

Americans who see the world through a monocultural lens, are not conceptually or emotionally prepared to accept diversity of appearance, belief and behavior as normal. Diversity may appear confusing, frustrating or simply uncomfortable. Americans haven't been acculturated to think that difference is valuable or worth understanding often because we are simply waiting for it to go away. We tend to emphasize individuality, i.e., "We're all alike under the skin. We're all just human beings" and ignore cultural or group differences. Diversity makes us feel incompetent. We don't know what members of non-dominant groups expect of us, how they want to be treated, what might offend them or why, in some instances, they act the ways that they do. The case of Sujata at the beginning of this chapter actually occurred on a New England campus. Sujata simply couldn't imagine disobeying her parents and her RA could not imagine seeing a change of major as posing a choice between life and death. As student affairs professionals, we have put ourselves through hundreds, if not thousands of diversity workshops in an effort to understand differences. White Americans have asked our colleagues of color to explain their experiences to us *ad nauseam*, until many of them have given up in frustration. In an even more sensitive area, heterosexual student affairs professionals have pushed themselves to understand their gay and lesbian colleagues and have experienced a great deal of discomfort in facing the ambiguity of their own sexuality.

To summarize, Americans of the dominant culture have difficulty in understanding, perceiving and experiencing diversity because:

- We're not used to it.

- We don't have a cultural perspective that values it.

- We work in bureaucracies that were originally designed to carry out standardized tasks with and for people with essentially similar needs. Diversity in this setting is a problem by definition. Our work environments mask the benefits of difference.

- We are unaware of many elements in our own culture and therefore have trouble knowing when our discomfort is related to the crossing of one of our "taken for granted" cultural boundaries. Interpersonal space, noise levels and assertiveness are three of the most obvious.

- Engaging cultural diversity, for Americans, is profoundly disorienting. It challenges our sense of self, our national values, our faith, our confidence and our ways of knowing the world.

It forces us to reexamine our most deeply held beliefs. We are asked to do this in a culture which believes that there is a right or best way to do everything and that values are hierarchical. Therefore, in our own self-examination, we may find things we don't like, don't believe are right or provoke shame. If we accept a new perspective, we may believe that we must reject one which we previously believed and trusted.

The last item in this list is probably the most significant and is the biggest reason why we as Americans and student affairs professionals are having so much difficulty in understanding and managing diversity. Experiencing a world in which diverse perspectives and cultures co-exist is frightening, disorienting and painful. If one is used to living in a world of hierarchical values and unitary ideas about goodness and acceptability, diversity throws everything into disarray. How will we know who we are, what is right, how to act, who to appreciate? If our personal lifestyle includes hidden elements which were previously devalued and might now be revealed such as sexual orientation, chronic dependency on persons or substances or chronic disease or disability, how will we know what is safe, what to reveal and under what circumstances? All of our unquestioned assumptions will be called into question. We will have to rethink everything. Asking Americans of the dominant culture to accept diversity is a task almost as great as asking medieval Christians to accept a world where the sun, not God or the earth, is at the center. When we began talking about equal opportunity and affirmative action we really didn't know where the road would take us. We didn't know the cost of assimilation for so many members of non-dominant groups. And we certainly didn't know that at some point members of these groups would no longer be willing to pay the admission price of cultural self-destruction (Cose, 1993).

MOVING TOWARD MULTIPLE LENSES

The student affairs profession and the higher education community in the United States are now faced with a daunting task—the need to develop a paradigm which assumes diversity in the culture and on our campuses as a permanent state of affairs. Failure to engage, understand and appreciate the implications of cultural diversity can now be seen primarily as a failure of courage and imagination rather than any set of technical or operational difficulties. It is time to reexamine the foundations of our profession. A paradigm which embraces and explains diversity will make it possible for us to educate students from many cultural backgrounds, collaborate with faculty and manage services for our multicultural populations. Angela Davis is partially correct in her comments about breaking down and beginning anew. We may not need to break down our organizations, but we do need to reexamine the roots of our professional philosophy and beliefs about education. If we understand the origins of our beliefs, we will develop a better sense of how they are currently helping us and how they may be hindering us in developing a sense of direction for working in global education and intergroup collaboration on our campuses.

REFERENCES

Almanac. (1993, August) *The Chronicle of Higher Education. XL.* (1).

Armstrong, K. (1993) *A history of God.* New York: Alfred A. Knopf.

Astin, A. (1993) Diversity and multiculturalism on the campus: How are students affected? *Change. 25.* (2), 44–49.

Bell, D. (1992) *Faces at the bottom of the well.* New York: Basic Books.

Bellah, R., Madsen, R., Sullivan, W., Swidler, A., & Tipton, S. (1985). *Habits of the heart: Individualism and commitment in American life.* New York: Harper and Row.

Boyer, E. (1990) *Campus life in search of community.* Princeton, NJ: The Carnegie Foundation for the Advancement of Teaching.

Capra, F. (1982) *The turning point: Science, society and the rising culture.* New York: Simon and Schuster.

Cose, E. (1993) *The rage of a privileged class.* New York: HarperCollins.

D'Augelli, A. (1991) Gay men in college: Identity processes and adaptations. *Journal of College Student Development. 32.* 140–146.

Davis, A. (1989, April) Rethinking alliance building. Paper presented at Parallels and Intersections: Unlearning racism and other forms of oppression conference. Iowa City, IA.

Faludi, S. (1991) *Backlash: The undeclared war against American women.* New York: Doubleday.

Gamson, Z. (1993) The college experience. *Change. 25.* (3) 64–68.

Garland, P. (1985) *Serving more than students.* (ASHE–ERIC Higher Education Report No. 7) Washington, DC: Association for the Study of Higher Education.

Gilligan, C. (1982) *In a different voice.* Cambridge, MA: Harvard University Press.

Gleason, P. (1992) *Speaking of Diversity: Language and ethnicity in twentieth century America.* Baltimore: Johns Hopkins Press.

Hamilton, K. & Samuels, A. (June 6, 1994) Hall: Not going peacefully. *Newsweek.* 45.

Harman, W. (1988) *Global mind change.* New York: Warner Books.

Ibrahim, F. (1991) Contribution of cultural world view to generic counseling and development. *Journal of Counseling and Development.* 70. 13–19.

Ivey, A., Ivey, M. & Simek-Morgan, L. (1993) *Counseling and psychotherapy: A multicultural perspective* (3rd ed.) Boston: Allyn and Bacon.

Kuh, G., Whitt, E. & Shedd, J. (1987) *Student affairs 2001: A paradigmatic odyssey.* Washington, DC: American College Personnel Association.

Lasch, C. (1979) *The culture of narcissism.* New York: W.W. Norton.

Margolis, M. (1979) *Viable democracy.* New York: St. Martin's Press.

McEwan, M., Roper, L., Bryant, D. and Langa, M. (1990) Incorporating the development of African-American students into psychosocial theories of student development. *Journal of College Student Development.* 31. 429–436.

Merelman, R. (1984) *Making something of ourselves: On culture and politics in the United States.* Berkeley, CA: University of California Press.

Minow, M. (1990) *Making all the difference: Inclusion, exclusion and American law.* Ithaca, NY: Cornell University Press.

Myers, L. (1993) *Understanding an Afrocentric world view: Introduction to an optimal psychology.* Dubuque, IA: Kendall/Hunt.

National Association of Student Personnel Administrators (1989) *Points of View.* Washington, DC: NASPA.

Phelan, P., Davidson, A. & Hanh, C. (1993) Students' multiple worlds: Navigating the borders of family, peer and school culture. In P. Phelan and A. Davidson. (Eds). *Renegotiating cultural diversity in American schools.* (pp. 52–88). New York: Teachers' College Press.

Poston, C. (1990) The biracial identity development model: A needed addition. *Journal of Counseling and Development.* 69. 152–155.

Reimers, D. (1992) *Still the golden door.* (2nd ed.) New York: Columbia University Press.

Schroeder, C. (1993) New students—New learning styles. *Change.* 25. (5) 21–26.

Scott, D. and Awbry, S. (1993) Transforming scholarship. *Change.* 25. (4) 38–44.

Takaki, R. (1993) *A different mirror.* Boston: Little, Brown & Co.

Terkel, S. (1992) *Race.* New York: Doubleday.

Todorov, T. (1982) *The conquest of America: The question of the Other.* (Richard Howard, Trans.) New York: Harper and Row.

West, C. (1993) *Prophetic thought in post-modern times.* Monroe, ME: Common Courage Press.

Ziman, J. (1978) *Reliable knowledge.* London: Cambridge University Press.

2

Telescopes and Kaleidoscopes: Lenses that Focus Our Vision

Earlier in the discussion three words were used almost interchangeably: paradigm, culture and lens. The words have very different meanings, but can be considered three ways of describing the process by which people make sense of information, organizing, interpreting and using it.

PARADIGM

A paradigm is a frame of reference, a set of assumptions through which to interpret the masses of data that we apprehend (Kolb, 1984) every day and to make sense of them. Paradigms can be described as "a distillation of what we think about the world (but cannot prove) " or as systems of ideas along with methods of learning and understanding (Lincoln & Guba, 1985, p. 15). The notion of paradigm and paradigm shift has been widely discussed in the physical sciences (Kuhn, 1970; Ziman, 1978; Zukav, 1979), the social and behavioral sciences (Caple, 1991; Caple, 1987a; Caple, 1987b; Lincoln & Guba, 1985) and business (Wheatley, 1994). Within student affairs, *Student Affairs Work 2001: A Paradigmatic Odyssey* (Kuh, Whitt & Shedd, 1987) contributed to professional understanding of this concept and efforts to bring our work into line with developments in related fields.

Kuhn (1970) used the term paradigm in two ways. It indicates the means by which legitimate problems in a particular field of study are defined. For example, the scientific paradigm defines problems as those which involve data and phenomena that can be observed, measured and replicated under defined circumstances. A scientific problem might involve studying the behavior of a virus in a particular environment, such as the human bloodstream. A legitimate problem in the social sciences would involve studying the behavior of voters in particular electoral regions or regarding specific political or economic issues. In student affairs, the study of factors affecting attrition and retention is a legitimate problem which is currently being investigated. The second aspect of a paradigm describes legitimate research methods used to generate reliable information about those problems, or to solve them. In studying a virus, standard laboratory procedures are used, and only data gathered using those procedures are considered reliable. In studying the HIV virus which causes AIDS, researchers use various inquiry methods to understand the biochemical structures of the virus, the means by which it replicates and experiment with various methods of disrupting replication as they search for a cure. No scientific AIDS researcher would take a vial of HIV-infected blood to the top of a mountain, tie it from a cord around her neck and fast and meditate on the mountain top for forty days as a means of finding a cure. A mystically-oriented scientist might do something comparable, for example, go on a retreat to think about the problem, but the results of the research would never be reported in those terms because the terms don't fit the accepted paradigm for scientific research. The results generated would not be considered valid, even if they were accurate. The scientist would return to the lab and test the insights, using the standard scientific methods. If the scientific research confirmed the mystical insight, then the results would be reported because scientific results, rather than mystical insights, are considered valid in the scientific paradigm.

The dominant paradigm in a discipline tells practitioners and researchers what to think about and how to investigate. In student affairs the dominant paradigm focuses on inquiry about student life outside the classroom, in such areas as psychosocial, cognitive and moral development; individual, interpersonal and group behavior; organized student activities, retention and so forth. Methods for investigating these issues tend to be derived from the same types of scientific, empirical methods widely used in other behavioral sciences. Standard statistical techniques are used to analyze data and present results in commonly accepted formats. For a paradigm shift to occur in this context, student affairs practitioners and researchers would have to change the types of phenomena we choose to investigate as well as our ideas about legitimate research methodology. Both these shifts are now under way. A great deal of discussion about qualitative research methods (Caple, 1991; Stage, 1992; Manning, 1992) is in progress. A focus on student learning in and out of the classroom has emerged as a significant area of concern (Schroeder, 1993). Examination of the effectiveness of peer tutoring through analysis of student journals (Mann, 1994), use of interviewing to describe transitions among adult women students (Breese & O'Toole, 1994) and naturalistic studies of leadership development among women students (Whitt, 1994) and community building on financially distressed campuses (Manning, 1994) are examples of some of the topics which are being investigated using new research paradigms. A focus on all aspects of a student's life and learning actually constitutes the reemergence of an earlier paradigm forcefully promoted by W. H. Cowley and Esther Lloyd-Jones in the 1920s and 1930s which achieved its official expression in the 1937 *Student Personnel Point of View* (Saddlemire & Rentz, 1986).

CULTURE

The dominant paradigm in a country shapes its national value system and indicates the ways in which citizens of that country are likely to interpret events. The paradigm is a product of national/ethnic history, religious belief systems, family values and an almost infinite number of other elements. It is almost synonymous with the term culture. Culture is discussed and defined extensively in the next chapter. For purposes of this discussion, culture signifies an understanding that people have of their universe which guides their interpretation of events as well as their expectations and actions in that universe (Ogbu, 1990). Culture, in this sense, emerges within any group that shares a common set of experiences in the larger world. The men who stormed the beaches on D-Day in World War II developed a common frame of reference about the world which was obvious in their remarks during the celebration on the 50th anniversary of their invasion. Many of them have not seen each other for fifty years, but their bonds, which were forged during the war, form a common thread to this day and shape their vision about America's role in the world. Their common "cultural" frame of reference is most visible to those who do not share it, the succeeding generations who had very different experiences as they grew up and developed very different assumptions about how to interpret events, what to expect and how to act in the world. The dissent about the appropriateness of President Bill Clinton's presence at the D-Day commemorations, given his non-combatant status during the Vietnam War, highlights culture as shaped by generation and life experience rather than ethnicity. The people who share a culture think of their perspective as common sense. Outsiders see it as a point of view.

LENS

Individuals see and interpret the world through a combination of paradigms. These paradigms, which include cultural, philosophical and personal elements, overlap, occasionally conflict and interact in a very broad frame of reference. In the United States the frame of reference, or national paradigm, is constructed by the elements described in the Roots section of the previous chapter. Lens is a metaphor for the particular paradigm an individual uses to view and interpret a situation at a particular time in a particular context. Lenses can be understood as the interpretive framework in which individual experience and cultural heritage combine. Ho has suggested the concept of internalized culture as a way to describe the processes by which lenses are created. "Internalized culture may be defined as the cultural influences operating within the individual that shape (not determine) personality formation and various aspects of psychological functioning"(1995, p. 5). Lenses can be changed as long as people know they are using them. Lenses exist, metaphorically, in arrangements that change in the same way that an optometrist changes the lenses in the diagnostic equipment when a person is getting a new prescription for glasses or contact lenses. The physician asks the patient to look through different lenses and asks the patient to compare. "Which one is clearer? Which one feels more comfortable? Which combination allows you to see the best?" Different elements of a cultural paradigm may become salient depending on the circumstances which a person is dealing with at a particular time.

Problems are likely to arise when an individual doesn't realize that he or she is using a lens to perceive and interpret a situation. This experience typically occurs when an individual believes that there is only one way to interpret a set of events and one set of criteria to use in analyzing or evaluating them. The person who doesn't know that she or he is wearing lenses believes that what she sees is what is "really there," and that anybody else who doesn't see it or interpret it in the same way is obviously wrong. Americans often don't realize that they are wearing lenses. People who think dualistically (Perry, 1970) and view the world as consisting of right and wrong ideas, don't know that lenses exist. These people often discount the value of other people's ideas, denigrate other ways of doing things and interpreting events, get into conflicts and cause difficulty in problem solving. They may also believe that anybody who acts like an American is an American without realizing what types of distortions and blindness their lenses are causing.

Lenses function unconsciously unless they are challenged or a contrasting view appears. Among people who share them, lenses are taken for granted. Information interpreted through personal lenses is believed to be "true," because the interpreter is often not aware of the interpretive process. Different lenses through which people viewed the tape of Rodney King being subdued (or assaulted?) by members of the Los Angeles Police Department led to dramatically different conclusions about responses to this situation. If Rodney King was seen as a dangerous criminal who might have assaulted the police with a gun at the first opportunity, then the police behavior made sense in terms of self-protection and maintaining the public order. If King was perceived as a Black man being beaten to unconsciousness by several heavily armed white men, the actions of the police were excessive and irresponsible since King did not constitute a danger to anyone at that point. Lenses probably included race, socio-economic status, residence in or outside South Central Los Angeles, acquaintance with anybody who did live there, political and religious belief systems and so forth.

PARADIGM CREATION

Lenses as Personal Constructs

Paradigms help people impose mental road maps on complex, confusing or novel situations. Kelly's (1955) theory of personal constructs offers a way of describing the process by which people develop personal lenses. Kelly describes the way people perceive and interpret events as the creation of a series of bipolar constructs such as good/bad, easy/hard, big/little. These constructs serve as hypotheses to explain what is happening, help the person compare this situation to previous similar situations, predict what is likely to happen next and decide how to respond. For example, when a person comes to a street corner and sees a traffic light, he or she views the situation as follows

> Red/green . . . Choose green; Go/stop . . . choose go; Safe/dangerous. . . . choose safe; on this corner, cars usually obey the light/don't obey the light . . . choose obey: *Action*: The person then crosses the street.

When perceiving another person walking toward him or her, the first person will also generate a series of bipolar constructs which compare this person to others and suggest subsequent actions:

> Familiar/strange . . . choose familiar; Pleasant/unpleasant . . . choose pleasant; Close friend/acquaintance. . . . choose acquaintance: *Action*: Say hi, wave and smile. Another construction might be: familiar/strange. . . . choose strange; comfortable/uncomfortable. . . . choose uncomfortable; larger than me/smaller than me . . . choose larger; same race/different race. . . . choose different race: *Action*: Look away, walk quickly, leave wide space between self and other person as they pass on the sidewalk.

The second person is similar enough to the stereotypes that the first person holds about unsafe people that she or he chooses to avoid the person based on previous experience or hypotheses about how that person is likely to act.

The culture or cultures in which a person participates, by birth, by choice or by life circumstances, shape that person's frame of reference, or paradigmatic lenses, through which she or he makes sense of the world. In Nova Scotia, for example, people believe that soft-shelled lobsters are indigestible and should not be eaten. On the coast of Maine lobsters are eaten regardless of the hardness of their shells. The only issue in Maine is the taste of the lobster and the amount of meat in the shell. Mainers eat soft-shelled lobsters and residents of Nova Scotia don't, practices which are determined by local culture and its construction of meaning. A march by members of a neo-Nazi group through Skokie, Illinois where many survivors of German concentration camps live would evoke powerful and painful memories for those survivors and possibly raise questions about their own safety. Presumably, a group of non-Jewish teenagers for whom World War II and Nazism are simply descriptions in history books, would have a much less intense reaction and might have little or no concern about how that group might affect them personally.

Paradigms serve as epistemological and ontological guides for individuals. That is, they give people a means to decide what is real and how reality can be known. In familiar situations, paradigms function below the level of awareness and appear as "common sense." In unusual situations, people create new personal paradigms for themselves based on previous sets of constructs about how to behave in comparable or fairly similar situations. Adolescent girls, for example, face the challenge of maintaining their friendships in the presence of interpersonal or moral conflicts which seem to increase in frequency as they mature and their lives become more complex. They develop a relationship paradigm which permits them to reconcile conflict and maintain friendship through extensive discussion of their values, their concern for each other and the models of balance each girl developed as she grew up in her own family (Gilligan, Lyons & Hanmer, 1990). Boys more frequently construct a paradigm based on justice and the use of abstract principles in making moral decisions (Kohlberg, 1969). In Moslem cultures, individuals often rely on precepts from the Koran in deciding how to make sense out of events, how to treat other people, how to dress, what to eat and so forth. Trying to understand and carry out the will of Allah in all events becomes paramount. In many Asian cultures, The Tao exerts a strong influence. People are likely to be patient because they expect events to follow a course which ought not to be interfered with. Ultimately, people who adopt The Tao as paradigm believe that balance restores itself. Whatever actions are taken should follow the natural flow of events, not contradict it. A Taoist would be likely to react differently to a corrupt politician than a member of the Democratic Party in the United States. In American jargon, the Taoist would see the politician as inevitably failing because corruption would catch up with him or her. The American Democrat would be more likely to "throw the scoundrel out" in the next election. An American Taoist might observe that "What goes around, comes around."

The ultimate paradigm might be considered the one which provides the broadest possible explanation for the very large number of facts that people have to understand and respond to in their lives. Historically, religion and philosophy have provided very general paradigms to help people make sense of their lives. In some times and places, monotheistic religions have served as governing paradigms. In other times and places, non-theistic, philosophical approaches have served the same ends. In the late 20th century Western world, the dominant paradigm is largely based on the principles of empirical science as they were developed during the Renaissance and Enlightenment by scientists such as Newton, Copernicus, Bacon, Galileo, and their heirs. These principles govern our ideas about reliable knowledge and inquiry methods. They contain underlying assumptions about order, predictability, cause and effect relationships, objectivity and single perspective explanations, the primacy of logic and the necessity of empirical evidence to substantiate beliefs. This paradigm achieved its highest level of utility and accuracy in the field of Newtonian physics (Capra, 1982). It is arguably the paradigm which most powerfully shapes our American frame of reference. To test the significance of this paradigm in your own thinking, try to imagine how you would make sense of a world in which any one of the elements described below were not considered "true" or "accurate".

The Scientific Paradigm

The Newtonian paradigm dominated physical and social science research throughout the late 19th and most of the 20th century. With its emphasis on prediction and control, it has been responsible for expanding our understanding of the material world, but this expansion has had a cost. The paradigm has established borders to our understanding and placed lenses on our perception which mask significant elements of the human experience, particularly those which arise from spirituality, interpersonal relationships, intuition and personal experience. These elements cannot be reduced to mathematical formulae. This paradigm dominates the cultures of the North Atlantic—Europe, the United States and Canada (West, 1993). Paradigms which emphasize understanding and unification are rooted in African and Asian worldviews. These paradigms tend to emphasize self-knowledge as the root of all knowledge and the connectedness of perception, knowledge, relationships and wisdom (Myers, 1984). An examination of the Afrocentric paradigm, which occurs in the next two chapters, highlights the borders of the scientific paradigm. Thus the assumptions of the scientific paradigm become clear as assumptions, not presentations of things as they "really" are.

The scientific paradigm has roots in various aspects of Western philosophy whose names have been used in confusing and interchangeable fashion. It has several elements which must be described separately , but which interact as people use them to expand knowledge, conduct research and understand and interpret data. Each of the aspects is defined below, followed by several questions. The questions are designed to focus the reader's beliefs about that aspect of the scientific paradigm.

1) This paradigm is objectivist. That is, it assumes that concepts or empirical categories can be defined by direct reference to "objects in concrete" (Lincoln & Guba, 1985, p. 20) or things that exist materially, in the physical world. Ontologically, objectivism assumes that reality is synonymous with physical reality. That which is real exists in the physical world and can be observed, measured and counted. Objectivism is sometimes described as empiricism or materialism.

Questions: What kinds of realities can you describe which are nonmaterial, or non-physical? Do they seem as real to you as tables and chairs? Your answer shows you how objectivism shapes your perspective.

2) The paradigm is positivist. Positivism assumes a separation between the observer and that which is observed. The world is assumed to exist independently of the observer. Events occur whether or not anybody is there to observe them. Point of view, perspective or frame of reference are not taken into account when reporting observations. Observers are considered interchangeable because the world exists "out there," and the observer, human, mechanical or electronic, merely records what is. Data exist independently of theory or interpretation in what is also called a "correspondence theory of truth" (Lincoln & Guba, 1985, p. 24). Truth is assumed to correspond to accurate descriptions of data. Positivist categories of analysis are assumed to be embedded in the data and discovered by the researcher. They are not seen as human constructs around which data is organized to create meaning. Positivism has been challenged in physics since the early 20th century (Capra, 1982; Capra, 1975) and more recently in the social sciences as well (Lincoln & Guba, 1985; Stage, 1992; Stigler, Shweder & Herdt, 1990). Challenges to positivism are based on the notion that reality is more complex than a single perspective explanation and that all observation is interpretive. "There is more to theory than meets the eyeball" (Hanson, 1958, p. 7).

Questions: If two people were standing in the forest and a tree fell, would they both hear the same sounds? If a Hindu and a Christian were walking in the woods and came upon a swarm of bees, would they both have the same experience or react the same way? If an African American and an Anglo-American student were sitting in the same classroom and the professor said, "let's call a spade a spade" would the sentence mean the same thing to both Americans? Does the phrase "get real" signify to you that you are thinking about the impossible or the unacceptable and that somebody who is "more realistic" is trying to get you back into the acceptable paradigm?

3) The paradigm is grounded in two valued logic in which all data are evaluated according to whether or not they fit into the theoretical interpretation. The goal of two valued logic is to develop categories of analysis which account for the largest amount of data and minimize the range of data which cannot be understood. Research based on eliminating the null hypothesis is organized in this fashion. Data, by contrast, are always three grounded. Some fit the theory and are included. For example, students who are struggling with choice of vocation or finding ways to develop intimate relationships fit into Chickering's theory of identity formation. Some data challenge the theory and are excluded. For example, students whose main concern is finding enough time to spend with their children while also working and going to school do not seem to fit into any of the categories related to identity formation and are therefore excluded from this theory. Finally, some data cannot be accounted for by the theory and are considered ambiguous or anomalous and are not discussed. For example, African American students may be creating an identity which includes developing competence and emotional control, but emphasizes spiritual development and relationships with family more strongly than traditional age Anglo-American students. African Americans display some characteristics in common with students described by the original theory and some concerns which are not accounted for. Ideally, a new theory should evolve which takes a previously unacknowledged group into its set of explanations (McEwan, Roper, Bryant & Langa, 1990). In constructing theory and making the transition from three grounded data to two grounded logic, distortions and errors always occur. Some information is simply ignored or discredited because it cannot be accounted for in the analysis. The goal is to develop categories which keep the undecided middle ground as small as possible (Ziman, 1978). In the

positivist, objectivist approach to categorization, issues of value, power and relative worth are not discussed. Scientists' values are assumed not to play a role in the process. Challenges to this point of view have been raised by feminists in particular and will be discussed in subsequent chapters.

Questions: What do you do when you have data you can't explain? Do you try to create an explanation, expanding your paradigm, ignore or discount it, or put it on hold until an explanation presents itself? How do you explain the presence of very bright students on campus who can't get grades above C's no matter how hard they try? Does intelligence level help us understand why women are so heavily outnumbered in engineering or men in nursing? Can people really know what God wants them to do or know who's on the phone before they pick it up? Why do nice guys sometimes rape women or other guys? What do you do when your theories or personal constructs don't satisfactorily explain what's going on in your world?

4) The paradigm has a number of other scientific characteristics. It uses deductive thinking, based on hypotheses which are developed logically and tested empirically (Patton, 1990). It assumes a uniformity of nature across time and space and does not acknowledge the effect of context. It assumes that the larger the data set, the more generally true and universally accurate the analyses may be. It also assumes that a universal scientific language can be developed to describe nature so that all scientists will understand descriptions in a similar fashion (Lincoln & Guba, 1985). It assumes cause and effect relationships which are incremental, mechanical and traceable backward in time (Caple, 1987a). It assumes that culture has little to do with perception and nothing to do with science. It asserts that "all aspects of complex phenomena can be understood by reducing them to their constituent parts" (Capra, 1982, p. 59).

The Limits of the Scientific Paradigm

The scientific paradigm, which has tremendous utility in helping people understand, predict and control their environments, has serious limitations when used to develop a system of morality and values for human societies or as the only means to understand and interpret human behavior (Ziman, 1978). When this paradigm governs research in the social sciences, humans are treated as data sets that are not significantly different from oth-

er physical phenomena whose behavior is governed by impersonal, universal laws. Sociology, for example, studies humans in
the aggregate and attempts to discover universal truths about
the behavior of humans in groups. The social and behavioral
sciences have "reified", or made things of, events and relationships, giving them the appearance of independent existence, separate from human interpretation. This approach reflects the
empirical or materialistic assumptions of the scientific paradigm.
It seriously distorts research data which fall into the middle category of "no explanation". This includes the data which are seen
through individual lenses and cultural paradigms, particularly
those related to faith, intuition, personal loyalty and other non-
materialistic phenomena. These beliefs exert powerful effects on
human behavior but are extremely difficult to quantify. In these
situations, the limits of the scientific paradigm, the boundaries
of its utility, are highlighted and made visible. It presents information with misleading certainty and often ignores information
because it does not fit in scientific categories. In other words,
this lens does not show us everything it purports to show. It is
better at showing us outcomes or effects of large trends on masses of people than it is on showing us the particular and individual processes by which people change or develop insight and
make meaning of their lives (Gamson, 1993). Data collected and
presented as "variables" are data reduced and taken out of context. The resulting picture is incomplete, failing to present the
whole picture of complex human experience.

This paradigm is so pervasive that it does not appear in day
to day life as a set of assumptions about the world. It appears
as "the way things are," reflecting an attitude about reality, objectivity and reasonableness. Positivist, empirical methods govern our understanding of what constitutes reliable knowledge.
As a culture, we believe in the trustworthiness of facts, pieces of
non-contextual information. We tend to believe data presented in
statistical form more than any other type of data. We ask for "the
bottom line" as measured numerically. We are reluctant to rely
on anecdotal evidence because we are not sure how valid it is,
i.e., how large a percentage of the total data universe it represents. People who solve problems by responding to "gut instinct"
are generally considered less reliable than people who operate
on the basis of facts. People who attempt to fund projects in
universities or elsewhere because they "know" what is needed,
without providing empirical evidence of both need and proba-

bility that their response will meet the need, generally do not receive the funds they request.

Seeing the world through the assumptions of the scientific paradigm, Americans often seem to rely on two valued logic illustrated by such phrases as, "America, love it or leave it" and "If guns are outlawed, only outlaws will have guns." Talk shows which present complex problems like domestic violence, human sexuality, gun control and hate speech flourish on day time television by pitting one oversimplified point of view against another. Campus hate speech regulations adopt an either/or approach which pits the rights of one person against another rather than attempting to judge the effect or intention of the speech in the context in which it occurred. This approach preserves the free speech of one group at the expense of the freedom of movement of another group. Despite the existence of a number of schemes of cognitive and moral development which describe the ability to manage complex and interacting ideas as the hallmark of sophistication and wisdom (Perry, 1970; Kitchener & King, 1994; Baxter-Magolda, 1993), a desire for right answers seems to dominate national discourse.

Our national belief that reality exists "out there" and that change occurs in a simple cause/effect process also reflects the domination of the scientific paradigm in the American cultural perspective. Marginal or non-dominant groups which view events differently are often ignored because their version of reality strains the paradigm. For example, from a materialist perspective, military security is more important than art. During the Reagan and Bush administrations several artists appeared before Congress to request that appropriations for the arts and humanities be increased. The artists clearly described how relatively small cuts in military spending could lead to relatively enormous increases in funding for the arts with no significant impact on military security. Maya Angelou suggested facetiously that, at the going rate for one nuclear submarine, Congress might request a design that was one foot shorter and fund the arts for an extended period of time with the money saved. Similar strategies have been attempted by women's groups in attempting to increase funding for nutrition programs and other human services by suggesting that the government fund human service programs and force the military to raise funds privately when it needed more equipment. The humor in both situations is a function of the extra-paradigmatic perspective. Nutritional needs cannot challenge military needs in the dominant paradigm.

The scientific paradigm examines facts as if they existed without context. As a result, when groups request that facts be examined in context (social, cultural, economic), they are accused of confusing the issue or refusing to take responsibility. They are also clarifying issues by describing their complexity and suggesting a wider range of approaches. Changing the context may well change the facts. Feeding infants may decrease the costs of special education years later. Providing safe public housing may decrease the prison population. Providing holistic support programs for disadvantaged students may ultimately decrease the strain on social security. All of these approaches depend on seeing information in context and envisioning a very complicated process of unfolding events. None of these approaches makes sense if it is presented in strict cause/effect terms. The potential success of each depends on the attitudes of those who participate in implementing solutions. Individual attitudes such as optimism, faith or belief in equal opportunity are generally not measured when setting government policy. The interpretive lenses of positivism and objectivism do not present the most accurate picture when viewing complex problems which include hopes and fears as well as empirical data.

The American paradigm frames significant differences as representing confusion, transition or error. Two valued logic requires that all data be assigned to permanent, mutually exclusive categories. As a nation of immigrants, our metaphor for acculturation was the melting pot, a metaphor which was based on the eventual elimination of cultural difference. People who could adapt to and adopt the national paradigm of American culture could find a way to fit in. People who could not adapt because of unchangeable characteristics or because the cost of changing their paradigm was too high, were excluded no matter how long they remained. English immigrants, predominantly male, defined American cultural paradigm in the earliest colonial days. They retained their own hierarchical social system, considered the native people savages, construed African slaves as non-human and presented their paradigm as objective reality. Jefferson and his peers considered darker skin color to be *prima facie* evidence of natural differences between the groups. These differences were extended to include a ranking of differential intelligence, passion, sensitivity and capacity for the other attributes of civilization (Takaki, 1993). Rather than formulate a concept of Africans and Native Americans as people who lived differently with different spiritual beliefs, different ways to conceptualize family and different methods of feeding, clothing and interacting with other groups, the Founding Fathers considered these people less than human and developed means to subdue and dominate them. They used the lens of eugenics which focuses on birth characteristics, rather than eunomics, which defines citizenship by participation in creation of a law-abiding society, as their guidelines for determining citizenship (Hannaford, 1994). They thus created a lens in which race played a large part and behavior a relatively small one.

The scientific paradigm, which has taken American culture so far technologically seems to have reached its limits in terms of its hegemonic status. The limits of this paradigm restrict our ability to understand or cope with the unprecedented cultural diversity of the late 20th century. Perceiving the world through this lens may cause a person of European ancestry to wonder how long a person with Asian features has lived in the United States even though the other person's family arrived a hundred years earlier than the European family. It may cause us to wonder why children of Indian immigrants are still so resistant to eating hamburger or dating, when Latino-Americans are going to realize that young people should leave their parents' home after completing their education or when recent immigrants from the Middle East are going to learn to be on time and get their business done efficiently without talking about family.

BORDER CROSSINGS AND NEW PARADIGMS

In the late twentieth century, the United States of America and its institutions of higher education are struggling to adjust to a world in which profound, apparently irreconcilable differences can no longer be avoided. We have reached the limits of the scientific paradigm as a frame of reference for understanding and coping with this complexity. We have arrived at the border of this paradigm which so heavily influences American culture. New perspectives, models and sets of interpretive constructs are necessary to take us across the border so that our country and our institutions of higher education can become multicultural. To cross the border, Americans must begin to understand the role of culture in shaping individuals—their perceptions, values, beliefs and behavior. We must begin to experience the reality of people from many other cultures as a personal experience, and go beyond intellectual understanding to others as presented in "objective" descriptions. We must be willing to tolerate the confusion this border crossing will inevitably provoke. As a nation and as a profession, we must begin moving from domination to participation, from assuming that we set the standards to realizing that, in this new world, we should be contributing to their creation.

REFERENCES

Barr, M. and Fried, J. (1981) Facts, feelings and academic credit. in J. Fried (Ed.) *New Directions in Student Services: Education for student development.* (pp. 87–102) *15.* San Francisco: Jossey–Bass.

Baxter-Magolda, M. (1993) *Knowing and reasoning in college.* San Francisco: Jossey–Bass.

Bordo, S. (1987) *The flight to objectivity.* Albany, NY: SUNY Press.

Breese, J. & O'Toole, R. Adult women students: Development of a transitional status. *Journal of College Student Development. (35)* 183–189.

Brislin, R. (1990) *Applied cross-cultural psychology.* Newbury Park, CA: Sage Publications.

Brooks, J. & Brooks, M. (1993) *The case for constructivist classrooms.* Alexandria, VA: Association for Supervision and Curriculum Development.

Caple, R. (1991) *Journal of College Student Development: Special Edition.* (32) 5.

Caple, R. (1987a) The change process in developmental theory: A self–organization paradigm, Part 1. *Journal of College Student Personnel. 28.* 4–11.

Caple, R. (1987b) The change process in developmental theory: A self–organization paradigm, Part 2. *Journal of College Student Personnel. 28.* 100–103.

Capra, F. (1982) *The turning point: Science, society and the rising of culture.* New York: Simon and Schuster.

Dalton, C. (1993) Introductory memo to students in Law, Culture and Difference course. Boston, MA: Northeastern University School of Law.

deTocqueville, A. (1956) *Democracy in America.* R. Heffner (Ed.). New York: Mentor Books.

Dewey, J. (1916) *Democracy and education.* New York: The Macmillan Company.

Friedman, J. (1991) Further notes on the adventures of phallus in blunderland. In L. Nencel and P. Pels (Eds.), *Constructing knowledge.* (pp. 95–113). Newbury Park, CA: Sage Publications.

Friere, P. (1985) *The politics of education.* Westport, CT: Bergin and Garvey.

Gailey, C. (1993) Lecture in Workshop on Multicultural Perspectives in Curriculum Development and Teaching Strategies. Boston, MA: Northeastern University.

Gamson, Z. (1993) The college experience: New data on how and why students change. *Change. 25* (3) 64–68.

Gilligan, C., Lyons, N. & Hanmer, T. (1990) *Making connections.* Cambridge, MA: Harvard University Press.

Giroux, H. & McLaren, P. (Eds.). (1994) *Between borders.* New York: Routlege.

Hall, S. (1990) The emergence of cultural studies and the crisis of the humanities. *October. 53.* 11–23.

Hannaford, I. (1994) The idiocy of race. The *Woodrow Wilson Quarterly. XVIII* (2). 8–45.

Harding, S, (1991) *Subjectivity, experience and knowledge: An epistemology from/for rainbow coalition politics.* Tenth Annual Fellows Lecture. Washington, DC: Society for the Study of Values in Higher Education.

Ho, D. (1995) Internalized culture, culturocentrism and transcendence. *The Counseling Psychologist (23).* 1. 4–24.

Howe, I. (1976) *World of our fathers.* New York: Harcourt, Brace, Jovanovich.

Keller, E. (1985) *Reflections on gender and science.* New Haven, CT: Yale University Press.

Kelly, G. (1955) *The psychology of personal constructs.* New York: Norton Press.

Kitchener, K. & King, P. (1994) *Developing reflective judgment.* San Francisco: Jossey–Bass.

Kohlberg, L. (1969) Stage and sequence: The cognitive developmental approach to socialization. In D. Goslin (Ed.) *Handbook of socialization theory and research.* Chicago: Rand McNally.

Kuh, G., Whitt, E. & Shedd, J. (1987) *Student affairs, 2001: A paradigmatic odyssey.* Alexandra, VA: American College Personnel Association.

Kuhn, T. (1970) *The structure of scientific revolution.* Chicago: University of Chicago Press.

Kuh, G. (Ed.) (1993) *Cultural perspectives in student affairs work.* Lanham, MD: American College Personnel Association.

Levine, A. (1980) *When dreams and heroes died.* San Francisco: Jossey–Bass

Lincoln, Y. & Guba, E. (1985) *Naturalistic Inquiry.* Newbury Park, CA: Sage.

Mann, A. (1994) College peer tutoring journals: Maps of development. *Journal of College Student Development (35).* 164–169.

Manning, K. (1994) Rituals and rescission: Building community in hard times. *Journal of College Student Development. (35)* 275–281.

Manning, K. (1992) A rationale for using qualitative research in student affairs. *Journal of College Student Development. (35).* 132–136.

Margolis, M. (1979) *Viable democracy.* New York: St. Martins Press.

McEwan, M., Roper, L., Bryant, D. & Langa, M. (1990) Incorporating the development of African-American students into psychosocial theories of student development. *Journal of College Student Development. (31)* 429–436.

Ogbu, J. (1990) Cultural models, identity and literacy. In R. Stigler, R. Shweder & G. Herdt (Eds.) *Cultural psychology.* (pp. 520–541) New York: Columbia University Press.

Patton, M. (1990) *Qualitative evaluation and research methods.* Newbury Park, CA: Sage.

Pederson, P. (Ed.) (1991) Multiculturalism as a fourth force in counseling. *Journal of Counseling and Development. 70.* (1).

Perry, W. (1970) *Forms of intellectual and ethical development in the college years.* New York: Holt, Rinehart and Winston.

Sabine, G. (1961) *A history of political theory* (3rd ed.).New York: Holt, Rinehart and Winston.

Saddlemire, G. & Rentz, A. (Eds.) (1986) *Student affairs: A profession's heritage.* Alexandria, VA: American College Personnel Association.

Schroeder, C. (1993) New students-New learning styles. *Change. 25.* (5) 21–26.

Stage, F. & Assoc. (1992) *Diverse methods for research and assessment of college students.* Alexandria, VA: American College Personnel Association.

Stigler, J. Shweder, R. & Herdt, G. (Eds.) (1990) *Cultural psychology.* New York: CUP.

Takaki, R. (1993) *A different mirror.* Boston: Little, Brown and Company.

West, C. (1993) *Prophetic thought in post-modern times.* Monroe, ME: Common Courage Press.

Wheatley, M. (1994) *Leadership and the new science.* San Francisco: Berrett–Keohler.

Ziman, J. (1978) *Reliable knowledge.* London: Cambridge University Press.

Zukav, G. (1979) *The dancing Wu-Li masters.* New York: Bantam Books.

3

Believing Is Seeing:
Culture as Paradigm

DEFINITIONS OF CULTURE

The term "culture" is more widely used than "paradigm" and probably has acquired many more definitions, interpretations, applications and emotional nuances. Culture has historically referred to the shared characteristics, values, behavior patterns, ideals, artifacts, language and cognitive categories that members of a particular group hold. These commonalities are transmitted to new members of the group and permit members of one cultural group to differentiate themselves from members of other groups (Brislin, 1990). Culture can include "demographic variables such as age, sex, status and affiliation . . . as well as ethnographic variables such as nationality, ethnicity, language and religion" (Pederson, 1991, p. 7). Members of cultural groups such as Castellano Spaniards, Puerto Ricans, Ibo, Brooklynites or Parisians, have historically had a common area of residence although there are notable exceptions. Many Jews, for example, have lived in Diaspora for more than 2,000 years while maintaining elements of a common culture.

Studying Cultures Through Different Lenses

In keeping with the scientific paradigm, recent discussions of culture in the student affairs literature have tended to reify the phenomenon in order to study it (Cheatham & Assoc., 1991; Eldridge & Barnett, 1991; Kuh, 1993). What is culture, in general?

39

This question is the beginning of a search for general principles which explain and categorize the available data. What are the contents of a particular culture? This begins the search for data that can be organized according to the principles, assuming separation of the observer and the observed. How can we be sure that we learn *about* different cultures? What is the *impact* of culture on development? Our metaphors for studying and understanding culture are non-interactive and reflect the positivist, objectivist research paradigm. Studies of students and their cultures attempt to establish categories of differentiation among students who are assumed to be members of different cultures so that we can understand how they think, what they value, how they behave, so that we can treat them appropriately and effectively. How can we establish valid, two valued categories so that we minimize anomalous data? In lay terms, how can we minimize ambiguity, establish theoretical certainty and be sure that we understand the phenomena "out there" and maintain control? How can we turn people into data?

Anthropologists and other constructivist researchers who use ethnographic and phenomenological methods are less likely to see culture as object and more likely to view it as process. They attempt to see the world *through* the perspective of the culture they are studying. They look inward and outward simultaneously, trying to understand different cultures and trying to understand how their own culture is simultaneously shaping their perception. They recognize that "there is no point in looking for foundations or using the language of absolute truth . . . [they] recognize the power of the environment to press for adaptation, the temporality of knowledge and the existence of multiple selves behaving in consonance with the rules of various subcultures" (Noddings, 1990, p. 12). They ask "What's going on here? How are the various elements in this situation interacting?" Culture, from this perspective, "is a process of negotiating power and creating shared meaning through talk" (Gailey, 1993). Shared meaning is an element which has appeared in previous definitions. Negotiating power is a new dimension which will be applied to analyses of the acculturation of students from non-dominant cultures to campus life and to relations among faculty members, students and administrators later in this chapter.

Cultural psychology which focuses on the interaction of culture and psyche, uses yet another definition. It is

the study of the way cultural traditions and social practices regulate, express, transform and permute the human psyche, resulting less in psychic unity for human kind than in ethnic
divergences in mind, self and emotion . . . [it studies] the ways
subject and object, self and other, psyche and culture, person
and context, figure and ground, practitioner and practice live
together, require each other and dynamically, dialectically and
jointly make each other up. (Shweder, 1990, p. 1)

To a certain extent Kuh acknowledges the interactions between
individuals and campus cultures as "simultaneous and mutually
shaping" (1993, p. 3), a perspective which acknowledges the dynamism of culture. However, Kuh focuses on cultural outcomes
such as artifacts, perspectives, values and assumptions while a
constructivist approach would be more likely to focus on the
process by which these develop and change meaning. Cultural
psychology assumes that all people live in uncertainty and
search for meaning by creating intentional worlds in which
"nothing real just is" (Shweder, 1990, p. 4). All meaning is constructed by people who are involved in events, observing them,
participating in them and reflecting on them. This contrasts with
the positivist objectivist assumptions that things exist independently of human perception and that organizing categories
emerge from empirical data with no particular regard for the
person who creates the categories.

Intentional worlds are sociocultural environments which exist, "as long as there exists a community of persons whose beliefs, desires, emotions, purposes and other mental
representations are directed at it and are thereby influenced by
it" (Shweder, 1990, p. 2). In intentional worlds, "human beings
and sociocultural environments interpenetrate each other's identity and cannot be analytically disjoined into independent and
dependent variables" (Shweder, 1990, p. 1). From an Afrocentric
perspective this interpenetration is expressed in the aphorism, "I
am because we are" (Myers, 1993, p. 20). In addition, "there is
no logical requirement that across intentional worlds the identity of things must remain fixed and universal" (Shweder, 1990, p.
3). In other words, a person who is considered deranged in one
culture might be considered inspired in another; a game played
with a ball by two competing teams might be a form of recre-
ation in one intentional world and a method by which serious
decisions are made about life and death in another.

The paradigm of intentional worlds in which "nothing real just is," provides a dramatic contrast to the scientific paradigm which seeks to discover universal truths that can be expressed in a universal language and remain constant across time and space. Intentionality is based on existential uncertainty and consciousness of human efforts to create meaning in a world of shifting circumstances. Science is based on the notion of a stable universe in which cause and effect relationships lead to inferences of unchanging principles. Monotheistic religion has also historically focused on applying unchanging principles to the vagaries of human life and attempting to discover the meaning of life through understanding these principles. Metaphorically, the contrast between scientific/monotheistic approaches and cultural psychology approaches might be compared to stages on the Perry scale, with science and its two valued logic falling toward the Dualistic end of the scheme and Intentionality with its multivalued logical/intuitive approach falling toward the Commitment in Relativism scheme (Perry, 1970). Even this metaphoric comparison is somewhat misleading. The Perry scheme is hierarchical, with the higher stages conveying a higher level of cognitive complexity and sophistication than the lower. To be higher on an hierarchy implies that one is better since hierarchies exist for purposes of tracking progress and determining value. The differences between bifurcated approaches and multifaceted, non-hierarchical approaches is more one of style than value. Both are capable of attaining high levels of complexity, albeit based on different approaches to valuing (Baxter-Magolda, 1993).

Positivism and Constructivism

Two branches of philosophy provide the basis for both positivist and constructivist approaches to research. Ontology is the study of the nature of truth and epistemology is the study of the relationship between the knower and the known (Lincoln & Guba, 1985; Ziman, 1978). In the scientific paradigm, truth is unchanging, and the knower observes, but does not interact with the known. The basic reality is physical and can be measured, counted and seen, touched or apprehended in some other physical modality, either by people directly through the senses or through use of instrumentation. In constructivist paradigms, subject and object are always considered interactively, and absolute truth is not a viable construct. Constructivism is grounded in the notion that

> We construct our own understandings of the world in which we live. We search for tools to help us understand our experiences . . . We construct through reflection upon our interactions with objects and ideas . . . Knowledge comes neither from the subject nor the object, but from the unity of the two. (Brooks & Brooks, 1993, pp. 4-5)

Constructivism focuses on relationships between people, events and all sorts of phenomena. The relationships tend to be non-linear, interactive and somewhat unpredictable. In this paradigm, change is often irreversible because it proceeds in a web-like process, not in a straight line (Allen & Cherrey, 1994; Caple, 1987). A constructivist tends to look for interactive patterns and trends rather than unidirectional cause and effect events. Constructivism generally seeks to understand the particular in depth, rather than to construct universal explanations for classes of events (Frye, 1990). From this perspective realities are social constructs which are related to tangible events and objects, but whose meanings are constructed by the persons who observe, organize and interpret them (Lincoln & Guba, 1985).

> Every cognitive act takes place at a point of intersection of innumerable relations, events, circumstances and histories that make the knower and known what they are, at that time. [It focuses on] the complex network of relations with which an organism realizes or fails to realize its potential, be they historical, material, geographical, social, cultural, racial, institutional or other (Code, 1993, pp. 269-270).

Constructivism constitutes an element of the philosophical foundation of the emergent paradigm (Kuh, et al. 1987) in which "*the* central aspect is a shift from objects to relationships and story telling supplants classical logic as a way of knowing" (Capra, 1989). The term is somewhat loosely defined and overlaps with the psychological concepts of "connected knowing," (Belenky, et al. 1986), contextual knowing (Baxter-Magolda, 1993) and with the notion that relationships and connection form the core of female moral development (Gilligan, et al. 1990). Constructivism undergirds naturalistic inquiry (Lincoln & Guba, 1985), feminist epistemologies (Alcoff & Potter, 1993), non-hierarchical models of identity formation (Myers, Speight, Highlen, Cox, Reynolds, Adams & Hanley, 1991) and experiential learning (Kolb, 1984).

Constructivist Perspectives on Science and Education

Constructivism reflects a revision of the scientific paradigm which began to appear in physics in the early twentieth century. In the work of Heisenberg, Einstein, Bohr, Bateson & Chew (Capra, 1982) subjectivity became part of the scientific process. A description of the observer and the observation instruments became essential to any presentation or interpretation of data. Heisenberg's uncertainty principle paved the way for an increased emphasis on subjectivity and the interaction of cognitive, affective and interpersonal elements in making meaning and interpreting events.

In his bootstrap theory, Chew proposed that "The universe is seen as a dynamic web of interrelated events. None of the properties of any part of this web is fundamental" (Capra, 1982, p. 93). No part of the "physical" world is necessarily reducible to any other part, or set of fundamental building blocks. In other words, "the basic structures of the material world are determined by the way we look at this world; . . . observed patterns of matter are reflections of patterns of mind" (Capra, 1982, p. 93). Chew and many other physicists have challenged our common sense ideas about physical reality and have demonstrated repeatedly that perspective shapes observation and that human thoughts about events are the determinants of reality, not the other way around. Chew's bootstrap approach to describing the universe, "opens up the unprecedented possibility of being forced to include the study of human consciousness explicitly in future theories of matter" (Capra, 1982, p. 95). More recently, Keller (1985) has discussed the relationships between gender and science and introduced ideas like dynamic autonomy, the notion that even events which appear to be separate actually exist in dynamic relationship to each other, reminding us of Kuh's comment (1993), cited earlier about mutually shaping events.

Developments in early 20th century physics paralleled developments in philosophy. In *Democracy and Education* (1916) John Dewey described an educational philosophy tailored to the needs of the dynamic, growing, multicultural American democracy. His approach would be considered constructivist in modern terminology because he emphasized active learning, the interaction of subject and object and the personal construction of meaning. He urged the teaching of scientific methods of observation and analysis, but also emphasized the role of the individual in making meaning from the data. He described democracy as, "a mode of associated living, of conjoint, communicated experience" (pp. 101-102) which repudiates the principle of external authority and continually searches for areas of common concern around which citizens can evolve responses suited to their best common interest. He observed that, "Education is a constant reorganizing or reconstructing of experience. It has all the time as an immediate end . . . The direct transformation of the quality of experience . . . in order to add meaning to the quality of the experience" (Dewey, 1916, pp. 89-90). John Dewey suggested that an extremely important task of education in a multicultural democracy was the creation of shared meanings among citizens. This approach is a contrast to recent educational philosophies which emphasize the study of a presumably static, historical American culture in order to integrate oneself into it, adopting its dominant perspective as one's own (Bloom, 1987).

Battles between positivists and constructivists have shaped higher education in this century. Taylor (1952) identified three philosophies of education which constantly struggled for dominance, the rationalist, the neo-humanist and the instrumentalist. Rationalist approaches fall into the scientific tradition, instrumentalists into the constructivist framework and neo-humanists somewhere in between. These three philosophies have shaped the struggle over the content and form of general education, a debate which began in the 1930s and has ebbed and flowed inconclusively since then (Crookston, 1973; Katz, 1988). Recent conflicts between constructivism and positivism have framed the debate over political correctness on campus. The positivist approach to the study of literature assumes that the *content* of Western culture can best be understood by studying an agreed upon canon of literary works, generally beginning with Plato, Aristotle and the Bible and proceeding through the works of the great Christian male writers of Europe like Shakespeare, Donne, Rousseau, Voltaire, Dante, Chaucer and so forth. Arriving at modern literature, a smattering of American Jewish and female writers was often included. Constructivist participation in this debate has appeared in many voices: feminism, African American studies, Asian and Latin American studies, gender studies, gay and lesbian studies, African writings and the oral traditions and artifacts of non-literary cultures such as the Inuit, African ethnic/tribal groups and native peoples around the world. Scholars from all of these groups speak from constructivist perspectives because they make the role of the observer and the effect of viewpoint central to their analyses (Simonson & Walker, 1988).

IT'S NOT *JUST* AN ACADEMIC DIFFERENCE OF OPINION

Unfortunately, the debate over the canon has been neither civil nor scholarly in many instances. As Sancho Panza allegedly commented to Don Quixote, "Whether the stone hits the pitcher or the pitcher hits the stone, it's going to be bad for the pitcher." Constructivist approaches make point of view explicit and identify biases and assumptions in the perspective of the observer. Constructivist scholarship often discusses power relationships and power differentials between the observer and the observed as well (Friere, 1985; Friedman, 1991; Giroux & McLaren, 1994; Harding, 1991). Positivist, objectivist approaches make different, and contradictory assumptions. Constructivists can afford, philosophically, to tolerate and even protect the expression of many different perspectives. Even when constructivists are emotionally committed to their own perspective and have difficulty remaining civil to contradictory perspectives, cognitively they believe that multiple interpretations ought to be permitted and cannot be denied the right to exist. Constructivists struggle with the problem of developing criteria for evaluating credibility or truth value (Scott, 1991; Bordo, 1987; Patton, 1990; Ziman, 1978) but they do not believe that one perspective ought to dominate or have hegemony. Constructivism can tolerate positivist objectivism as one perspective but the reverse is not true.

Positivism assumes that the most valid perspective ought to dominate until a better interpretation, which accounts for more data, is articulated. Therefore, the positivist approach cannot logically validate or accept multifaceted constructivist approaches. Whether the stone hits the pitcher or the pitcher hits the stone, it's going to be bad for the pitcher. Positivism doesn't accept the validity of multiple perspectives as a permanent state of affairs, but rather views multiplicity as a transitional phase in progress toward unitary explanations. Constructivists tend to believe that multiple explanations can co-exist and ought to be respected for the complementary understandings they suggest. When they are under pressure to make sense out of a disrespectful and frustrating world constructivists are often accused of dominating or making attempts to impose politically correct views on others. This behavior can be viewed as an instance in which emotional needs for expression and a sense of being listened to overwhelm the capacity for intellectual discourse rather than as aspect of the philosophical approach *per se.* "When the universe becomes unmanageable, human beings became absolutists" (Bordo, 1987, p. 17). In constructivist philosophy as in life, categories are not simple, neat or abstract (Scott, 1991). Differences must be understood, experienced and occasionally resolved in dialogue which involves intellectual, emotional and interpersonal elements along with differences in access to power and other resources. A noted thinker in the field of cultural studies, a field of social, educational and political analysis which is shaped by constructivist philosophy, commented, "We came from a tradition entirely marginal to the centers of English academic life, and our engagement in the questions of cultural change . . . we first reckoned within the dirty outside world" (Hall, 1990, p. 12). When constructivist proponents of cultural studies began their work, they withdrew from the traditional centers of higher education because their marginalization was so profound that they were not taken seriously in academic discourse (Giroux & McLaren, 1994). They refused to use two valued logic, to assume that knowledge was stable or categories permanent. They generated the equivalent of Chew's bootstrap theory for human/cultural studies.

Both / And

Although positivism and constructivism often have difficulty co-existing, both paradigms have utility in understanding the human experience. In the following sections of this work, we will examine culture and its function as paradigm for interpreting human experience from positivist and constructivist perspectives. First, the content of American culture will be examined with special attention to the intersection between the scientific paradigm, monotheism and other elements of Anglo-American culture. Secondly, the processes by which culture changes at its borders will be examined, particularly with reference to interactions between the scientific culture of American universities and the various constructivist cultures of different student groups and the student affairs profession. Finally, we will examine one particular point of intersection of these two cultures—the college classroom which is dominated by faculty trained in the scientific tradition and populated by students who represent many different paradigmatic perspectives but are generally trained to believe in the hegemony of one. The problem is that the modern classroom has come to resemble a Tower of Babel. The Tower was a construction project described in the Bible. Many languages were spoken on the project, but no common language was used for conducting public business or making decisions. Nobody was trained in enough languages or skilled enough in utilizing context to bring about mutual understanding. The project was abandoned.

THE ANGLO-AMERICAN CULTURAL PARADIGM: A POSITIVIST INQUIRY

In keeping with the strengths of the positivist approach, it is useful to examine the components of American history, society and culture which contribute to the Anglo-American cultural paradigm. What general principles govern the typically American perspective on the world? What can be discerned by studying and classifying the data? The major categories to be examined are 1) our monotheistic heritage; 2) our scientific, materialist belief system; 3) our assimilationist ideology and 4) our belief in liberal democracy and the supreme importance of the individual. In addition, our experience of geographic isolation has led us to construct a world view in a relatively isolated setting, unchallenged by other perspectives. These categories, described briefly in a previous chapter, will now be described in more depth, with particular attention paid to the American historical experience.

Monotheistic Heritage

The western hemisphere was "discovered" by Europeans who were searching for gold and the opportunity to spread Christianity (Todorov, 1982). The United States was settled by people searching for personal opportunity and religious freedom. Our national mythology enshrines freedom of religion as one of the most important national values. Our constitution forbids the state to establish or favor any particular religion or denomination. Debates about the propriety of permitting "moments of silence" in schools, providing federal support for services to students in church-related schools or allowing religious groups to use public facilities are on-going in the courts. What is often overlooked, however, is that the founders of this country wanted freedom to practice their own religion in their own way, without interference from others. They did not tolerate atheism. They generally attempted to convert the Native People to Christianity. The only group tolerated, however imperfectly, was the Jews because they allegedly worshipped the same God even though they ignored His Son and the Holy Spirit. Christian denominations founded separate colonies (Maryland, Connecticut, Massachusetts and Rhode Island) in order to establish religious hegemony in their own territory.

The Anglo-European settlers did not value religious diversity in the sense that we use the term today. They considered Christianity the True Faith and all other beliefs were considered the Devil's work (Todorov, 1982). They shared a belief in a Christian God and came from various groups which had historically persecuted or avoided members of other Christian groups, and, in some instances, Jews. They shared a history of monotheism believed in the commandment to "have no other Gods before Me." Although each monotheistic group had slightly different beliefs about the nature of God, how God ought to be served and how humans ought to live under the "fatherhood" of God, they all believed they were right and attempted to convince others to believe the same way they did. The Christian articulation of God evolved from the Jewish articulation of a God who killed His enemies, including other gods and their idols, and then instructed His followers to destroy the holy places of the competing religions (Armstrong, 1993). Although the United States has a public philosophy of religious toleration and supports many interfaith organizations and ecumenical, humanitarian good works, those who believe in Judaism or Christianity are generally trained to believe that their faith is the True Faith and their God, the One God. The Zen saying, "There are many roads up Mt. Fuji (one of Japan's sacred mountains), but the view from the top is the same," is not reflective of monotheism in America.

Scientific Materialism

The second element of the American cultural paradigm is scientific materialism. The scientific component is an amalgam of the positivist objectivism described earlier. Scientists and most Americans interpret data according to pre-existing theoretical frameworks, whether they are implicit or articulated. For example, in the United States, logical reasoning has more credibility than intuition or experiential "ways of knowing," such as exploring dreams for hidden meaning or going on a vision-quest to help make a decision or set a life direction in most contexts. Arguments which are supported by data are more powerful than arguments supported by religious beliefs or value statements. Empirical evidence, be it financial, behavioral, political or geological, typically has more credibility than omens, inspirations or contacts from disembodied spirits. Large amounts of data which support existing theories, belief systems or values have the most credibility of all. Sociologists, political scientists, economists and other interpreters of mass amounts of data are listened to endlessly. They provide us with culturally acceptable truths in culturally credible form.

In 1993-1994, the United States experienced the most costly natural disasters in its history, the floods in the Mississippi basin, Hurricane Andrew in Florida and the Los Angeles/Northridge earthquake. In addition, the Northeast had the coldest, wettest winter in 30 years and Los Angeles experienced the human tragedy of rioting and pillage after the Rodney King decision. Deaths from AIDS climbed steadily and have exceeded the death toll from the Vietnam war. These phenomena bear a profound resemblance to the Biblical Four Horsemen of the Apocalypse whose arrival predicted the end of the world. Scientific explanations abound and are given high visibility in the news media. During earthquakes, hurricanes, blizzards and floods, people are glued to their television sets looking at isobars, fault lines, shoreline erosion and reports of wind speeds and barometric pressure as if they were looking at omens and searching for reassurance. Data comforts us even when it cannot protect or reassure. The Four Horsemen are not mentioned even if they might provide a more cogent sense of how to avoid repeats of these disasters or what may happen to us when they are finished. In the dominant culture, religious explanations tend to have much less credibility than scientific ones when discussing natural disasters. Barbara McClintock, a Nobel laureate geneticist presents an interesting contrast to our national assumptions about interpreting data within pre-existing, unchallenged belief systems. McClintock discovered genetic transposition, the process by which "genetic elements can move, in an apparently uncoordinated way, from one chromosomal site to another" (Keller, 1985, p. 159). Her discovery challenged the dominant Mendellian dogma of genetic theory. Because McClintock was a philosophical and methodological deviant for most of her career, her work is considered marginal and controversial. Rather than search for data which confirm her hypotheses and demonstrate the validity of existing theory, McClintock asserts that nature is much too complex and variable to be forced into singular theoretical interpretations. She tries to "listen to the material." In an interview with Keller, McClintock asserted, "Trying to make everything fit into a set dogma won't work . . . There's no such thing as a central dogma into which everything will fit" (Keller, 1985, p. 162). She warned investigators not to ignore exceptions or aberrations and thus miss important clues to understanding. "The important thing is to develop the capacity to see one kernel (of maize) that is different and make that understandable" (Keller, 1985, p. 163). She tries to imagine the processes by which difference occurs, to understand the process and then to explain it. "Exceptions are not there to prove the rule. They have meaning in and of themselves" (Keller, 1985, p. 163). She challenges the dominance of two valued logic (either/or, subject/object, mind/matter) and the search for unifying principles, preferring to maintain a respect for difference and appreciation of "multiplicity as an end in itself" (Keller, 1985, p. 163). Barbara McClintock's approach to genetics is comparable to cultural psychology. Instead of "thinking through culture" she thinks through corn.

When asked how she finally came to understand the variations in corn kernels, McClintock remarked that she tried to think like a kernel of corn. This remark reflects a constructivist approach, that of a person who enters the situation, engages it from the perspective of the major participants and adopts that perspective in an effort to understand. Constructivists engage a phenomenon, join with it and try to find the appropriate perspective for understanding. Positivists disengage, observe and analyze and try to fit their observations into a theory or to exclude them, using two valued logic on three valued data. Constructivists focus on the "undecided" category of data and evoke its unique processes and meaning. Positivists focus on the "yes" or "no" categories and use preconceived ideas about meaning and relationships to explain what they see.

University administration and faculty also employ these two approaches. People who see others as members of categories and treat them according to their categorical, or stereotypic, descriptions, are operating from a positivist perspective. People who see others as individuals with a variety of attributes, some of which are related to categories of race, ethnicity, gender, sexual orientation, age and so forth, and try to understand the individual needs of the person are operating from a constructivist perspective. Generally speaking, most people can use either perspective and often try to adopt the more appropriate one in any given situation. This is one way of explaining why all bureaucracies have people who are empowered to make exceptions to the rules.

Materialistic Assumptions

Materialism has several complementary meanings in this discussion. The first refers to the hegemony of empirical data over all other types. The second refers to an emphasis on acquiring material goods and evaluating a person's worth by the amount of material he or she accumulates. (Recent bumper sticker, "The boy who dies with the most toys wins.") A wealthy person is generally considered a successful person. In the United States, more is considered better, as evidenced by the rapidly filling garbage dumps. In the absence of material accumulation, having a lot of anything is virtuous, such as having earned many awards, written many books, visited many countries, made many motion pictures and so forth. Value accrues from having things which can be counted and measured. Historically the emphasis on materialism is connected both to the scientific tradition and the mercantile practices which characterized the early period of American history. In addition, Puritans emphasized hard work and believed that idleness or laziness was sinful. These historical threads combined to connect virtue and money in American culture (Eibling, Jackson & Perrone, 1974). Poverty has been associated with blame worthiness. We tend to "blame the victim" when it comes to ascribing character flaws to people on welfare. Evidence that the majority of people on welfare are white and get off welfare in less than two years (*New York Times*, 1994, June 19, p. 4E) does not stop many Americans from complaining about "welfare queens" and assuming that the majority of people on welfare are women of color who abuse drugs and willfully neglect or harm their many children.

A final element of materialism involves the national emphasis on physical appearance as a key indicator of personal worth. The national preoccupation with attractive physical appearance can be easily discerned in a review of advertising in the mass media. "You can't be too thin or too rich," asserts an ad for an expensive wrist watch. The media bombards the public with a stream of advertising designed to change every conceivable aspect of one's physical appearance from teeth to hair to body weight, shape and musculature to eye color. In addition, what cannot be changed can be covered or disguised by a variety of outer and undergarments. The goal of this transformation is to bring the consumer closer to the American ideal of beauty, an ideal which can be observed in almost any magazine on the shelf of the local supermarket, but which is exceedingly difficult to find in a natural human form.

A second manifestation of concern with appearance is preoccupation with race as identified by skin color and physical features. Race as designator of status began before slavery in America. Benjamin Franklin warned the founders to take care of the "lovely whites" and protect them from the Blacks and Tawneys (Takaki, 1993). Earlier, in 1554, Englishman George Best was preoccupied with the skin color of some Africans who had been trained as interpreters for English traders and observed that their skin color seemed to proceed from some natural infection (Takaki, 1993). The United States continues to struggle with its racist heritage as we define and redefine our affirmative action categories, our theories of racial identity formation (Atkinson, Morten & Sue, 1989; Hall, Cross & Freedle, 1972; Hoare, 1991; Smith, 1991) and biracialism (Poston, 1990) and the internal racism in the African American community which also classifies people according to skin color.

Materialism is a significant part of the American cultural paradigm. This is not necessarily a sign of decadence or decay. It means that Americans believe that the most credible evidence for any argument or set of beliefs must be grounded in physical evidence, material things which can be counted, measured and accumulated or replicated. Some humanists, for example, are quite materialistic in that they believe that life begins and ends with the physical body. Nevertheless, organizations such as the American Humanist Association and the Society for Ethical Culture attend to the life of the mind, matters of public morality, compassion and care for the planetary ecosystem through their publications and activities. Some wealthy people use their money for self-indulgence and others for public benefit. Materialism is simply one element in the national belief system. It can be extremely beneficial when it values the provision of income support, food for poor children and access to education. Materialism can become dangerous if it is emphasized to the exclusion of other equally significant aspects of the culture.

Assimilationist Ideology

Assimilationist ideology has been a central part of our national thinking (Gleason, 1992). Our motto is *E Pluribus Unum*. Since our beginnings, we have attempted to bring unity from the diverse groups of people who arrived here as immigrants and to assimilate and deculture the Native People who were here before the Europeans. The earliest settlers in what is now the United States came from England. As soon as Africans began to be imported into the colonies as slaves, race became a defining element in American identity. Race became increasingly more important throughout the 17th century and was embedded in the Constitution when slaves were defined as property, and counted as 3/5 of a human being for census purposes (Takaki, 1993). Difference has always mattered in this country—visible difference as described by skin color and cultural difference as described by variations in emotional expressiveness, time orientation, family orientation, work ethic and emphasis on the relative value of materialism and spirituality. Immigrants whose living patterns most closely approximated those of the English blended in the most easily.

The immigration process of Jews from various parts of Europe illustrates this point. The earliest settlers were generally Spanish Jews who were "close in cultural style" to Protestant Americans (Howe, 1976, p. 51). The Ladinos, as they were called, were quiet, reserved, kept family matters to themselves and presented a courteous, distant facade to others in public. The waves of German Jewish immigration presented a bit of a challenge to assimilation because Germans were seen as a little too loud and pushy, but they practiced a form of Judaism which closely resembled Unitarianism, conducted most of their services in German and dressed like the rest of society. They maintained a strong work ethic and placed a very strong emphasis on secular education and training their children for the professions.

By the time the largest wave of Jewish immigration arrived in the United States, the Germans had assimilated into the dominant society (Birmingham, 1967) and were desperate to avoid attracting attention to their less-educated brothers and sisters who were arriving from Poland, Russia and the rest of Eastern Europe in unprecedented numbers. These immigrants brought their entire families and intended to remain, hoping to create better lives for their children. They came from rural ghettos, were used to living in religious communities and having access only to religious education, were emotionally expressive and were trained in the loud and noisy style used to debate Judaic law. In addition, many of them wore clothing which was unusual in the United States, had very large families and shared a tradition in which the women managed the home and worked to bring in money while the men retired, as young as possible, to a life of study and prayer (Howe, 1976). Their modern counterparts are the Hasidic Jews who live in Crown Heights, Brooklyn and several other self-contained communities in New York. To Americans, the women appeared far more aggressive than the men, and thus were seen as behaving inappropriately in their roles as wives and mothers. The Jewish mother of stage, screen and stereotype was born from this experience. The settlement house movement, along with efforts to improve public education and hygiene in the City of New York during the late 19th and early 20th century, were motivated by the strong need of assimilationist German Jews to Americanize their brethren as quickly as possible. Colorful differences were embarrassing, People who had arrived and assimilated earlier were desperate to avoid a new round of anti-Semitism.

The major waves of immigration among most ethnic groups were motivated by economic necessity, although political and religious factors often played a role. Migrants were admitted and recruited when the United States had unmet labor needs, for building railroads, agricultural work, urban construction, mining and other types of backbreaking labor (Takaki, 1993). German Jewish refugees from Hitler's Reich were generally admitted when and if they could contribute to American war research. Boatloads of religious refugees were turned away, just as boatloads of Haitians and Chinese are currently being rejected because the economy is now burdened by surplus labor. As quickly as possible, refugees have been encouraged to stop speaking their native languages and learn standard, unaccented English, to give their children American first names, to adopt American ways of life and to move into the dominant culture. From the earliest Jewish immigration to the most recent refugees from Southeast Asia, families have been torn apart by their own efforts to move into the American Way of Life, leaving behind the cultural roots which had permitted so many to survive for so long under far less favorable economic and material circumstances. Many hyphenated Americans were raised in and continue to support the melting pot tradition.

Liberal Democracy and Individual Rights

The fourth key element of the American cultural paradigm is our belief in liberal democracy and individual rights (Bellah, Matson, Sullivan, Swidler & Tipton, 1985; 1991; Matsushida, Lawrence, Delgado & Crenshaw, 1993). Liberal democracies are based on two assumptions: 1) The welfare of the individual is of paramount importance and 2) "The relationships between individuals in a community are irreducibly moral relations" (Sabine, 1961, p. 745). Conceptually, there is no conflict between attending to the needs of an individual and maintaining a community because human beings are social beings and therefore cannot exist outside community. Operationally, one major role of government is to balance the needs of any particular individual or group against the needs of the larger community in order to maintain both. The tension is continuous and therefore leads to a corollary, which is the profound reliance of liberal democracies on the value of free speech and the marketplace of ideas as the means by which solutions to all problems can be sought. These democracies also employ constituent assemblies and elected government officials who conduct business in public and are responsible to the voters.

Individual interests have traditionally been considered the most important interests in liberal democracies. The source of morality in these democracies is the assumption that persons are to be treated as ends in themselves. Persons may not be considered means to ends. "A community exists because the people in it do more or less recognize each other as ends or sources of value and therefore as beings having rights, with a moral claim on the obligations that those rights impose" (Sabine, 1961, p. 744) Since liberalism arose as part of the Enlightenment, it also asserts that individuals act rationally, in their enlightened self-interest. This assumption leads to the emphasis, in democratic societies, on education, free access to information and freedom of speech. This belief in behavior based on enlightened self-interest underlies the theory of the free market capitalism and the science of economics which also assume that if "economic man" [sic] operates in his enlightened self-interest, economic markets will prosper. In this century the Republican party and economic conservatives have been the strongest advocates of this position. Although liberalism began as an effort of the developing middle classes to generate a power base for themselves (Sabine, 1961) it has, in modern times served conservative interests very effectively by emphasizing the role and power of the individual and de-emphasizing class, ethnic and other group interests which, in modern society, can easily overwhelm individual interests.

Liberalism differentiates between society and government. Society is pluralistic, filled with many groups which command allegiance from their members and have shared interests that contradict the interests of other groups. Society is disorganized and not structured according to any overarching principles. Government is much more limited. It is organized for the purpose of keeping options open for individuals (Margolis, 1979). deToqueville (1956) was describing American society rather than American democratic government when he called individualism an erroneous judgment which originated from deficiencies of the mind. Individualism causes people to sever themselves from the community and to leave society at large to itself. deTocqueville observed that Americans had the tendency to focus on individualism as the pursuit of self-interest, in a manner that sapped the virtues of public life and ultimately degenerated into selfishness. This tendency has ebbed and flowed throughout our history (Levine, 1980) and has been in a period of ascendancy since the 1970s. "American cultural traditions define personality, achievement and the purpose of human life in ways that leave the individual in glorious, but terrifying isolation," asserts the group which authored Habits of the Heart (Bellah, Matson, Sullivan, Swidler & Tipton, 1985, p. 6).

American belief in the primacy of the individual amplifies the positivist belief in facts without context and the objectivist belief in the observer's separation from events observed. "This ideal of freedom has historically given Americans a respect for individuals . . . sometimes even made them tolerant of differences . . . (but it) leaves Americans with a stubborn fear of acknowledging structures of power and interdependence." (Bellah, Matson, Sullivan, Swidler & Tipton, 1985, p. 25) It also leaves Americans with a naiveté about the effects of culture in shaping perceptions, values and behavior. Americans tend to believe that all choices are individual choices, made with little awareness of history, context or culture.

The American legal system has codified this dimension of our cultural paradigm (Reidy, 1991). Legal conflicts are couched in the language of conflicting rights and resolved by establishing the primacy of one set of rights over the other. Legal discourse is governed by rules of logic and evidence. Issues of hate speech and first amendment rights of free speech are particularly difficult to resolve in this format because context and impact must be reduced to the language of individual rights. Although legal scholars in the critical legal studies movement have attempted to place the law in a broader social, political and historical context, their work has gone largely unnoticed by the American public and remains highly controversial among legal scholars (Bell, 1987; Minow, 1990). The attacks on the work of Lani Guinier (1994), who was briefly a candidate for Director of the Civil Rights division of the Department of Justice, indicate the level of controversy which surrounds such analyses. Efforts to regulate speech on campus as a means of decreasing intergroup conflict have been unsuccessful thus far because of this focus on conflicting rights and the primacy of the individual right to free speech, however widely misunderstood (Dalton, 1993).

In short, our cultural focus on individualism makes the very notion of group-oriented identity difficult for Americans to comprehend. This undermines our ability to see ourselves as members of communities without perceiving our membership as a threat to our freedom. It impedes our ability to understand the effect of cultural groups on the creation of communities, perceive each other as complex cultural beings or recognize that our inevitable conflicts often have origins which are much broader than simple interpersonal dislike (Carter, 1990). The legal structure by which we maintain order reinforces individualism and provides very little support for balanced notions of individual and group responsibility (Etzioni, 1993). The historical emphasis on personal mobility and independence, the scientific training which emphasizes non-contextual data, the materialist focus which differentiates according to appearance and ignores non-material data all interact to produce individuals who see the world through a lens called "I" which is shaped by personal experience and limited to the perspective developed in a single life-time.

Geographic Isolation

The final important element of the American experience is our geographic isolation "from sea to shining sea". The American historical experience has been one of separation from other cultures, domination or extinction of native cultures which antedated the arrival of the Europeans and more recently ignoring subdominant cultures in the United States. Recent efforts to designate English as the official language reflect the desire to suppress an important component of other cultures, particularly Spanish speaking groups along the southern rim of the country. In the eras which preceded widespread and rapid international travel, most Americans remained at home. This relative isolation has strengthened the dominant cultural paradigm since competing paradigms appeared slowly, in small pockets and tended to transform themselves into compatibility with the dominant culture. Competing paradigms or cultural belief systems never achieved sufficient strength to make the American worldview visible by contrast. This national experience of relatively slow assimilation has led to the current perspective which assumes that the "American way," however defined, is "normal" and that all other worldviews, perspectives and behaviors are somehow not normal.

In the current era two circumstances have radically altered our isolation: increased travel and instantaneous international communication. Even Americans who never leave the country can know what's going on almost anywhere in the world through CNN on television or the BBC on National Public Radio. A third circumstance which affects our awareness of the global events is extended visitation or semi-permanent immigration to the United States. Even people who now immigrate to this country can regularly return to their homelands if they can afford it and their relatives can visit them in this country. This makes maintenance of the home culture in the United States possible and creates many new forms of multiculturalism depending on which elements of the dominant culture the immigrants choose to include in their own. In addition, executives of international businesses often live in the United States for several years or live and work in the United States for months at a time. Finally, the United States remains a beacon for students from all over the world, many of whom bring their spouses and children with them and remain here for a year or more, increasing the cultural interaction already underway.

PRINCIPLES OF THE AMERICAN
CULTURAL PARADIGM

After examining this subset of data about American culture, a number of principles emerge:

1. Monotheism, science and assimilationism have at least one element in common. They all support the notion that *there is always a best answer or explanation*, and that it is singular rather than complex. Monotheistic religions believe that their explanation of the universe and man's [sic] place in it is the right one, even when there is a *de facto* history of toleration of other beliefs. They tend to prescribe behavior and belief and, with greater or lesser intensity, demand compliance (Armstrong, 1993). Science looks for unifying principles behind the data and assumes that these principles should be discovered, rather than invented (Minow, 1990). Science emphasizes those characteristics which are shared and results which can be replicated and predicted. It throws out anomalies. The assimilationist approach to immigration and Americanization also focuses on helping immigrants integrate themselves into the dominant culture. We do not accept people as they are when they are different from the dominant image of Americans. We demand that they change themselves as a precondition for acceptance. This approach worked fairly well when citizens had Northern European roots. Since we "tend to draw distinctions . . . on the basis of race, gender and other fixed personal traits" (Minow, 1990, p. 17). It works far less well when citizens don't have the physical characteristics of Northern Europeans or when they believe that they can retain

their mixed ethnic, "hyphenated American" status indefinitely (Cose, 1993; West, 1993).

2. Because of the two valued logic which dominates science and religion, the American cultural paradigm supports *hierarchical thinking*. This means that Americans often have trouble thinking both/and rather than either/or. This thought process causes a dilemma of assuming that if one idea, or experience or thing is good or worthy, its opposite must be bad or worthless. We have trouble promoting high self-esteem without thinking that we are comparing ourselves to others who are less good. If white is good, black must be bad. If logic is good, feelings must be less good. If rich is very good, poor must be terrible. If there is a dominant way to be a good American, anything which challenges the hegemony of the image must be incorrect or bad.

3. Materialism, empiricism or positivist objectivism—whatever term is used to describe the frame of reference—has trained Americans to *trust physical evidence and doubt all other evidence*. Truth values are discovered through examination of physical data, whether they are columns of numbers, piles of things or observable interactions in test tubes or petri dishes. Truth has been equated with the ability to predict and explain events with high levels of certainty and separated from any sense of morality (West, 1993). In our scientific culture, truth is associated with empirical accuracy, and is considered unchangeable, once established. This perspective leads to such commonplaces wisdom as "You can't argue with the bottom line," or "Let the facts speak for themselves," without anybody feeling entitled to challenge the values by which the bottom line was determined or defined.

4. Individualism and a powerful *emphasis on rights as opposed to responsibilities* has left Americans with a strong mistrust of any force which suggests that some aspect of individual freedom or gain should be sacrificed for the common good or to the benefit of the less fortunate, except in times of crisis like war, flood, fire, hurricane, earthquake and other human or natural disaster.

5. Individualism, in combination with materialism and positivism, implies that a *person can do whatever he or she wishes to the environment, physical or human* because that person is an agent acting on an object. This behavior can be permitted to continue

until an equally powerful opposing force stops it. Mutual shaping or reciprocity is not assumed unless accompanied by fairly drastic confrontation. This point of view has been translated into "Freedom to swing your arm ends where my nose begins," or "Looking out for Number #1." This perspective encourages Americans to see themselves as alone, responsible for themselves, acting without regard to or awareness of context or consequences. It is a cause and effect mode of thinking which is linear and exists only in laboratory experiments where all the "confounding data" of human complexity can be controlled. This perspective also contributes to the American tendency to blame the victim for his or her circumstances and to assume that it is within the victim's power to change his or her situation unilaterally. It allows disrespect for individuals, including women and members of many non-Anglo groups, because they define themselves as members of families whose opinions must be taken into account and which are often considered to have the right to tell the individual what to do.

6. Americans also believe, for the most part, that *reality is "out there,"* to be discovered, not "in here," in the mind of the observer, able to be articulated. Reality is singular, exists externally from the observer and has to be accepted once it is discerned. This tends to make Americans quite naive about viewpoint and its role in shaping perception. Many Americans who see the world through the dominant cultural paradigm simply don't realize that culture shapes their point of view even though they are quite aware of their own opinions about specific issues. Listening to a BBC broadcast, or even more to the extreme, a Russian broadcast about events in Somalia, Bosnia or Chechnya would probably be quite confusing because Americans would want to know which broadcaster was telling the truth. Because of all the factors discussed in this chapter, Americans tend to think that they are observing and reacting to a world which exists beyond themselves, whose meaning they have no part in constructing, and which, for the most part, they are powerless to change.

SUMMARY

These six principles—assuming that there is a singular, correct interpretation of events, that logic is two valued, that values are hierarchical, that truth means physical evidence, that freedom means separation, and that reality is out there without regard to viewpoint—can be considered major dimensions of the American cultural paradigm. As with all paradigms, this one shapes a frame of reference, provides a set of ideas through which events can be interpreted and gives guidance to those who believe in it about how to act and feel as well as think. This paradigm has enormous implications for the ability of the United States to create a truly diverse society, one which accepts the existence of multiple perspectives without needing to decide which one is true. It also has implications for the ways we think about and engage in education and the ways in which student affairs professionals relate to other members of campus communities as we conduct our professional lives.

REFERENCES

Alcoff, L. & Potter, E. (Eds.) (1993) *Feminist epistemologies*. New York: Routledge.

Allen, K. & Cherrey, C. (1994) Shifting paradigms and practices in student affairs. In J. Fried (Ed.). *Different voices: Gender and perspective in student affairs administration*. (pp. 1-11) Washington, DC: National Association of Student Personnel Administrators.

Armstrong, K. (1993) *A history of God*. New York: Alfred A. Knopf.

Atkinson, D., Morten, G. & Sue, D. (1989) *Counseling American minorities*. (3rd ed.). Dubuque, IA: William C. Brown.

Barr, M. & Fried, J. (1981) Facts, feelings and academic credit. In J. Fried (Ed.). *Education for student development*. (pp. 87-102). *New Directions in Student Services*. 15. San Francisco: Jossey-Bass.

Baxter-Magolda, M. (1993) *Knowing and reasoning in college*. San Francisco: Jossey-Bass.

Belenky, M., Clinchy, B., Goldberger, N. & Tarule, J. (1986) *Women's ways of knowing*. New York: Basic Books.

Bell, D. (1992) *Faces at the bottom of the well*. New York: Basic Books.

Bellah, R., Madsen, R., Sullivan, W., Swidler, A., & Tipton, S. (1985). *Habits of the heart: Individualism and commitment in American life*. New York: Harper and Row.

Birmingham, S. (1967) *Our crowd*. New York: Harper and Row.

Bloom, A. (1987) *The closing of the American mind*. New York: Simon and Schuster.

Bordo, S. (1987) *The flight to objectivity*. Albany, NY: SUNY Press.

Brislin, R. (1990) *Applied cross-cultural psychology*. Newbury Park, CA: Sage.

Brooks, J. G. & Brooks, M. (1993) *The case for constructivist classrooms.* Alexandria, VA: Association for Supervision and Curriculum Development.

Caple, R. (1987) The change process in developmental theory: A self-organization paradigm, Part 1. *Journal of College Student Personnel. 28.* 4-11.

Capra, F. (1989) *Uncommon wisdom.* New York: Simon & Schuster.

Capra, F. (1982) *The turning point: Science, society and the rising of culture.* New York: Simon and Schuster.

Carter, R. (1990) The relationship between racism and racial identity among white Americans: An exploratory investigation. *Journal of Counseling and Development. 69.* 46-50.

Cheatham, H. & Associates. (1991) *Cultural pluralism on campus.* Alexandria, VA: American College Personnel Association.

Code, L. (1993) Taking subjectivity into account. In L. Alcoff & E. Potter (Eds.). *Feminist epistemologies.* (pp. 15-48). New York: Routledge.

Cose, E. (1993) *The rage of a privileged class.* New York: HarperCollins.

Crookston, B. (1973) Education for human development. In C. Warnath. (Ed.). *New directions for college counselors.* (pp. 47-65). San Francisco: Jossey-Bass.

Dalton, C. (1993) Introductory memo to students in Law, Culture and Difference course. Boston, MA: Northeastern University School of Law.

deTocqueville, A. (1956) *Democracy in America.* R. Heffner (Ed.). New York: Mentor Books.

Dewey, J. (1916) *Democracy and education.* New York: The Macmillan Company.

Eibling, H., Jackson, C. & Perrone, V. (1974). *Two centuries of progress: United States history.* River Forest, IL: Laidlaw Brothers.

Eldridge, N. & Barnett, D. (1991) Counseling gay and lesbian students. In N. Evans & V. Wall (Eds.). *Beyond tolerance: Gays, lesbians and bisexuals on campus.* (pp. 147-178). Alexandria, VA: American College Personnel Association.

Etzioni, A. (1993) *The spirit of community.* New York: Crown.

Friedman, J. (1991) Further notes on the adventures of phallus in blunderland. In L. Nencel & P. Pels (Eds.). *Constructing knowledge.* (pp. 95-113). Newbury Park, CA: Sage.

Friere, P. (1985) *The politics of education.* Westport, CT: Bergin & Garvey.

Frye, M. (1990) The possibility of feminist theory. In D. L. Rhode. *Theoretical perspectives on sexual difference.* (pp. 174-184) Yale University Press.

Gailey, C. (1993) Lecture in Workshop on Multicultural Perspectives in Curriculum Development and Teaching Strategies. Boston, MA: Northeastern University.

Geertz, C. (1983) *Local knowledge.* New York: Basic Books/Harper-Collins.

Gilligan, C., Lyons, N. & Hanmer, T. (1990) *Making connections.* Cambridge, MA: Harvard University Press.

Giroux, H. & McLaren, P. (Eds.). (1994) *Between borders.* New York: Routlege.

Gleason, P. (1992) *Speaking of diversity: language and ethnicity in twentieth century America.* Baltimore: Johns Hopkins Press.

Guinier, L. (1994) *The tyranny of the majority.* New York: The Free Press.

Hall, S. (1990) The emergence of cultural studies and the crisis of the humanities. *October.* 53. 11-23.

Hall, W., Cross, W. & Freedle, R. (1972) Stages in the development of Black awareness. In R. I. Jones (Ed.). *Black Psychology* (pp. 156-165). New York: Harper and Row.

Harding, S, (1991) *Subjectivity, experience and knowledge: An epistemology from/for rainbow coalition politics.* Tenth Annual Fellows Lecture. Washington, DC: Society for the Study of Values in Higher Education.

Hoare, C. (1991) Psychosocial identity development and cultural others. *Journal of Counseling and Development.* 70. 45-53.

Howe, I. (1976) *World of our fathers.* New York: Harcourt, Brace, Jovanovich.

Katz, J. (1988) *A new vitality in general education.* Washington, DC: Association of American Colleges.

Keller, E. (1985) *Reflections on gender and science.* New Haven, CT: Yale University Press.

Kolb, D. (1984) *Experiential learning.* Englewood Cliffs, NJ: Prentice-Hall.

Kuh, G. (Ed.). (1993) *Cultural perspectives in student affairs work.* Lanham, MD: American College Personnel Association.

Kuh, G., Whitt, E. & Shedd, J. (1987) *Student affairs work, 2001: A paradigmatic odyssey.* Alexandria, VA: American College Personnel Association.

Levine, A. (1980) *When dreams and heroes died.* San Francisco: Jossey-Bass.

Lincoln, Y. & Guba, E. (1985) *Naturalistic Inquiry.* Newbury Park, CA: Sage.

Margolis, M. (1979) *Viable democracy.* New York: St. Martins Press.

Matsushida, M., Lawrence, C., Delgado, R. & Crenshaw, K. (1993) *Words that wound.* Boulder, CO: Westview Press.

Minow, M. (1990) *Making all the difference: Inclusion, exclusion and American law.* Ithaca, NY: Cornell University Press.

Noddings, N. (1990) Constructivism in mathematics education. *Journal for Research in Mathematics Education. 4.*

New York Times. Welfare as we've known it. (June 19, 1994) The Week in Review. 4E.

Patton, M. (1990) *Qualitative evaluation and research methods.* Newbury Park, CA: Sage.

Pederson, P. (Ed.). (1991) Multiculturalism as a fourth force in counseling. *Journal of Counseling and Development. 70. (1).*

Perry, W. (1970) *Forms of intellectual and ethical development in the college years.* New York: Holt, Rinehart and Winston.

Poston, C. (1990) The biracial identity development model: A needed addition. *Journal of Counseling and Development. 69.* 152-155.

Reidy, D. (1991, Winter) The law, dominant paradigms and legal education. *University of Kansas Law Review.* XXX. 415-459.

Sabine, G. (1961) *A history of political theory.* ((3rd ed.). New York: Holt, Rinehart and Winston.

Scot, M. (1991) Naturalistic research: Applications for research and professional practice with college students. *Journal of College Student Development. (32)* 416-422.

Shweder, R. (1990) Cultural psychology—what is it? In J. Stigler, R. Shweder & G. Herdt. (Eds.). *Cultural psychology: Essays on comparative human development.* (pp. 1-46). New York: Columbia University Press.

Simonson, R. & Walker, S. (Eds.). (1988) *Multicultural literacy: Opening the American mind.* St. Paul, MN: Greywolf Press.

Smith, E. (1991) Ethnic identity development: Toward the development of a theory within the context of majority/minority status. *Journal of Counseling and Development. 70.* 181-188.

Takaki, R. (1993) *A different mirror.* Boston: Little, Brown and Company.

Taylor, H. (1952) The philosophical foundations of general education. *General Education.* Washington, DC: National Society for the Study of Education. Fifty-first yearbook.

Todorov, T. (1982) *The conquest of America: The question of the other.* (R. Howard, Trans.). New York: Harper & Row.

West, C. (1993) *Race matters.* Boston, MA: Beacon Press.

Ziman, J. (1978) *Reliable knowledge.* London: Cambridge University Press.

4

Borderlands: Fear of The Other and Cultural Differences

From the European perspective, America has always been a country of immigrants. Although there were large numbers of native people in North America when the settler/conquerors arrived, many English immigrants saw them as barely human. They defined, or constructed, their view of the native people as Other, a process which occurs when one group perceives another group to be so different from themselves that the differences become extremely significant. The definers use the defined to draw the boundaries of their own humanity and group membership. In the 16th century, Europeans defined the Other as anyone who was not European and not Christian (McGrane, 1989). The mores and values of the Indians were incomprehensible to the settlers. The native people did not use an intricate monetary system, own personal property or cultivate land individually. They had different and contrasting ideas about family, child rearing, spirituality and learning. They were seen as pagans and were described by the new arrivals as people who lived without faith (Todorov, 1982).

Almost immediately, the English began to construe the native people as a point of contrast to themselves, using their unfamiliarity with native ways as a means of defining that which was uniquely English and civilized. They created a lens through which the native people were seen as totally and permanently Other. Their Otherness was defined from a combination of physical characteristics and observable behavior. Once the category was established, it was assumed to describe a natural distinction between the immigrants and the natives, a phenomenon which the English noticed and described, but did not create. "As exiles

living in the wilderness far from civilization, the English used
their negative images of Indians to delineate the moral requirements they had set up for themselves" (Takaki, 1993, p. 41). As
AngloEuropean Christians, the Puritans saw the non-Christian
native people as incarnations of the Devil. They warned against
the degeneracy of Indian ways, citing their sexual and ritual behavior as examples of Devil worship. They believed that, "Interracial cavorting threatened to fracture a cultural and moral
border, that of Puritan identity. Congress of bodies, white and
'tawny' signified defilement—a frightful boundlessness" (Takaki,
1993, p. 42). This early attitude about cavorting with the Indians
extended to marriages which crossed racial lines and was later
codified in the miscegenation laws of the American south. Trans-
gressions were punished harshly, often without waiting for formal litigation. Billie Holiday's powerful song "Strange Fruit"
refers to one product of mob justice in the American South,
Black men suspected of transgressing some racial boundary, usually sexual, were hung in trees as evidence of what happened to
Black people who didn't stay in their place.

Anthropologists have devoted much effort to understanding
the processes by which a given society constructs the Other (Harrison, 1991a; McGrane, 1989; Diamond, 1974) and attempts to
understand difference. McGrane traces the construction of the
non-European Other through several centuries. Definitions of the
Other changed from the Other as non-Christian (16th century),
to the Other as Ignorant, a person who explains the world in
non-scientific concepts (Enlightenment Era), to the Other as some
one whose world view represents an earlier perspective in time,
a frozen representation of the forces of human evolution (19th
century) to the current explanation of the Other as one whose
culture is different. More recently Other has come to signify "the
negative of the socially affirmed self" (Kovel, 1984, p. XXIX).
Since difference is a comparative term, it implies that there is a
standard from which each culture varies, even if that standard
is as yet undiscovered or unconstructed. For example, the term
Oriental implies East, but the rest of the construction, the location of West, is assumed rather than defined. Feminists in anthropology, literary criticism and philosophy have also been
particularly active in this area (Eisenstein and Jardin, 1980). Harrison describes the study and construction of difference in terms
of feminist scholarship, stating that feminists have gone through
three distinct phases in their attempts to understand the social
construction of "woman" as a category of human experience.

First scholars studied women, then they studied gender and finally they have begun "deconstructing sameness and understanding differences, understanding for example, how race and class shape and divide gender, identity and experience" (Harrison, 1991a, p. 4).

Given their propensity to look at physical phenomena for evidence of a natural and Divine order (Rossi, 1980), the English defined differences between themselves and the Indians as indicative of God's order, differences which could not be overcome by any human effort. Although skin color became the most visible indicator of difference, behavioral differences were also troublesome. "The English possessed tremendous power to define the places and peoples they were conquering. As they made their way westward, they developed an ideology of 'savagery' which was given form and content by the political and economic circumstances" (Takaki, 1993, p. 44). They construed the Indians as subhuman savages, lower in values, aspirations and capacity than the English. As a people struggling to develop a sense of identity which valued the old ways but was set in a new environment, the English colonists established borders between themselves and the native people as a means of confirming a sense of their own community and their own individuality in a new world (Erikson, 1966). They maintained their construction of the Indians as savage Others for pragmatic reasons associated with violence and the unwillingness of the Indians to do what the settlers wanted them to do. These pragmatic reasons were rationalized by the construction of the Other as a child whose values were radically different and therefore could not be trusted to care for their resources properly (Todorov, 1982). This included the Indians' refusal to see the land, the sky, the water and the "two legged, four legged and winged" co-inhabitants of the earth as potential objects for possession, and, more importantly for sale or exploitation.

Since so many of the early immigrant groups intended to establish their own version of the Kingdom of God in North America, they believed that they had a mandate to wipe out oppositional groups if those groups could not be civilized according to their categories and definitions (Todorov, 1982). The settlers often construed their destruction of human life as part of the civilization of the continent, the new Eden. This perspective is replicated frequently in American western films, where the Indians have been represented as untrustworthy savages who rape, murder and start wars to kill the God-fearing white people. Only recently in such films as *Little Big Man* and *Dances with Wolves* and television shows like *Dr. Quinn, Medicine Woman* has the behavior of the white settlers been presented in mass culture from a perspective which is somewhat more balanced. The current portrayals humanize the Indians, acknowledge the harsh sides of the settlers and portray some of the complexity involved in relationships between the two groups. Until the civil rights movements of the 1960s including the American Indian Movement (AIM), the white perspective of American Indians dominated mass culture, leading to enormous emotional damage and physical destruction among the Indian communities in the United States. Recently, economic and cultural changes such as the success of several tribes at prosecuting land claims and the enormously profitable gambling complex run by the Mashantucket Pequots have begun to reverse this 400 year trend.

As North America was settled, or invaded, by Europeans, the assimilation process continued, suppressing differences among immigrant groups and encouraging the development of similarities. People who looked, spoke and acted like the first immigrants had the easiest task of assimilating into American culture. To the degree that people looked different from the English and northern European immigrants and spoke differently than the standard setters, they found and continue to find it more difficult to be considered American regardless of the length of time that they and their families have lived in this country (Takaki, 1993). Race and physical appearance, continue to be an American pre-occupation. The question of "What are you, *really?*" continues to haunt children of biracial marriages (Poston, 1990). Americans continue to create borders and categories based on physical appearance and behavioral characteristics and then use those categories to decide who's in and who's out.

CULTURAL PLURALISM AND MULTIPLE BORDERS

To this point, culture has been defined as an ethnic phenomenon with common language, place of residence, religion, values, behavior patterns, ideals and/or other cognitive categories as central characteristics. A broader definition of culture follows:

> an understanding that a people have of their universe—social, physical or both—as well as their understanding of their behavior in that universe. The cultural model of a population serves its members as a guide in their interpretation of events and el-

ements within their universe; it also serves as a guide to their expectations and actions in that universe or environment. (Ogbu, 1990, p. 523)

This definition describes the human construction of self in a particular context, the human and the physical environment. Ogbu describes how cultures tend to produce "folk theories" of how the world works, based on the collective historical experience of the group. These theories develop in the context of those elements which a group has in common and tend to evolve with the social experience of the group. Patricia Turner, a folklorist, has written about the role that rumors play in African American communities commenting that even when rumors have no basis in fact, they are particularly tenacious because "something about them rings true . . . they pique something in the imagination that people are concerned about (and) they serve as tools of resistance for the people who share them" (Macmillan, 1994, p. A6).

Using Ogbu's description of culture, cultural groups can emerge from particular collective experiences in specific times and places and do not necessarily involve a common ethnic experience. This definition includes the "gay, lesbian and bisexual" culture (which often refers to itself as BiLaGa) which has been shaped by a common understanding of themselves as outsiders in the heterosexual world, and common experiences of exclusion, harassment, invisibility and other forms of victimization. The culture continues to evolve in response to events in public life such as the national debate over domestic partnership as a legitimate form of commitment comparable to marriage and the AIDS crisis and evolving social and medical responses to it. Other groups which can been considered as cultures in this definition include deaf and hearing impaired people, homeless people, survivors of domestic, particularly sexual, abuse members of age cohorts (Howe & Strauss, 1993; Strauss & Howe, 1991) as well as males and females. The student affairs profession also shares some elements of a culture in terms of this definition, because of its chronic outsider status in the academy (Lloyd-Jones, 1938; Kuh, 1993), its set of identifiable values (Young & Elfrink, 1991), the traditions and rites associated with national organizations and professional preparation programs, and its recognition of the borders between itself and other cultures on the campus (Barr & Fried, 1981; Kuh 1993).

It is clear from this expanded definition of culture that all people are members of multiple cultures and that the folk theories and explanations of a particular culture may be more or less salient for each person depending on the situation in which the person finds herself at a specific time and place. For example an African American female engineer might find her gender to be most salient at a job site, her profession most salient at a social event with her husband and her race most salient at a workshop for recruiting "minorities" into the construction industry. The salience of each set of cultural perspectives and characteristics affects how a person will perceive, interpret and behave in a situation. That experience may permit the person to contribute to the changing stream of information and interpretation which constitutes the evolving folk theories of the group. If ten Black women engineers are treated with respect and taken seriously at a national meeting, the folk wisdom related to their status and value in the profession may begin to change, thus changing the experience for the next cohort. Is it possible to separate Anita Hill, the Yale alumna and attorney from Anita Hill, the African American government employee or Anita Hill, the daughter of hard working, impoverished southern farmers who raised a large family, sent many of them to college and raised them all in the Christian faith? Who was Anita Hill when she testified in the Clarence Thomas confirmation hearings? Which culture was salient for her? For the diverse audience who watched her on national television?

Ogbu's definition of culture permits us to move beyond ethnicity and race and to investigate culture as a created and very fluid phenomenon which affects all Americans including all people involved in student affairs and higher education. Each of us is a member of a particular work culture and various professional cultures which shape our understanding of the worlds in which we live and work and serve as guides to behavior as we attempt to make our way successfully in these intentional worlds (Shweder, 1990). Every time a member of a student affairs staff serves on a committee which also includes faculty members, academic administrators and/or students, that student affairs professional brings cultural assumptions with him or her to the meeting and guides his or her behavior accordingly as the committee conducts its business. Some of these assumptions coincide with those of others on the committee and some contradict the assumptions that others make. The student affairs staff member probably assumes that student welfare should take precedence in any decisions. The faculty member may well assume that departmental status or curricular priorities are most important. Students have very different ideas of what they might need for their own welfare. These ideas are shaped not only by student status, but also by gender, ethnicity, race, sexual orientation, disability status and age, to name a few key factors.

POWER AS AN ELEMENT OF CULTURE

Many cultural critics and commentators add an additional factor into the discussion of culture, that of differences in power between groups (Nieto, 1994; Harrison, 1991a; Giroux, 1994). Power can be defined as the ability to advance one's goals and achieve one's ends in a particular social, political, economic or cultural context. The group that has the most power heavily influences or determines definitions of value, truth, good, justice and other elements of morality, affecting social relationships in situations where they have hegemony. This is true whether the situation involves relatively few people, such as a church group or a social club or millions of people, such as a nation. The values which dominate culture in the United States have been discussed previously. Groups which support other value systems have a great deal of difficulty getting equal time and equal respect for their beliefs in the world outside their own group. "Class, gender, racial and ethnic differences cannot be reduced to 'cultural diversity,' especially when the latter is a smoke screen behind which power disparities and economic polarization lie unaddressed or inadequately treated" (Harrison, 1991a, p. 3). Harrison calls the emphasis on cultural diversity, separate from any awareness of power differentials, "a notion of cultural critique that is largely limited to giving privileged Americans the benefits of cross-cultural knowledge" (Harrison, 1991a, p. 5). Painfully, her description of cultural diversity seems to mirror the vast majority of those efforts at diversity training or education which are conducted on American campuses. Extending her insight into our committee meeting, we must ask ourselves which culture prevails as we define or attempt to understand the problems of the modern college or university? Whose definitions of value and truth prevail when a college begins to create a University 101 Freshman Seminar? What kind of knowledge deserves credit? What kind of teaching and learning are considered academically legitimate? Who is entitled to teach? Cultural differences impact all of these decisions. Which cultural values dominate?

As discussed earlier, the power to define those elements of

our common American culture has been largely held by descendants of the Anglo-European settler/conquerors whose perspective is shaped by hierarchical thinking, scientific, materialistic truth values, heterosexual norms and an emphasis on individual autonomy. This perspective is also characterized by a belief that there are universal truths to be discovered which can provide accurate information about classes of data, including groups of people. When power to dominate operates by defining knowledge and truth, validating some aspects of human experience and devaluing or ignoring others, it constitutes an extremely subtle and malignant form of oppression, because it undermines people's confidence in their own ability to make sense of their world(s) (Friere, 1994). This hegemony of meaning can and does lead to self-hatred, lack of self-confidence, resentment and hostility within groups and between the non-dominant and the dominant group. People who are defined as Other within the dominant culture become relatively powerless.

Take for example, the powerful American belief in the capacity of the individual to rise above oppressive conditions like poverty, inadequate education or discrimination. If an individual who is a member of an non-dominant group in this culture, perhaps an impoverished Mexican-American farm worker who has had little formal schooling and inadequate nutrition for most of his life, takes this belief in decontextualized individual achievement as the standard for human worth, he would be very likely to fall into despair and blame himself for not getting out of poverty. He would internalize the idea of blaming himself for his circumstances. If that same person comes to understand how group oppression operates, the difficulty of trying to improve one's economic situation in a capitalist society without economic support, the sacrifices one often is expected to make in leaving family to "make your own fortune" in the world, that person can develop a very different view of his situation and a very different idea about choice and self-worth.

Another example can be found among gay and lesbian people who cannot reconcile the wonderful experience of falling in love with the dominant social interpretation of the meaning of that particular type of love, i.e., that it is unacceptable, abnormal and despicable (Obear, 1991) and the fairly widespread belief that people can overcome those "abnormal" impulses if they try hard enough. The abnormally high rate of suicide among gay teenagers is but one example of the consequences of internalized self-hatred derived from believing the dominant view of normal sexual behavior and feeling. A final example of this type of distorted thinking has occurred extensively among adolescents of color in the nation's inner cities. Accepting the virtues of the "culture of consumption" (West, 1993, p. 16), many choose to sell drugs and commit crimes in order to achieve financial status in their communities and often to support their families as well. What standard of individual achievement exceeds that of accumulating wealth in this culture? What destruction and poverty of spirit has this standard wrought? Might poverty be construed as one sign of Otherness in American culture?

Americans have historically been resistant to thinking about power differences between groups, particularly class differences, because American belief in the power of the de-contextualized individual to achieve anything he or she wants is so strong in the national mythology (Bellah, Madsen, Sullivan, Tipton & Swidler, 1985). Americans in the dominant culture seem to have a vested interest in blaming dominated people for their condition, rather than looking at the context in which their oppression exists. Two valued logic also contributes to this construction of the problem. Rather than viewing an individual in context, able to affect some aspects of his or her life and not able to affect others, many Americans tend to see "individuality" and "autonomy" as operating to the exclusion of contextual effects. This phenomenon is powerfully demonstrated in *A Class Divided* (Woodruff, 1970) a film depicting a classroom experiment conducted in an Iowa elementary school in the 1960s and since replicated in many training programs. In response to the racial violence which erupted after the shooting of Martin Luther King, a third grade teacher divided her class into two groups, according to eye color. One day the blue-eyed group wore identification collars and were treated as if they weren't as bright, worthwhile or acceptable as the brown-eyed group. The second day the process was reversed and the blue-eyed students were the privileged group. Within a single school day, the oppressed group in the experiment began to lose confidence in itself, to do less well on standard spelling drills, to demonstrate hostile behavior toward the dominating group and to isolate themselves from the others in fear. When the collars were switched, the behavior reversed itself. In the commentary following, the teacher described how a group of healthy, active and intelligent third graders turned into terrorizers and terrorized less than an hour after being put into a context of oppression. If this process occurs so quickly among a group of children who are friends, there is much to be learned about the power of context and group perception for all of us.

PERSPECTIVE, UNDERSTANDING
AND POWER RELATIONSHIPS

A person's perspective about events and their meaning is profoundly affected by the cultural groups to which that person belongs, the one(s) which is/are salient in relation to the specific events and the power of the salient group in relation to the dominant group in terms of establishing definitions, categories, meanings and truth values. This approach to understanding culture, meaning and hegemony reconfigures our understanding of the importance of perspective in any interpretation of human events. It makes claims to universal truth and objectivity not only misleading and inaccurate, but disrespectful and possibly dangerous (Harding, 1993a; Code, 1993). Describing the claim of universality as "the God trick," Harding (1993b, p. 57) asserts that objectivity is an illusion which is part of the scientific American belief system. Even relative fairness or impartiality cannot be achieved unless the perceiver/definer makes his or her standpoint, and thus his or her biases in perception clear, a process she describes as "the emerging logic of multiple subjects " (Harding, 1993a, p. 2). Phenomena which were formerly believed to have objective existence, independent of human observation must now be considered as

> a relation rather than a thing or an inherent property of people. Race, gender, ethnicity and sexuality do not designate any fixed set of qualities or properties of individuals, social or biological, such that, if one possesses these and only these properties then one is a man, African American and so forth. Instead, masculinity is continuously defined and redefined as 'not femininity,' 'colored,' 'not white' and so forth (Harding, 1993a, p. 2).

Thus, a complex understanding of human phenomena involves awareness of one's own standpoint and its biases, awareness of the events described and awareness of the interactions between them. Contributing to one's perspective and interpretation are the cultural lenses through which events are observed and the power differentials between the various cultures and perspectives which interact in the particular situation.

Even a person's understanding of who he or she is in a particular situation can change as events unfold. A dominating student leader, perhaps a pledge master in a fraternity, may be harassing to pledges, submissive to the chapter president and deferent but non-compliant with the IFC advisor who is a woman and a member of the student affairs staff on campus. If the pledge master is sent to an IFC meeting to discuss rush, advocates for his group's position on some subject and is unable to defend the group's position successfully, how is he likely to be seen by his brothers, the other members of IFC and the advisor? Every observer's perspective on the pledge master's personality and the events at the meeting is likely to be affected by the group perspective which is salient in the situation and the power relationships among the groups. Did he sell out to the administration? Was he a victim of historical resentment among fraternal groups? Efforts to determine what "really" happened at the meeting are likely to prove fruitless. If the same set of events, as defined behaviorally, occurred in the Pan Hellenic sorority council, or if the fraternity council involved only white fraternities and a separate council existed for historically black fraternities, the events themselves and their interpretations by multiple subjects would be expressed somewhat differently, according to different values and power relationships which were salient among the women's groups or the African American groups. As Harding once again observes

> for Europeans knowledge seeking is a process of first separating the observer (self) from what is to be known and then categorizing or measuring it in an impartial, disinterested, dispassionate manner. In contrast, Africans know reality predominantly through the interaction of affect and symbolic imagery . . . (which) requires inference from or reasoning about evidence . . . (but) refuses to regard as value free what is known or as impartial, disinterested or dispassionate, either the knower or the process of coming to know (Harding, 1987, p. 302).

Harding also observes that there is a curious coincidence between women's values, as she understands them, and African values. Her description of the values women tend to hold has been supported elsewhere in the literature, particularly in the writings of Gilligan (1982; 1990) and the group which wrote *Women's Ways of Knowing* (Belenky, et al. 1986). One clear area of similarity between African and women's values is in the strong emphasis on relationships and the creation of shared meaning. Thus there are at least two different perspectives operating in this situation about how to describe and define events, how to interpret the behavior of the pledge master and all the others involved and whether or not to conclude that a fair decision was reached. If group perspectives or relative power of groups in relation to each other changed, both outcome and interpretation would also change. The final question becomes who has the right and the power to define the situation and describe it to the community at large? Whose perspective dominates meaning making in this situation? A more poignant and painful example of this type of problem is that of initiation practices used by some historically Black fraternities. What does the symbolism of the chain and the brand mean to young African American men? What does it mean to white students? What does it mean to university administrators? The meaning of these two symbols is very powerful. They are both related to the historical experience of African slavery in the United States. Whose meaning dominates?

BORDER CROSSINGS AND BIFOCAL PERSPECTIVES

It is now apparent that all people, and certainly all Americans, are members of multiple cultural groups, and that perspectives which are shaped by group membership may be operative and conflicting in any specific situation. Therefore border crossings are both intrapersonal processes in which any person might engage as context changes and interpersonal processes which occur when members of one group have to do common business with members of another group. Border crossings involve changes in understandings of events, in self-perception and in power relationships. They are frightening, de-centering and fascinating. They operate differently for members of the dominant culture than they do for members of all other cultures.

Intrapersonal Borders

Intrapersonal borders emerge when people move from one setting to another and a new aspect of their cultural background becomes salient. People from working class backgrounds cross a border when they attend college or begin to work in a profession. The norm in working class families is to think about work as hourly wages. Work is what you do to earn money. Work is done either well or poorly, but is rarely considered an intrinsic motivator. Work is a means to an end. On the other hand, work among professionals carries intrinsic motivations, implies a service ethic, relevance to social values and shared culture and assumes continuous, creative thinking about means by which the quality of one's professional work can be improved (Carpenter, 1991).

When race is the salient issue, as it often is in discussions of cultural diversity, Anglo-Americans must move across an intrapersonal border from viewing white as the normal experience of humanity to viewing black as another normal experience of humanity. White people must begin to transcend cultural stereotypes about race, as well as their internalized racism, their fear of The Other, as constructed around race. "Identity is always a temporary and unstable effect of difference" (Grossberg, 1994, p. 13). Given the racist heritage of the United States, when a white person seriously attempts to experience a black person as fully human, and, to the degree that humanity shares common characteristics, similar to him or her, that white person must reshape his or her identity and de-emphasize race as a key component. In a culture which prizes individuality this can be an extremely frightening experience. Changing the relative importance of a significant element of one's individuality has the potential to cause disintegration among the other, less important elements. Other cultural differences are also important, with or without the element of skin color as a contributing factor. It is often difficult for Americans to get beyond their discomfort with non-Anglo physical characteristics, differently accented English, different priorities around family relationships, different levels of emotional expressiveness and voice volume, religious practice and so forth. In the United States, race seems to dominate as the defining factor, but many significant differences evoke images of The Other, the person whose humanity is different from Anglo-American humanity.

The practice of border pedagogy has arisen as an approach to helping people make intrapersonal border crossings. Grossberg and others teach by showing students how to "examine their own conditions of existence" (Grossberg, 1994, p. 13) by stepping outside their own cultural conditioning and examining how their ideas about themselves and others have been created by the culture—in the media, the arts, religion, schooling and so forth. These cultural critics and teachers use an approach called

"interpretive rationality", a process by which students are asked
to examine how various differences come to be defined in a society, which differences are acknowledged and which are ignored. Within the framework of the problematic approach, the
meaning of events, the questions asked and the questions which
remain unasked become the subjects of the discussion and inquiry (Giroux, 1981). Interaction between content and process,
knowing facts and creating meaning is explored. For example, a
discussion might address question of race, class, appearance,
sexual orientation and so forth: Why has race become such an
important point of difference and whom does this construction
of difference serve? Why is physical appearance, particularly
weight, so important and whom does this construction serve? Do
differences based on family income matter? Are they emphasized? Differences in sexual orientation, in religion and so forth
are equally compelling and frightening (Giroux, 1981). A significant purpose of border pedagogy is to help people learn where
borders have been established, explore the forces that established
them, how each person is defined by a range of borders which
may be invisible to him or her and whether or not people feel
comfortable and competent with the borders that define them.
The exercise in the paragraphs below is an exercise in discovering borders.

✳   ✳   ✳   ✳   ✳

Read this exercise as a pause during which you take time to
think about your own ideas, attitudes and opinions about Otherness.

*Think of yourself as a person of another culture. If you are white,
try thinking of yourself as African American; if you are African American think of yourself as a member of an Asian culture or as a white
American; if you are heterosexual, think of yourself and homosexual or
bisexual and vice-versa. Try to make an inventory of your feelings,
your thoughts, what you might gain from the change and what you
might lose. Continue this exercise over the next several weeks and keep
a journal of your reactions. Place yourself in situations where people
of another culture constitute the majority and pay careful attention to
your reactions. Pay attention to your non-dominant status. Try to
empathize with the feelings of students of color on predominantly white
campuses. Go to an African American church, a mass conducted in
Spanish, a Buddhist temple or an orthodox Jewish synagogue. Attend
events conducted by African American, Asian-American or Latino or*

predominantly white student groups. Talk to your friends about their lives as members of their particular culture in the United States. If you don't have friends in other cultural groups, ask yourself why? Pay attention to your feelings as you think about initiating such a conversation. Read Race *(Terkel, 1992),* Race Matters *(West, 1993),* Typical American, *(Jen, 1991) or* Pigs in Heaven *(Kingsolver, 1993) or the poetry of Audre Lord, a Black lesbian who speaks of the experience of multiple oppressions in the language of feeling and imagery. Try to understand and experience what you can about being a member of a non-dominant culture in America. Contrast that experience to being a member of the dominant culture. You may be a person of many cultures, giving you a great deal of insight into cultural interactions in the larger American society. As you begin to see yourself and your race as constructions of this culture, you have begun your own border crossings.*

*   *   *   *   *

The exercise in the paragraph above is an exercise in discovering borders. The process of border crossing itself pushes many Americans over another border. Suddenly "reality" is experienced as a construction which varies with perspective and perceiver, not a "thing" external to the individual, which is there to be discovered. This border crossing goes from positivist empiricism to subjectivist constructivism, a border crossing of enormous significance which will be discussed in the next chapter.

Border Crossings from Anthropology to Psychology

Border crossings have been described in the language of intellectual and moral development (Baxter-Magolda, 1992; King and Kitchener, 1994) as progress which students make when they learn to infer meaning from context and organize data to support values and perspectives. When King and Kitchener discuss reflective judgment and wisdom, they are describing the elements of intellectual and moral development which permit people to manage the "unavoidable, difficult problems that are inherent in adult life, "problems that do not have clear-cut solutions, where people need the ability to "recognize the uncertainty of knowing and [possess] the ability to find shared meaning that allows a wise judgment" (1994, p. 219). In that process, students learn the skills to untangle facts from meanings, and realize on an emotional as well as an intellectual level, that all reality is not "out there." When students realize that construction of reality is a process in which they engage daily, they become capable of crossing, creating, moving or eradicating borders. They are able to differentiate between a range of perceived skin tones and the social construction of race and Otherness. Having visited their internal borders, they can "go beyond the empty pluralism that always racializes the Other, but never makes whiteness visible" (Giroux, 1994, p. 41). Border pedagogy "decenters as it remaps" (Aronowitz & Giroux, 1991, p. 119), breaking down the dominant narratives by which reality has been constructed and often accepted unquestioningly by students, faculty and administrators in higher education, just as it has been widely accepted by most Americans, particularly those who benefit.

The process of decentering and remapping which Aronowitz and Giroux (1991) discuss is internally frightening and disorienting. If identity is constructed in relation to a particular social reality, when the map of that reality changes and is seen as a human construction, identity can be distorted or reshaped, possibly to the point of disintegration. Who am I if I don't know who I am in relation to my environment, my friends, my goals and so forth? If my ideas about the permanence of Truth have been so disrupted that Truth may not be stable or may not start with a capital "T", how do I know what knowledge to trust? Perry (1970) described the process of moving from a belief in an external Authority that supplies standards, to the crisis induced by a perception of no objective, external standards to the realization that one chooses one's standards and then makes commitments to live by one's choices. Perry's work on intellectual and ethical development described the border crossings of Harvard students in the 1960s and has become a classic work for student development educators. Progress along Perry's scheme of intellectual development allows people to become aware of perspective, to look within for the assumptions which shape perspective and to loosen their hold on the search for absolute Truth. Higher levels of intellectual development as described by Perry permit intellectual understanding of "the logic of multiple subjects" (Harding, 1993, p. 2), and enable people to imagine the borders which can be crossed if they have the courage.

The process by which people create their identity changes as they move through the various developmental stages. Drum (1980) divides this process into three stages, basic, expansive and refined. At the basic levels, students ask Who am I? Initially this is experienced as Who do the adults in my life expect me to be? or Who am I supposed to be? The expansive stage transmutes the questions to Who do I happen to be? in the middle stages of the process. In the refined stage the questions are Who do I want or choose to be? or Who might I become? As individuals move through this process, they tend to experience their locus of control shifting from external to internal and to feel as if they have more power in their lives. Researchers continue to investigate the connections between intellectual development (Baxter-Magolda, 1992), reflective judgment and moral judgment (Kitchener & King, 1994), as well as relationships, morality and sense of self (Gilligan, Lyons & Hanmer, 1990). Although each of these areas of inquiry describes different aspects of human thinking and feeling, it is clear that all of them address the process by which a person conceives of him or herself in context and how those ideas about self-in-context change as context changes. Advanced levels of development permit a person to take different types of information into account and develop viable criteria by which that information can be judged for utility, truth value and moral guidance in a given situation. In other words, the more well-developed a person's ability to think through complex, unstructured problems, the more capable that person will be of making border crossings because he or she has the tools with which to understand what is happening.

The process of making the initial border crossing, from naive positivism to constructivism, from belief in Authority as given to Authority as constructed and changing, is different for members of the dominant cultural group in the United States than it is for all other groups. Members of all other groups have to cross borders constantly. They do not have the luxury of believing that one standard fits all situations. Members of the dominant group have this luxury because they are far less likely to need to adapt in foreign "territory" to survive. Students of color who succeed on predominantly white campuses do so by learning appropriate behavior for the setting—how to act in class, how to respond on tests, how to study, what to study, how to behave in public, how to make friends with white students and so forth. To the degree that their upbringing has been shaped by different standards and expectations than that of their white peers, they know that the way they act at school is learned behavior designed to bring them success in that environment. When gay and lesbian students don't talk about their personal lives or pretend that they have intimates of the opposite sex, they know where the border is and when they have crossed it. When women leaders learn to talk about men's sports or cars, they have crossed a border into a world of white male culture and they know it. When student affairs professionals meet faculty members and discuss student development in both theory and practice, they are opening doors for faculty from other disciplines to cross into the cultural arena of student affairs. When they discuss the scholarship of the faculty member, they have crossed the border in the other direction. When they talk about parking lots or complain about student behavior, both are wandering in a demilitarized zone and may not know where the border is, much less how to cross it.

All non-dominant groups must know where the borders are because moving into the territory of the dominant group defines them as Other and subjects them to the likelihood of cultural erasure at best, disrespect or violence at worst. Members of the dominant group can remain oblivious to borders because their version of reality, value and truth dominates wherever they are. They represent the hegemonic belief system even when they don't constitute the numerical majority. Through their domination of the major sources of ideological indoctrination in this country, the press, the church, the schools, the arts and so forth, they validate their perspective and ignore or devalue others (Giroux, 1981). This phenomenon is operative when an all white department can't find a "qualified" member of an affirmative action group to hire because they can't differentiate between professional qualifications and personal discomfort with difference (Sagaria, 1988). It occurs when members of a positivist, behavioral psychology department won't hire a new faculty member whose expertise is in qualitative research on human subjects because they believe her scholarship isn't sufficiently rigorous. It occurs when members of a departmental curriculum committee refuse to consider awarding academic credit for a freshman seminar or a resident assistant course because there is too much experiential learning involved in the program even though the syllabus meets departmental criteria for acceptance. The faculty members who represent the scientific objectivist paradigm which dominates most American universities generally do not need to rethink their epistemological standards because they retain the power to set the standards. Their perspective dominates and it assumes that one perspective, presumably the one which leads to the "best" explanations of events, is the one that should dominate. Multiplicity of perspectives, or the logic of multiple subjects is not part of the value system. The existence of "multiple and frequently contradictory knowings" (Harding, 1993, p. 5), is at best a state of confusion which, according to scientific perspective, will one day disappear when more of the facts are known.

Crossing Borders and Border Conflicts

Existentially, intrapersonal border crossings may be more difficult than interpersonal ones, but they are less visible and generally less physically violent. Interpersonal and intercultural border crossings are the ones we see daily on campus as we wonder why the Puerto Rican students only eat with other Puerto Ricans, why Taiwanese students always hang out together or marvel at how multicultural basketball teams seem to be. The phenomenon of white students hanging out with other white students never seems to command the same level of attention.

Two issues make intergroup border crossings extremely problematic in the United States. First, America lacks an ideology of legitimate difference associated with group membership. Americans do not have a language to discuss differences between groups in non-hierarchical ways. We are too enmeshed in hierarchical judgments of worth, in emphasis on individual autonomy, too wedded to our historical ideology of the melting pot to teach our young people how to converse about group related differences honestly (Mohanty, 1994). We often treat our differences as family secrets. As with all family secrets, that which is not discussed becomes a matter of shame, a matter of pretending that the situation does not exist, a matter of confusion and dishonesty (Terkel, 1992). The various theories of racial and gay, lesbian and bisexual identity formation reflect this problem as they correlate an individual's progress toward a positive sense of self with affirming or non-judgmental acceptance of difference (Cross, 1978; D'Augelli, 1991; McEwan, Roper, Bryant & Langa, 1990; Poston, 1990; Troiden, 1989). Within the various cultures created by students of color, there are numerous subdivisions based on non-racial categories such as national origin, class, date of family migration, primary language and so forth which have typically been ignored in discussions of student culture. The racial lens is the easiest, most familiar one for Americans of the dominant culture to use in working with these students. However, the lens distorts perception and leads to isolation of some groups from the mainstream of campus life because of the perception that they are all being lumped together and not treated with respect of understanding. How can we expect our students to understand each other's cultural differences if they don't have the language and the confidence to discuss the issue, if there is no extensive public discourse about the content of the many different cultures which must coexist in the country? If we restrict these conversations to the various cultural celebratory months and weeks, members of the groups who are celebrated remain exotic Others. They are never seen by the dominant group as Americans who are college students, similar in many ways to themselves, people who are complete human beings entitled to act on their world, reflect on its problems and transform it as they wish (Friere, 1990). Cultural difference becomes entertainment rather than relationship—not a situation which is conducive to deepening intersubjectivity (Giroux, 1981) or mutual understanding.

This cultural taboo against discussing difference is slowly beginning to erode. Cracks have appeared in popular culture The film "White Men Can't Jump" introduced the phrase, "It's a Black thing" to white audiences. Finally the mass media admitted that there was such a thing as a black thing. How many cultural "things" do we need to talk about, particularly the not-too-pleasant cultural things such as the portrayal of rigid family restrictions and family ghosts in *The Joy Luck Club* (Tan, 1989), or the depiction of the violence and arrogance of some Hasidic Jews in *Sotah* (Regan, 1993) or the often irresponsible and abusive behavior of black men in *Waiting to Exhale* (McMillan, 1992). Novels such as these three provide an invaluable service to the dominant culture in American society by showing their perspective on their own culture and giving all their readers permission to talk about what they don't understand. Film is a more powerful medium than literature in our culture. John Singletary's *Boyz in the Hood*, shows living conditions in South Central Los Angeles, hope and hopelessness, unavoidable violence, senseless death and the never-ending sound of the police helicopters. The comparison between South Central and an occupied war zone is unavoidable. The drone pervades the viewer's awareness. South Central is not suburbia. If we are all citizens with equal rights and opportunities, then something is terribly wrong in our society. The inability of the larger society to discuss real differences between groups as a precondition to discussing our common life as Americans is reflected in our students' inability to carry on the conversation as well. When students can't talk about difference, particularly irritating differences, they either ignore them or fight about them (Carter, 1990).

The second issue flows from the first. Most differences between groups involve power differences, which are a crucial part of cultural differences. A complete understanding of culture must include "antagonistic lived experiences" (Giroux, 1981, p. 27) within particular historical and social settings. These experiences involve the efforts of different cultural groups to make sense of their lives within the situation where cultures co-exist and imply continual struggles to make power relations equitable among groups. Under the best of circumstances, groups strive for balance and equity. Under the worst, each strives for domination. Conflicts emerge when different groups command different levels of resources in the environment and some are thereby disadvantaged, materially, emotionally or in any other area. For example, disadvantage can occur when groups need differential levels or types of academic help, when they perceive that the environment ignores their social/cultural needs, when they are exposed to overt harassment or a when patterns of unequal opportunity exist. Disadvantage can also occur when a group attempts to identify an unmet need and that need is not perceived as significant by the people in power, the people whose perspective defines "reality." These people often say, "We know you need or want X (or that X would be desirable) but the *bottom line* is, we can't afford it." The values under which financial decisions are made are thus buried beneath the unquestioned value of the "bottom line." Opportunities to question the means by which the bottom line is created are rare because these opportunities would expose the value system on which the institution is managed and the perspective of the managers as a perspective rather than the truth or reality.

When exposed, power differences can easily provoke conflict. In any given situation, the group with the greater power has the ability to define normal vs. deviant, acceptable vs. unacceptable, what's worth spending money on and what's not.

> The central issue, then, is not one of merely *acknowledging* difference; rather the more difficult question concerns the kind of difference that is acknowledged and engaged. Difference seen as benign variation (diversity) for instance, rather than as conflict, struggle or the threat of disruption, bypasses power as well as history to suggest a harmonious, *empty* pluralism [emphasis supplied] (Mohanty, 1994, p. 146).

The majority of diversity education programs on American campuses seem to treat difference as empty pluralism, as if there were no history to the differences. The history of difference in the United States is long and painful. Failure to acknowledge this denies the context from which it continues to arise. It also contributes to the inability of many Americans to perceive the consequences of these problems or feel responsible for addressing them. For example, *most African Americans came here as prisoners; Large numbers of Japanese-Americans were interned in concentration camps during World War II; Many Catholics believed that Jews were responsible for the killing of Christ until the Pope recently instructed Catholics to give up this belief; The white power structures in the Northeast and the Southeast permitted great violence to occur during attempts at integration; Many Korean-Americans today are frightened for the safety of their families every time there is some sort of tension in dozens of ethnic ghettos all over the United States; The income levels of African American college graduates are still lower than white American high school graduates; There are more Black men between the ages of 18 and 25 in prison than in college; The college graduation rate for Puerto Ricans and American Indians is a fragment of the rate for white Americans; Domestic violence, particularly by men against women continues; Arab-Americans are increasing targets of violence.* These are problems of cultural difference. They are group problems related to group perspectives, not individual difficulties.

Americans seem particularly unwilling to discuss differences in power between groups. "The ideal of freedom has historically given Americans respect for individuals . . . but it is an ideal of freedom that leaves Americans with a stubborn fear of acknowledging structures of power and interdependence in a technologically complex society dominated by giant corporations and an increasingly powerful state" (Bellah, et al. 1985, p. 25). America lacks a history of class struggle with the exception of early labor union conflicts. Our history has been one of economic opportunity for so many people for so long, that our belief in the unlimited potential of the individual to succeed economically has never been seriously challenged (Giroux, 1981).

Discussions of inequalities among groups in a democracy are problematic. They carry the assumption that if one talks about them, to be fair, one becomes obligated to do something about them. In the area of human rights, after many years of conflict in the streets and the courts, power differentials which cause unfairness for individuals have been adjudicated in large numbers. Affirmative action, OSHA legislation, voting rights, tenant rights, judgments about discriminatory dress codes and hair styles and equal access to many single sex educational institutions are all examples of efforts to redress historic differences in power which have disadvantaged certain groups. However, there has been relatively little specific legislation or litigation which addresses group issues that spring from historical injustice. Two notable exceptions are the increasing ability of Indians to win land rights claims and the reparations which Congress voted for survivors of the Japanese prison campus who had all their property confiscated during World War II. To admit that some groups have more power than other groups in the United States would be to deny the national mythology of equal opportunity for all, autonomy for the individual, the irrelevance of history in shaping the life experience and limiting or expanding the opportunities of members of one group or another. This admission would decenter the American cultural map and shine spotlights on the borders.

Discussing power differences between groups would almost certainly provoke conflict as well. In a system which pretends to equality, power differences ought to be temporary and subject to elimination. In a system of majority rule, whoever is in the minority simply cannot have equal opportunity to affect national or local policy. de Tocqueville (1956) called this the tyranny of the majority. Lani Guinier (1994) called it unfair and suggested means to eliminate permanent disenfranchisement of some groups. She was denounced in Congress and in the press as a quota queen, a term which suggested similarity with welfare queen, even though her writing never discussed quotas, but requested equalization of opportunity. In a student programming board which uses majority rule, the chances of a non-dominant group getting enough money to stage a major event is often quite small, not necessarily because of malevolence, but because of competition for limited resources and the need to provide programming which is acceptable for the greatest number, the hegemonic group. The complaint is often heard that if people of color, or gays and lesbians, want money for programming, they should get people on the programming board and get the votes. The problem is that these groups may never constitute a majority—even though collectively they can become a powerful force in campus politics. How do we remediate historical inequalities using the principal of majority rule, when the majority generally does not give up its privileges voluntarily?

There are numerous examples of intergroup differences which can easily lead to conflict and are therefore often suppressed.

When cultural groups want to form campus organizations such as an African American Business Students Association or an Asian-American Psychology Club, a women's center or a social service organization for gay, lesbian and bisexual students, these efforts often provoke controversy. This is a particularly acute problem in residence arrangements where students from similar backgrounds want to live together. When members of non-dominant groups attempt to focus on their own needs and create their own environments, they cannot exclude members of other groups *de jure*. They are often perceived as excluding those people *de facto*. From the perspective of the dominant group, this is accurate. Why would a white person want to live in an Afrocentric residence hall? The discomfort, insecurity and social isolation could easily be acute. From another perspective, why might a member of a non-dominant group want relief from living in a residence hall occupied by predominantly white students? They might be subjected to questions about their personal grooming, their dress, their dietary preferences or their home country from people who they do not consider close friends. They might be exposed to uncomfortable levels of noise, the presence of members of the opposite sex or the use and behavioral consequences of alcohol or illegal drugs. The question is not simply one of separatism or discrimination, but one of focusing on the perspective from which the "problem" is viewed in the first place.

Standpoint epistemology (Harding, 1993), the practice of labeling one's point of view, could be extremely helpful in this situation. Standpoint can be illuminated by asking questions such as: What messages does the conflict bring to the administrator? Whose interests does the current situation serve? Whose interests might be disrupted if the situation were framed differently or circumstances changed? Who will face the most discomfort if the students get what they ask for? Harding, talks about the need for men to try "to see themselves as they appear from the perspective of women's lives" (1993, p. 4), thus illuminating their own contrasting standpoint and realizing that efforts to understand a situation inevitably involve "multiple and frequently contradictory knowings" (1993, p. 5). People who are accustomed to looking for a unitary truth will undoubtedly feel quite uncomfortable with this approach.

A recent discussion of the problems faced by a white professor of African American history is illustrative. Students objected to having a white woman teach African American history, despite her extensive academic credentials. The African American students and staff at the university organized a sit-in in her class to protest. "In my own case, the administrative response evolved through three phases: at first, administrators tried to make the controversy go away as quickly as possible; then they tried to keep a lid on it by reacting in an *ad hoc* fashion to whatever the Black Student Alliance did; finally, they followed university rules and procedures. It is the last response that offers any administration the greatest chance of successfully charting a course through controversy" (Pope, 1994, B2). The author discusses the students' concerns, her own isolation, the failure of the administration to support her or inform her of her rights in the situation and so forth. She has a reasonable understanding of her students' anger and frustration, their non-dominant position on campus and their sensitivity to exclusion and stereotyping. However, she clearly highlights the failure of will showed by administrators in finding any productive means by which to create dialogue in an effort to address the issues raised by the students and subsequently by the professor. When power to suppress didn't work, they resorted to legalistic means which worked better but didn't necessarily increase understanding.

Arthur Levine, in an address to the American College Personnel Association (1994), reported the results of a survey conducted with 300 college presidents in the United States. When asked to identify the major issues facing their own campuses, the majority named cultural diversity as a very important issue. When asked to define diversity, their responses were confused and confusing, according to Levine. When asked what they wanted to do about the problem, they informed him that they wanted it to go away.

Border Blockades

Why don't we have more successful, spontaneous border crossings? Border crossings generally involve confusion, shifting power relationships, and a vague inability by most participants to understand how to achieve their goals and feel competent in the situation. When border crossings are complicated by fear of The Other, a belief that the dominant way is the normal way and other ways are not, it is difficult to care about the other group's interests and needs as much as you care about your own.

Some difficulties are directly related to the age or life circumstances of students. Students are still faced with the developmental dilemmas of learning to manage their emotions and develop competence (Chickering & Reisser, 1993). Our understanding of the scope of these emotions has changed significantly in the past

25 years. In addition to learning to manage sex and aggression (Chickering, 1969), they now must face and manage increasing pressure in the form of fear, anxiety, depression, anger, guilt and shame. Students' lives have become much more complex because of societal changes, economic changes, the increased age range they represent and the increased family responsibilities which many bring to college with them. When students are attempting to manage large debt burdens, the expenses of daily life, crowded classes and an insecure job future, they probably don't have a lot of energy left to seek out uncomfortable situations in their "spare time" on campus or to make friends with strangers whose behavior makes them uncomfortable and who represent the competition for jobs during and after college (Howe & Strauss, 1993). Under these stress-filled circumstances, if students have time to make friends on campus, they will probably seek out people who are very similar to them and with whom they feel comfortable.

Administrators don't seem to encourage meaningful border crossings. In fact, such crossings are often ignored or suppressed when they occur as Pope's experience illustrated. They can be disruptive and embarrassing to the institution or the department. They can force administrators to rethink business as usual or to see an issue from another perspective. Border crossings highlight the differences between student and institutional perspectives and challenge the status quo. Legalistic responses to disruption are often ineffective as demonstrated by the continuing inability of campuses to write speech codes which simultaneously protect freedom of speech and preserve an individual's right to be free from harassment (Fried, 1994). Conflict filled border crossings are very labor intensive to manage and the outcome of negotiations is never guaranteed. Safety zones must be established at the borders if these crossings are to occur.

CONCLUSION

Honest border crossings in which one group of people who see the world from a particular perspective attempt to understand and negotiate with another group of people might reorder the foundations of higher education, and that would be very disruptive for everybody involved. People with more power would be obligated to see the world from the perspective of people with less power and to step outside their perspective of benevolent authority. Angry people would have to step outside their anger and try to understand the fear that their anger engenders in others. White Americans would have to consider the benefits of whiteness and the implications of real affirmative action, experiencing the losses and the gains. Faculty members would have to make efforts to understand students' lives and learning processes, splitting their focus between subject matter and relationships with their students. Many of them would have to reconsider their ideas about academic rigor and legitimate learning.

Student affairs administrators would have to give up their perceptions of problem students as Other, people who somehow need to be controlled in order to avoid professional embarrassment. They would have to develop relationships with students which manifest both caring and control in a mutually respectful way (Noddings, 1988). They would have to cross the border from fear to courage and compassion when dealing with angry students and be willing to examine the system for procedures which might be unfair to groups. Simultaneously, they would have to attempt to understand the university from the perspective of many other groups who have equally strong vested interests in community welfare and the teaching/learning enterprise, but who behave differently and make decisions from different perspectives because they have different roles in the institution. Student affairs professionals would have to develop a new idea of their profession committed to border crossings in all directions. This is a move beyond "cultural diversity" to the creation of a civil community in which conflict is acknowledged and addressed, in which differences are respected even in the absence of agreement and students, faculty and administrators share power in pursuit of common goals. This is frightening to contemplate. This is border pedagogy (Aronowitz & Giroux, 1991) and learning how to do it is essential to the re-creation of higher education for citizens of our democracy in the next century.

REFERENCES

Aronowitz, S. & Giroux, H. *Postmodern education.* Minneapolis, MN. University of Minnesota Press.

Barr, M. & Fried, J. (1981) Facts, feelings and academic credit. In J. Fried (Ed.). *Education for student development.* (pp. 87-102). *New Directions for Student Services. 15.* San Francisco: Jossey-Bass.

Baxter-Magolda, M. (1992) *Knowing and Reasoning in College.* San Francisco: Jossey-Bass.

Belenky, M., Clinchy, B., Goldberger, N. & Tarule, J. (1986) *Women's ways of knowing.* New York: Basic Books, Inc.

Bellah, R., Madsen, W., Sullivan, W., Swidler, A. & Tipton, S. (1985) *Habits of the heart.* Berkeley, CA: University of California Press.

Carpenter, D. S. (1991) Student affairs profession: A developmental perspective. In T. Miller, R. Winston and Assoc. (Eds.). *Administration and leadership in student affairs.* (pp. 253-279). Muncie, IN: Accelerated Development, Inc.

Carter, R. (1990) The relationship between racism and racial identity among white Americans: An exploratory investigation. *Journal of Counseling and Development. 69.* 46-50.

Chickering, A. & Reisser, L. (1993) *Education and identity.* (2nd ed.) San Francisco: Jossey-Bass Publishers.

Chickering, A. (1969) *Education and identity.* San Francisco: Jossey-Bass.

Code, L. (1993) Taking subjectivity into account. In L. Alcoff & E. Potter (Eds.) *Feminist epistemologies.* (pp. 15-48). New York: Routledge.

Cross, W. Jr. (1978) The Thomas and Cross models of psychological Negrescence. *The Journal of Black Psychology. 5.* 13-31.

D'Augelli, A. (1991) Gay men in college: Identity processes and adaptations. *The Journal of College Student Development. 32.* 140-146.

de Tocqueville, A. (1956) (R. Hefner, Ed.) *Democracy in America.* New York: Mentor Books.

Diamond, S. (1974) *In search of the primitive.* New Brunswick, NJ: Transaction Books.

Drum, D. (1980) Understanding student development. In W. Morrill and J. Hurst. (Eds.). *Dimensions of intervention for student development.* (pp. 14-38). New York: John Wiley and Sons.

Eisenstein, H. & Jardin, A. (Eds.). (1980) *The future of difference.* New Brunswick, NJ: Rutgers University Press.

Erikson, K. (1966) *Wayward Puritans: A study in the sociology of deviance.* New York: Wiley.

Fried, J. (Ed.). (1994) *Different voices: Gender and perspective in student affairs.* Washington, DC: National Association of Student Personnel Administrators.

Friere, P. (1994) Remarks made at Northeastern University, Boston, MA.

Friere, P. (1990) *Pedagogy of the oppressed.* New York: Continuum.

Gilligan, C. (1982) *In a different voice.* Cambridge, MA: Harvard University Press.

Gilligan, C., Lyons, N. & Hanmer, T. (1990) *Making connections.* Cambridge, MA: Harvard University Press.

Giroux, H. (1994) Living dangerously: Identity politics and the new cultural racism. In H. Giroux & P. McLaren. *Between Borders.* (pp. 29-55). New York: Routledge.

Giroux, H. (1981) *Ideology, culture and the process of schooling.* Philadelphia: Temple University Press.

Grossberg, L. (1994) Bringin' it all back home: Pedagogy and cultural studies. In H. Giroux & P. McLaren (Eds.). *Between borders*. (pp. 1-28). New York: Routledge.

Guinier, L. (1994). *The tyranny of the majority.* New York: The Free Press.

Harding, S. (1993a) Subjectivity, experience and knowledge: An epistemology from/for rainbow coalition politics. Washington, DC: Society for Values in Higher Education.

Harding, S. (1993b) Rethinking standpoint epistemology. In L. Alcoff & E. Potter. (Eds). *Feminist Epistemologies.* (pp. 49-82) New York: Routledge.

Harding, S. (1987) The curious coincidence of feminine and African moralities. In E. Kittay & D. Meyers. (Eds.) *Women and moral theory.* (pp. 296-315). Totowa, NJ: Rowman and Littlefield.

Harrison, F. (Ed.). (1991a) *Decolonizing Anthropology.* Washington, DC: Association of Black Anthropologists.

Harrison, F. (1991b) Anthropology as an agent of transformation. In F. Harrison (Ed.) *Decolonizing Anthropology.* Washington, DC: Association of Black Anthropologists.

Howe, N. & Strauss, W. (1993) *13th gen.* New York: Vintage Books.

Jen, G. (1991) *Typical American.* Boston, MA: Houghton-Mifflin.

King, P. & Kitchener, K. (1994) *Developing Reflective Judgment.* San Francisco: Jossey-Bass.

Kingsolver, B. (1993) *Pigs in heaven.* New York: HarperCollins.

Kovel, J. (1984) *White racism: A psychohistory.* New York: Columbia University Press.

Kuh, G. (Ed.) (1993) *Cultural perspectives in student affairs work.* Lanham, MD: American College Personnel Association.

Levine, A. (March, 1994) Learning environments. Keynote Speech, presented at the annual convention of the American College Personnel Association. Indianapolis, IN.

Lloyd-Jones, E. (1938) *A student personnel program for higher education.* New York: McGraw Hill.

McMillin, L. (1994, March 24) The power of rumor. *The Chronicle of Higher Education.* pp. 6, 7, 15.

McMillan, T. (1993) *Waiting to exhale.* New York: G. K. Hall & Company.

McEwan, M., Roper, L., Bryant, D. & Langa, M. (1990) Incorporating the development of African-American students into psychosocial theories of student development. *The Journal of College Student Development. 31.* 429-436.

McGrane, B. (1989) *Beyond Anthropology.* New York: Columbia University Press.

Mohanty, C. (1994) On race and voice: Challenges for liberal education in the 1990s. In H. Giroux & P. McLaren (Eds.). *Between Borders.* (pp. 145-166). New York: Routledge.

Nieto, S. (1994) Moving beyond tolerance in multicultural education. *Multicultural Education. 1* (4). 9-12.

Noddings, N. (1988) An ethic of caring and its implications for instructional arrangements. *American Journal of Education. 96.* 215-230.

Obear, K. (1991) Homophobia. In N. Evans and V. Wall. *Beyond tolerance.* (pp. 39-68). Alexandria, VA: American College Personnel Association.

Ogbu, J. (1990) Cultural model, identity and literacy. In J. Stigler, R. Shweder and G. Herdt (Eds.). *Cultural psychology.* (pp. 520-541). New York: Cambridge University Press.

Perry, W. (1970) *Forms of intellectual and ethical development in the college years.* New York: Holt, Rinehart and Winston.

Pope, C. (1994, March 30) The challenges posed by radical Afrocentrism. *The Chronicle of Higher Education.* B1-B3.

Poston, W. S. (1990) The biracial identity development model: A needed addition. *Journal of Counseling and Development. 69.* 152-155.

Ragen, N. (1992) *Sotah.* New York: Crown.

Rossi, I. (Ed.). (1980) *People in Culture.* New York: J. F. Bergin Publishers.

Sagaria, M. (1988) Administrative mobility and gender. Journal *of Higher Education. 59.* 305-326.

Shweder, R. (1990) Cultural psychology—what is it? In J. Stigler, R. Shweder & G. Herdt. *Cultural psychology: Essays on comparative human development.* (pp. 1-46). New York: Columbia University Press.

Strauss, W. & Howe, N. (1991) *Generations.* New York: William Morrow and Co.

Takaki, R. (1993) *A different mirror.* Boston: Little, Brown and Company.

Tan, A. (1989) *The joy luck club.* New York: Putnam Publishing Group.

Terkel, S. (1992) *Race.* New York: Doubleday.

Troiden, R. (1989) The formation of homosexual identities. *Journal of Homosexuality. 17.* 43-74.

West, C. (1993) *Prophetic thought in postmodern times.* Monroe, ME: Common Courage Press.

Woodruff, J. (1970) *A class divided: Frontline.* Boston: Corporation for Public Broadcasting.

Young, R. & Elfrink, V. (1991) Values education in student affairs graduate programs. *Journal of College Student Development. 32.* 109-115.

5

Border Pedagogy: Reshaping Our Ideas of Teaching and Learning

Note: *There are more italicized sections in this chapter than there have been in previous chapters. The purpose of these sections is to engage the reader in the process of examining the ideas presented for both conceptual and personal meaning. As the discussion moves more deeply into constructivist and experiential education it becomes important for readers to consider these ideas in personal as well as theoretical context. The italicized sections represent an opportunity for the reader to do so.*

STUDENT AFFAIRS WORK AS TEACHING AND LEARNING

If a tree falls in the forest and no one hears it, does it make a sound? This is an old and well-discussed question in philosophy. If a person teaches and no one learns, has teaching occurred? Teaching can be defined as "causing people to learn" (Kuethe, 1968, p. 2) but it is often associated with the activities of people who are considered teachers without regard to outcomes in learning. "I taught it to them, but they didn't learn," is a sentence which makes logical sense, even if the assumptions it suggests about teaching and learning can be challenged. Conversely, learning often occurs without teaching or a designated teacher. Children learn to walk when they have the coordination, strength and imagination to stand up and move. Often they have help. They may also walk on their own and be discovered in the act. People learn all kinds of skills and information from experience, reading, vicarious experience and observation.

Although the student affairs literature does not contain a broad discussion of teaching, it is filled with discussions of

97

learning, emphasizing the conditions under which learning is likely to occur, rather than the activities of teachers. In 1934, Esther Lloyd-Jones described the evolving profession of student personnel work as

> the systematic bringing to bear on the individual student all those influences, of whatever nature, which will stimulate him [sic] and assist him, through his own efforts to develop in body, mind and character to the limit of his individual capacities for growth, helping him to apply his powers so developed most effectively to the work of the world. (Saddlemire & Rentz [Eds.], 1986, p. 21)

Shortly afterward, W. H. Cowley defined the student personnel perspective as

> a philosophy of education which puts emphasis upon the individual student and his [sic] all-round development as a person rather than his intellectual training alone and which promotes the establishment in educational institutions of curricular programs, methods of instruction and extra instructional media to achieve such emphasis. (Saddlemire & Rentz [Eds.], 1986, p. 69)

Cowley observed that his definition had two parts, the underlying emphasis and the approaches and techniques through which the emphasis, or point of view, was expressed (Saddlemire and Rentz, [Eds.], 1986, p. 69). Both Cowley and Lloyd-Jones believed that the student personnel profession needed to articulate and promulgate its philosophy of education as part of its efforts to make itself understood in the broader higher education community. The *Student Personnel Point of View,* published in 1937, incorporated a phenomenological perspective which asserted that each student ought to be understood in his [sic] uniqueness (Schetlin, 1968) and that the purpose of the student personnel profession was to help each student "vitalize" his education, making it personally meaningful as well as academically credible.

The first official definition of the student personnel profession was published by the American Council on Education. The SPPV asserted that

> One of the basic purposes of higher education is the preservation, transmission, and enrichment of the important elements of

culture—the product of scholarship, research, creative imagination and human experience. It is the task of colleges and universities so to vitalize this and other educational purposes as to assist the student in developing to the limits of his potentialities and making his contribution to the betterment of society.

This philosophy imposes upon educational institutions the obligation to consider the whole student—his intellectual capacity and achievement, his emotional make-up, his physical condition, his social relationships, his vocational aptitudes and skills, his oral and religious values, his economic resources, his aesthetic appreciations. It puts emphasis, in brief, upon the development of the student as a person rather than upon his intellectual training alone. (Saddlemire & Rentz [Eds], 1968, p. 76)

Both the Cowley statement and the *SPPV* share two assumptions, that philosophy and application are two aspects of the same phenomena and that the student should be considered holistically, learning in many contexts and aspects of personal life.

In the 1970s the holistic approach to education and learning was reaffirmed by Crookston who emphasized the need to understand the dual focus of philosophy and implementation in education. He suggested that *student development*, as a position title, should be a used to describe concepts, philosophies, underlying theories and methodologies associated with the profession (1986). The goal of student development education is to "move the student toward fulfillment as a realized person and an effective contributing citizen of the community and the world" (1973, p. 56). Crookston also used the phrase "education for human development" which he defined as, "the creation of a human learning environment within which individuals, teacher and social systems interact and utilize developmental tasks for personal growth and social betterment" (1973, p. 57).

Crookston, Cowley and Lloyd-Jones shared a common perspective on the learning process. They emphasized an holistic approach in which intellectual learning could not be separated from experiential learning and which, under ideal circumstances always involved a dynamic interaction between action and reflection. All of them also expressed concern over the schism in higher education which divided intellectual from experiential learning, and the evolving profession of student personnel from the rest of the educational enterprise. Finally, all of them saw the student in context, as a member of a college community, a circle of friends, a family and a democratic society. Education, from their perspective, worked most best when it gave the student the skills and knowledge to function effectively in all these contexts. Crookston asserted that "The relationship between the individual and society should be symbiotic, that is, mutually growth producing" (1973, p. 57). His goal was to help students develop *affective rationality*, the ability to "recognize feelings and translate them into rational action" (1973, p. 59).

PHILOSOPHIES THAT SHAPE
TEACHING AND LEARNING

Ideas about learning and credibility of knowledge are shaped and influenced by a branch of philosophy known as epistemology. Epistemology is the logical analysis of knowledge (Scheffler, 1965), the means by which we decide what can be known and what knowledge is reliable (Ziman, 1978). Rationalism, empiricism and pragmatism are three schools of epistemological thought. Rationalism and empiricism have dominated American higher education. Pragmatism has always occupied a secondary place in the credibility hierarchy. Lloyd-Jones, Cowley and Crookston based their ideas on a pragmatist approach and relied on the work of John Dewey, the eminent American pragmatist, for much of their philosophy. A brief description of the other two approaches follows as a point of comparison to the dominant epistemological view in student affairs.

Rationalists hypothesize the existence of self-evident truths and derive their beliefs about reliable knowledge from these basic principles, using deductive logic. The model for this approach is mathematics. The standard approach for proving theorems in Euclidean geometry is an example of rationalist thinking. Empiricists use science as their model. Reliable knowledge is based on observations of data. The data are ordered and arranged into categories from which general principles about the data sets are derived. The goal of empirical epistemology is to generate principles which yield reliable predictions over the widest possible field of data. Much social science research is based on empiricist epistemology. Most of what we officially know about students is generated through this type of research. Pragmatism emphasizes the experimental character of empirical science and elevates the role of the mind as the "active capacity for generating ideas whose function is to resolve the problems posed to an organism by its environment" (Scheffler, 1965, p. 5). Empiricists view the mind as a *tabula rasa* on which sense data are impressed. The mind organizes the data, but empiricists assume that the logic of organization is more or less embedded in the data and that the accurate observer records the implicit organization.

Pragmatists emphasize the role of the mind as highly active in the creation of patterns and the description of problems. Action research and formative evaluation are processes built on pragmatist epistemology. Pragmatism also involves active experimentation or problem solving in a human rather than laboratory context. People are assumed to interact with data for purposes of discovering how to solve problems and discern truth. "The idea of Truth is not a stagnant property . . . Truth *happens* to an idea. It *becomes* true; it is *made* true by events. Its verity *is* in fact an event, a process: the process namely of veri-fying itself—its veri-*fication*" (James, 1910, p. 210).

John Dewey is the most well known American pragmatist, a highly respected philosopher who spent a great deal of his career examining the relationship between educational philosophy, educational psychology and the need to prepare students to become effective citizens of our democracy. Dewey asserted that "Education is a constant reorganizing or reconstructing of experience. . . . (whose) purpose is to add to the meaning of that experience (and) increase the ability to direct the course of subsequent experience" (1916, p. 89). Dewey emphasized the interaction between people and their environment, describing the processes by which people transformed the environment as they learned about it, thus expanding their ability to learn. "The educational process is a continuous process of growth, having as its aim at every stage an added capacity of growth" (Dewey, 1916, p. 63). He believed that the purpose of education was to develop dispositions or patterns of behavior in which the individual was to acquire knowledge firsthand, reflect on its uses and consider its long-term implications (Frankena, 1965, p. 144) Dewey described this reflective disposition as character, which he defined as "an abiding identification of impulse with thought, in which impulse provides the drive while thought supplied the consecutiveness, patience and persistence, leading to a unified course of conduct" (Dewey, 1960, p. 36).

Deweyan pragmatism discounts the rationalist tradition, incorporates the empiricist tradition and emphatically adds the role of the experimenter as the person who shapes knowledge, uses knowledge and creates meaning. "An ounce of experience is better than a ton of theory because it is only in experience that any theory has vital and verifiable significance" (Dewey, 1916, p. 169). In this Dewey sounds remarkably like many student affairs practitioners who are quite impatient with "pure" theory and are constantly seeking ways to apply theory to problems in order to increase their understanding of situations and solve problems. Dewey refuses to be trapped in either/or thinking as it applies to the relationship between theory and experience. "Experience is primarily an active/passive affair; it is not primarily cognitive . . . The measure of the value of an experience lives in the perception of the relationships or continuities to which it leads up. It includes cognition in the degree in which it is cumulative or amounts to something or has meaning (p. 164) . . . The separation of 'mind' from direct occupation with things throws emphasis on things at the expense of relations or connections" (p. 167). Dewey's pragmatism is a process oriented approach to learning in which life becomes the laboratory and every thinking person a scientist. Truth is a function of the interaction between the person who knows and that which is known. Truth is directly related to the context in which it is discerned and is modifiable as context, value and meaning change via the person who discerns. Dewey's language antedates the modern constructivism which asserts that, "Knowledge comes neither from the subject nor the object, but the unity of the two" (Brooks & Brooks, 1993, p. 5).

Dewey prefigures many of the major developments in science, philosophy, education and management which have occurred in the last half of our century. His constructivist approach parallels theoretical developments in physics (Capra, 1989; Capra, 1982), feminist and Afrocentric philosophy (Alcoff & Potter, 1993; Myers, 1993) and cultural approaches to teaching, learning and educational administration (Friere, 1985; Friere, 1990; Giroux, 1981; Giroux & McLaren, 1994; Maxcy, 1994)). The changes in these disciplines reflect a number of common themes. They all focus on context and process. They assume interaction of observer and observed (Capra, 1989). They assume that scientific objectivity is a goal which can be approximated, but never fully achieved. Constructivists in all these disciplines assume that objectivity is based on the inaccurate assumption that one observer's perspective can be generalized to reflect a universal point of view. Constructivists prefer to describe their own perspective and discuss how their perspective shapes their perceptions, a process which Harding calls strong objectivity (1993). Constructivists tend to have political or social agendas for their disciplines. Rather than assume the facade of neutrality, they prefer to make their values explicit.

Constructivists in education emphasize the role which education plays in transmitting social values and serving the needs of the dominant economic groups. In the dominant approach the goal of education is to prepare technically skilled but politically naive workers who provide a labor force which contributes to economic productivity without challenging the system by which profits are distributed (Giroux, 1981). In 1916 Dewey expressed his objection to any type of vocational education which did not prepare workers to exercise their own ingenuity and initiative. He wanted industrial work to involve democratic processes and workers to be involved in key decisions. In current language, Dewey wanted vocational education and work conditions to empower workers (Westbrook, 1991). The process Dewey described has emerged during the past fifteen or so years under the labels of total quality management, profit sharing, downsizing, principled leadership (Covey, 1989), working smarter not harder and the learning organization (Senge, 1990).

FRAGMENTATION OF KNOWING AND LEARNING

Since Dewey's era the divisions between philosophy, science, education and management have become more distinct. Much of the separation between disciplines is directly connected to empiricism as it has shaped scientific research in this century. The social sciences have attempted to discover sharp, clear categories by which human behavior can be understood and predicted, minimizing the amount of data which does not fit into the established categories of analysis. Many philosophers have adopted a scientific stance in regard to the development of knowledge and alleged that knowledge itself is discovered rather than constructed and is therefore value neutral (Ziman, 1978). The epistemological assumptions embedded in the scientific approach have become the paradigm which shapes the understanding of modern Americans about reliable knowledge. This is particularly true among people who work at universities and have been trained in empirical research methodology. Dewey would probably be horrified at this narrow definition. It appears that the only officially reliable knowledge in our universities is that which has been derived from empiricist assumptions, using scientific methods of inquiry even though, "The phenomenon of scientism and parascientism arises as people attribute powers of social, moral and behavioral sensibility to a body of knowledge whose domain of validity is really limited to a much narrower range" (Ziman, 1978, p. 183). In other words, scientific methods are valuable for investigating problems in science, but not necessarily in other domains of life—and there are domains of life which are not scientific, namely those grounded in intuitive, affective and spiritual domains.

From a student affairs perspective, this means that knowledge derived from personal experience or intuition from conversations with individual students and work with groups of students, has little to no legitimacy when discussing what to do about problems or how to develop new approaches to teaching and learning. This knowledge is derived interpersonally rather than impersonally and would be considered valid within naturalistic research paradigms, but not in empiricist paradigms (Baxter-Magolda, 1992). This knowledge is considered anecdotal, not true across all classes of data or too particular to be useful. In attempting to use knowledge derived from personal and professional experience, the problem is not that other colleagues refuse to grant veracity to what we know. The problem is that they discount what we know because this knowledge is based on the truth values of pragmatism rather than the truth values of empiricism. The knowledge is not contradicted. It is devalued. It is not considered reliable or generalizable.

In describing naturalistic or "new paradigm" research, Scott (1991) clarifies the source of mistrust which empirically oriented researchers hold about data generated through constructivist or pragmatist methods. Naturalistic methods involve "more holistic concepts of human behavior". . . "a greater sense of context". . . [and a] "description and understanding of the world as seen by the persons themselves" (p. 416). No theory adequately explains the complexity of human experience so theories must be constructed as a consequence of researchers' efforts to understand how the research participants, or "subjects," construct their own realities. Questions and explanatory ideas are considered emergent rather than embedded and new explanations of processes develop as more data are generated. Rather than completing the entire investigation protocol before beginning the investigation, naturalistic researchers frame their initial questions and then devise subsequent questions and investigatory procedures in response to data. These methods acknowledge subjectivity and do not attempt to force data into preexisting theory. Rather than try to create generalizations which are universally true, they attempt to understand the specifics of particular situations in ways which accurately represent the viewpoints of the participants in the situations.

For example, if a career services office on a particular campus were being underutilized, the traditional "theory first" approach might involve referring to Chickering's theory of identity formation (1969), reasoning that third and fourth year students are the ones most likely to be interested in use of the career center and creating a campaign to inform these students about career services available through intensive publicity in upperclass residence halls. Additional marketing might be done with faculty who advise juniors and seniors. Freshmen and sophomores would probably not be targeted for the campaign because they were thought to be working on issues of managing emotions and developing competence. A more naturalistic, theory-emergent approach might involve speaking with those freshmen and sophomores who actually do use the career center and asking them what their priorities are at that point in their college career. Subsequent conversations might be held with students from the traditional age group who do not use the center, freshmen and sophomores who are older than average, married students and so forth. Having inquired about the needs of non-users at all levels, new approaches to developing programs for all students might emerge. In order to be considered research, data-gathering approaches must be systematic (Scott, 1991). However, student affairs professionals talk to students constantly about all kinds of issues and generate data which is useful for framing questions about program planning and service delivery even if it is not formally considered research. These are the types of data which are frequently discounted or ignored as anecdotal when they might actually be indicative of a larger trend or point toward a serious issue which has begun to emerge in student life.

The border between rationalist and empiricist epistemologies and pragmatist epistemology is profound. The first two traditions assume separation between a subject who thinks and observes and an object which is thought about or observed. Rationalist and empiricist epistemologies assume unidirectional cause and effect relationships. Neither tradition assumes mutual interaction or mutual shaping effects which occur between participants in a situation. In the pragmatic/constructivist tradition, there is constant mutual shaping between agent and situation. The person engages with aspects of the environment in order to effect a change. A change occurs (or does not occur). The person thinks about the events and their significance and either persists in the course of action or changes its direction. Events which occur subsequent to the action shape the pragmatist's ideas about what is desirable, what should happen next, the utility or value of her or his ideas about what ought to happen and the process continues.

The border between rationalist/empiricist epistemologies and pragmatic epistemologies exists in their understanding of the relationship between people and their environment—outsiders who manipulate and organize or insiders who interact and engage in a holistic process. It is highlighted in their understanding of the utility and credibility of knowledge. In the two similar traditions, knowledge is most valuable when it is most general. In pragmatism, knowledge can be equally valuable and reliable when it provides accurate insight into the particular. In commenting about the subject-object split which pervades Western epistemology, the revered Indian philosopher Krishnamurti, proposed the following synthesis, "*First*, you are a human being . . . *then* you are a scientist. First you have to become free, and this freedom cannot be achieved through thought. It is achieved through meditation—the understanding of the totality of life in which every form of fragmentation has ceased" (Capra, 1989, p. 29). In other words, the subject/object split does not have to be construed as a split. It can be construed as a dynamic synthesis in which each aspect of a phenomenon contributes to the understanding of the other elements and the whole. The subject/object split is a creation of human thought, a set of categories used to understand the world. We need Isaac Newton who observed events from the outside and we also need Barbara McKlintock who tried to observe them as a participant. Carl Rogers presented this integrative point of view in person-centered counseling and learning (1951; 1969a). His work was pragmatic since it emphasized the interaction between client, counselor and the data of the client's life. It was phenomenological in philosophy since it focused on the counselor's efforts to understand the client's perspective rather than impose a theory-shaped idea about how to solve the client's problems or address his or her concerns.

Rationalist/Empiricist Teaching

Our traditional ideas about teaching and learning are shaped by rationalist/empiricist epistemologies. In academic content, this means that credible learning consists of learning theories which explain categories of data, learning how to generate data and conduct analysis which permits organization of data into

categories, learning to critique, test and revise theories and ultimately learning to predict what will occur when certain circumstances prevail. In sociology, students learn theories about urban
development for example. They study the conditions which encourage the development of cities, the conditions necessary for
cities to flourish, the social and economic value of cities, the
dynamics of relationships between groups in cities and conditions which contribute to the decline of cities. On a final exam,
the students in this course might be asked to describe the conditions which lead to the decay of cities and then to analyze a case
study of a declining city in terms of its conformity to these principles or its anomalous conditions which cannot be accounted for
by the general principles or theory. In a biology course, students
might be expected to learn the stages of embryonic development,
the *in utero* conditions which might interfere with development,
the stages at which particular birth defects might occur if development is interrupted and so forth. They might be asked to examine anomalous cases and attempt to explain why the predicted
changes did not occur. Thus an important part of their education is dedicated to learning the process of theory revision and
theory building for purposes of explaining more and more data
and generating more universal explanations. Even in the humanities, in the very particular study of poetry for example, a ratio-
nalist/empiricist approach is often used. A student paper might
analyze the use of solar and lunar imagery in the work of Wallace Stevens to explain the general meaning which Stevens attributes to these symbols. If the student can identify an extensive
number of examples in which Stevens uses the sun to signify
concrete reality and the moon to signify imagination, then she
has developed a theory of solar and lunar imagery which subsequent readers can use to shape their understanding of Stevens'
poetry.

Rationalist/empiricist approaches to teaching and learning
have several common elements. Students and teachers are assumed to be studying material from an objective or universal
perspective. They are attempting to develop a universal understanding about the material. That is, they create a notion of truth
which will be accurate for all future students of this material
unless more data are generated which change the configuration
of the explanation. Their explanations do not take into account
the perspective of the observer or analyst. That is assumed to be
universal. To the degree that they permit their particular point
of view to "interfere" with their understanding, they lose their
objectivity and presumably their accuracy of interpretation.

These approaches rely heavily on logic and presentation of empirical data (facts). Arguments in support of a particular point of view are presented, data are provided which support the arguments and then counter arguments and counter arrangements of data are presented. The view which prevails is the one that marshals the most data with the strongest logic such that the opponents of the view are convinced or overwhelmed and unable to provide convincing counterarguments. The purpose of these discussions is to identify the correct or most generally valid perspective on the issue under discussion. Referring to this approach as an adversarial paradigm for inquiry, Moulton asserts that the goal of all such discussions is to establish the dominant perspective and discredit other interpretations. Further, it is very difficult to tell the difference between competence and aggression in the midst of these discussions since, "The best way of evaluating work in philosophy (a rationalist enterprise) is to subject it to the strongest or most extreme opposition" (1983, p. 151, 153) and then to provide the most absolute, deductively certain reasons for the validity of a specific interpretation.

Given the epistemological assumptions embedded in traditional approaches to teaching and learning, the rationale which structures traditional classroom processes becomes visible. If there is always a best way to interpret data or understand phenomena, then an expert who has mastered the interpretive processes must be present to act as authority and referee. If there is always a best interpretation, then finding and articulating it becomes a competitive process. As in any other competition, the one who reaches the goal first or with the best form wins. The contest must have an expert referee to insure fairness and adherence to the rules. The focus is on individual achievement and the referee decides who wins. This is obviously an oversimplification, a line sketch of classroom processes described as the empirical data of student/teacher behavior. This oversimplification strongly resembles "separate knowing." Separate knowing was described by Belenky and her colleagues (1985) as a method of learning which involved independent acquisition of information and competition between students. Classroom discussion resembles debate as students establish a classroom hierarchy based on scoring points for correctness of information and domination of adversaries. Connected knowing, in contrast, involves joint acquisition of information and cooperation among students as they attempt to understand each others' points of view and expand the total knowledge base available to the entire group.

Separate knowing seems to be characteristic of male students and connected knowing is characteristic of female students. In their research, the Belenky group discussed the processes by which women learn to use separate knowing. Separate knowing has become a way of describing dominant teaching learning style in college classrooms, an approach which many female students believe they must master in order to compete effectively, but which few find comfortable.

Pragmatist Approaches to Teaching and Learning: A Student Affairs Perspective

Pragmatist approaches to teaching and learning have never achieved comparable credibility in higher education. Pragmatist approaches tend to be used in experiential settings like cooperative education and fieldwork. Pragmatist approaches are usually suspected of "lacking rigor," which generally means failing to use in scientific methodology for generating and testing knowledge under controlled, replicable circumstances. Pragmatism is context dependent and does not always yield universal explanations or generalist approaches to truth. Pragmatism constantly attempts to reorganize or reconstruct experience (Dewey, 1916). Pragmatism operates very effectively in indeterminate zones where the most effective thinkers can make sense out of confusion and "work out useful integrations of conflicting views and interests" (Schon, 1987, p. 12). Indeterminate zones tend to appear in all areas of student life outside the classroom, where all the variables can be neither known nor controlled. Referring to the education of reflective practitioners, Schon describes the process of pragmatic inquiry and experimentation as artistry, turning the problem upside down, experimenting with different perspectives from which to understand and intervene. Pragmatism asserts that the environment itself is the medium through which much education is accomplished (Dewey, 1916). Pragmatism emphasizes the particular, understanding the details of a specific situation and the role of the observer/experimenter in creating meaning and knowledge.

Pragmatism can be a very frustrating way of approaching knowledge to the person trained in the rationalist or empiricist traditions because very little knowledge remains static. All knowledge is time and context related and thus subject to change. Pragmatism lacks the satisfaction available to rationalists and empiricists who believe that they *know* and that their knowledge is stable and reliable over time and across contexts. Pragmatists must acknowledge the role of their own values and perspective, and indeed personal interests, in arranging information and discussing meaning. They have few pretensions to universality. When an empiricist observes a pragmatist, she or he may very well see or construct a person who doesn't know what he believes, can't present the facts about the situation in an orderly manner and may have trouble predicting what's likely to happen or justify her predictions based on theory or data. When an empiricist meets a pragmatist at a meeting to determine student status, i.e., who should be put on academic probation and who should be dropped from the student rolls, the two schools of thought often collide. The empiricist looks at the data on the academic record. The pragmatist looks at the student's life circumstances and thinks about the potential effects of intervention on increasing the likelihood of student success. The empiricist appears to be sure, making decisions on solid data and accurate prediction formulae. The pragmatist appears to be soft, easily dissuaded from "high" academic standards, unable to guarantee with any certainty whether or not a particular intervention will succeed.

Pragmatism transcends several more borders which have remained relatively impermeable in rationalism and empiricism. Pragmatism allows for the possibility that knowledge may be derived in part from a transcendent source implying a notion of spiritual worth (Dewey, 1916). It is not exclusively materialistic, relying for all its knowledge on sense data. It also suggests that character development is a key goal of the learning process (Kolb, 1984; Loxley & Whiteley, 1986; Westbrook, 1991) and that knowledge ought to be used for improvement of the human condition, guided by common social concerns and the need to evolve a continuing consensus about social priorities (Dewey, 1916). Rather than pretending to be objective and value neutral, it makes values clear and balances perspectives which can easily come into conflict.

PRAGMATIST EPISTEMOLOGY
AND STUDENT AFFAIRS VALUES

Student affairs is a profession based on pragmatist epistemology. Our founders adopted a pragmatist approach to individualizing education and helping students develop the skills and knowledge to be self-supporting, reliable and responsible citizens of the American democracy. At the time Lloyd-Jones, Cowley and Dewey were writing, American society was struggling with the dual problems of accommodating waves of European immigrants and maintaining full employment. They emphasized the role of education as a means to address both sets of problems teaching people work skills, citizenship skills and integrating them into American society. Esther Lloyd-Jones wrote about the need for democracy in management and education, stating that "stern, indomitable . . . leadership . . . is recognized as inimical to the best development of personalities" (Lloyd-Jones, 1934, in Saddlemire & Rentz, p. 23). Lloyd-Jones also indicated her sense of the incompatibility of the student personnel approach to education with rationalist/empiricist approaches when she defined the role of student personnel as applying to "all university-student relationships aside from formal instruction", including "efforts to develop (the student) in body, mind and character to the limit of his individual capacity for growth and helping him [sic] to apply his powers so developed most effectively to the work of the world" (Lloyd-Jones as cited in Saddlemire & Rentz, p. 21). The work of the world is a much larger construct than "the work world," as it is currently used to describe college/vocational education and indicates a much broader vision of the goals of education than the technical training of students in skills which make them intellectually, manually or interpersonally competent (Chickering, 1969).

Student personnel has always been a profession which does not separate education from administration, focusing on the creation of educational environments rather than on the formal teaching process. Student affairs operates from a constructivist framework rather than a rationalist or empiricist point of view. Student affairs manages and educates simultaneously even though most settings emphasize one more heavily than the other. Student affairs staff members teach by setting policy, advising student groups, arranging service delivery, setting budget priorities, supervising staff members, soliciting student input, resolving interpersonal disputes, counseling, consulting and engaging in some formal teaching and training activities. Student affairs activities in classrooms are often considered suspect by academic faculty and generally considered the least legitimate sphere for the profession because of their location on a professional border. "We came from a tradition entirely marginal to the centers of . . . academic life and our engagement in questions of cultural change . . . we first reckoned with the dirty outside world . . . in the field of education outside the university, in extramural departments and adult working class courses" (Grossberg, 1994, pp. 2-3). This description of the cultural pedagogy movement in the 1970s clearly overlaps with a description of work in student affairs, in residence halls, intramural sports, student activities and all the other settings where students' lives shape the learning process.

> And yet, relation appears,
> A small relation expanding like the shade
> Of a cloud on sand, a shape on the side of a hill
> Connoisseur of Chaos
>
> (Stevens, 1964)

Stevens' poetic description describes the growing awareness of the educational nature of the "non-educational" activities of student services. Crookston bemoans the "historical separation of student personnel work from the academy" (1973, p. 51), and goes on to state, "What is needed is to transform education so that it neither focuses on subject matter requirements and syllabi, nor attempts to fit the student into a cultural heritage, but becomes a model of human development that teaches students the processes of discovering what is known and applying that knowledge to a deeper understanding of self, of enhancing the quality of relationships with others and of coping effectively with their world" (1973, p. 52). This is a pragmatic, constructivist description of education which is context based, takes individual and group perspective into account and exists in the "messy outside world," where truth is more often specific than general and the environment is naturalistic rather than controlled. The boundaries in student affairs are constantly moving and they are drawn in rather different locations than boundaries in academic areas. The understanding of expert shifts as requirements for expertise shift. Sometimes the student is the expert and the student affairs professional learns a great deal. Student affairs exists as an intentional world, where nothing real just is and where "realities are the product of the way things get represented, embedded, implemented and reacted to" (Shweder, 1990, pp. 3-4). In this intentional world "human beings and sociocultural environments interpenetrate each other's identity and cannot be analytically disjoined into independent and dependent variables" (Shweder, 1990, p. 1). The kind of teaching which student affairs professionals provide is comparable to Friere's notion of literacy education in which students learn to read not only the text, but also the environment around them of which the text is a product (1990).

As with all non-dominant groups that create their intentional worlds within larger, dominating cultures, student affairs professionals can see academic rational/empiricists because their power shapes our borders, the domain within which we operate. They, however, do not see us as clearly. Their academic borders establish disciplinary lenses through which other systems and intentional worlds are seen narrowly. Overlapping areas have historically been limited to disruptive student behavior, parking spaces, the quality of the campus food service and pension plans. Academicians rarely discuss their research with student affairs professionals and we rarely discuss our educational activities with them. Even when we discuss student learning, we generally do not think of what we do as teaching because we tend to accept the academic rational/empiricist definition of teaching and we define our behavior in those terms. Our failure to perceive each other clearly can be inferred from these bits of conversations I have had with a student and a colleague.

"I don't want to teach," one of my students recently said to me.
"Do you want your students to learn from you?" I asked her.
"You're not a teacher. When are you going to realize that?" one of my supervisors said to me. "You'll never know who I am," I thought.

Whose definitions prevail? One definition of oppression is permitting the dominant group to define a non-dominant group and for the non-dominant group to believe the definition. This may be labeled internalized racism, anti-Semitism or homophobia, self-blame for obesity, poverty or disability. It can also appear as failure to appreciate the educational role of student affairs because teaching does not occur as it is traditionally defined or recognized.

Shifting Borders: Student Affairs and Cultural Pedagogy

The educational processes which student affairs specialists manage, provoke or create are generally invisible as education, but often become visible when described differently or seen through other lenses. We are seen as managing the campus environment, particularly the housekeeping tasks of maintaining buildings, upholding order and entertaining students. We are known to counsel students, a remedial rather than educational activity, to collect money and dispense financial aid, to admit, retain and discharge students and to help them find jobs or make choices about majors and then about careers. We also advise a wide range of student groups and help students overcome obstacles to academic success.

Through an empiricist lens with its clear and separate categories, these are management and support activities which enable students to participate fully and effectively in educational activities. Through a pragmatist lens, these are activities which are important parts of the students' total learning environment in which myriad opportunities for the teaching/learning process present themselves to those who see them. Esther Lloyd-Jones called this teaching students social competence (1940). The terminology is different, but the message is clear. Those activities for which student affairs staffs are responsible, no matter how managerial or administrative they appear through the empiricist lens, are an essential part of undergraduate education. Many years later, Crookston called for higher education to include the development of affective rationality. He wanted "the individual to use his [sic] brain to deal with his feelings; to put emotion to work; to recognize creative, growth-producing impulses and be able to set them free; to recognize destructive impulses and learn not only to understand and control them but perhaps even to convert their energy into growth producing experiences" (1973, p. 59). As a Dean of Students during the tumultuous 1960s when buildings were burned and students regularly demonstrated against most aspects of traditional education, Crookston was quite familiar with the educational and managerial benefits of teaching students how to use their brains to deal with their feelings and funnel their destructive impulses toward growth producing experiences.

OTHER PEDAGOGIES–DIFFERENT BORDERS

To this point we have been discussing various approaches to epistemology or ways of knowing in terms of the Western schools of thought and their expression in American universities. Two additional lenses which have much in common with Western pragmatism but are less familiar to many people in higher education provide insight into the teaching/learning process. The two lenses are Afrocentric perspectives and feminist perspectives, both of which are quite different from the Anglocentric, empiricist, rationalist, objectivist perspective which has been described throughout this text.

Feminist Pedagogy and Student Development Education

Feminist perspectives have been described as "constructivist" elsewhere in this volume. Although feminist epistemologists and teachers (or pedagogues) differ from each other in many ways, they share a belief in developing knowledge in context, taking the perspective of the observer into account when describing knowledge or information. They place a heavy emphasis on the role which relationships play in the learning process. They also emphasize the social construction of reality, or constructivism, an approach which is comparable to Shweder's notion of creating intentional worlds. They continually call attention to the means by which people create meaning from data and ascribe significance to events rather than discovering meaning or significance within events. This emphasis places responsibility on people for making their values, politics and perspectives clear in any discussion. Feminist research tends to use naturalistic paradigms (Lincoln & Guba, 1985). It emphasizes in-depth understanding of the particular and tends to look for explanatory patterns but not rigid categories (Baxter-Magolda, 1994). Feminists discuss "marginality and epistemic privilege" (Bar On, 1993) which signifies the position of women as outsiders in a male-defined society and the mixed virtues of that position. As outsiders, women are not permitted the legitimacy of their own perspectives or interpretations of events. They are often made to feel stupid or incompetent because of the ways they interpret situations (Raymond, 1985; Stetson, 1985). Conversely, women have the advantage of a relatively clear view of the ways that the dominant group operates, defines and values because women's perspectives provide a contrast to those values, making them more visible (Gray, 1982).

Many authors have discussed female learning and classroom process. Belenky and others (1985) compare connected and separate ways of knowing. They discuss women's ideas about learning by understanding what other people are attempting to convey vs. learning by debating and challenging. Learning by empathic understanding is the preferred mode of the women in the study, but many also learn to use the procedure of debate, challenge and domination. They simply prefer not to use it and often find it boring or meaningless. In comments about "taking women students seriously" Rich remarked, "I see my function here today as one of trying to *create a context*, [*emphasis supplied*] delineate a background, against which we might talk about women as students and students as women" (1979, p. 237). Russell suggests that effective approaches to teaching women, and in her situation, African American poor women, should include the following: discuss one subject at a time, each from an interdisciplinary perspective; encourage story telling which presents knowledge in the context from which it is created; connect political values to daily life—meaning power dimensions of larger social issues rather than narrow political party issues; speak in the students' idiomatic language as well as the language of the dominant social group i.e., proper English; use everything; be concrete; have a dream (Russell, 1985). Her approach is a constructivist one—to help her students realize that they are living in a social, cultural, political and historical context in which they are survivors who have power even though the power structure continually tells them that they have relatively little worth. Friere calls this process the development of critical consciousness— helping people to see and understand the circumstances by which they have been immobilized and learned to have contempt for themselves. Friere's goal in situations like the one described by Russell is to help the students learn to engage in praxis, the cycle of action and reflection in which people learn to transform their environment and see themselves as agents in creating their own lives (Friere, 1990).

Feminist pedagogy discusses relationships among students and between students and teachers as they affect the learning process. This interpersonal situation is not typically considered part of the academic side of higher education, although Carl Rogers' discussions of teaching and learning (1969a; 1969b) provide a notable exception. Rogers' approach was such a dramatic departure from business as usual. He quotes the effects which his approach to teaching had on one of his students who was a professor as well.

> To say that I am overwhelmed by what happened only faintly reflects my feelings . . . I, for my part, never found in a class-room so much of the whole person coming forth, so deeply involved, so deeply stirred. Further, I question if, in the traditional setup, with its emphasis on subject matter, examinations, grades,

there is, or there can be a place for the 'becoming' person with his deep and manifold needs as he struggles to fulfill himself [*sic*]. (1961, p. 313).

These comments presume what we have been describing as a pragmatist approach—one which assumes that it is appropriate, even necessary and beneficial, for the whole person to be involved in the learning process in higher education. This approach also assumes that learning is holistic, involving behavior, affect and cognition. It springs from a combination of phenomenology, which asserts that each individual views the world from an individual perspective and that each view is entitled to understanding and respect, and existentialism which emphasizes paying attention to the here-and-now of experience. Both of these philosophical perspectives are often present in pragmatist education.

More recently Noddings (1994; 1984) has discussed the appropriateness of morality as an aim of education when morality is understood to address the ethics of human relationships and mutual care in the context of open dialogue, modeling by teachers and among students, practice and confirmation. Noddings suggests that "Teachers treat students with respect and consideration and encourage them to treat each other in a similar fashion. They use teaching moments as caring occasions" (1994, p. 177). Noddings refers to Dewey's comments on the need to address the growth of students as a matter of crucial importance in education. She further suggests that, "If we were to explore seriously the ideas suggested by an ethic of caring for education we might suggest changes in almost every aspect of schooling: the current hierarchical structure of management, the rigid mode of allocating time, the kinds of relationships encouraged the size of schools and classes, the goals of instruction, modes of evaluation, patterns of interaction, selection of content" (1994, p. 175). She indicates that all these subjects are worthy of attention, but that the role of helping students to care for each other and respect each other while they learn is so central that it becomes primary.

What most feminist educators have in common is their focus on the context of learning, the wholeness of the human experience as described by cognition, affect and behavior and their emphasis on minimizing rigid power differences in the teaching/ learning process. Among student development educators, the description of feminist approaches is probably best known through the work of Carol Gilligan and her associates. *In a Different Voice* (1982) and *Making Connections* (1990) discuss female moral development and women's learning about decision-making, caring for self and others, resolving interpersonal conflicts, exercising leadership, balancing conflicting needs and values and achieving maturity. Learning is considered holistically, providing valuable insights into the ways women think and learn in all domains.

Baxter-Magolda has also provided valuable insights into patterns of learning by describing the differences between interpersonal and impersonal patterns of knowing, independent knowing in which people attempt to understand but then subordinate others' ideas and contextual knowing in which people learn to integrate their own and others' ideas (Baxter-Magolda, 1992). Baxter-Magolda's work describes learning patterns which are associated with gender and describes optimal ways to help students learn in each pattern. Her approach assumes that both sexes can learn in both modes, but that women seem to cluster in the interpersonal and contextual modes while men seem to cluster in the impersonal and independent modes. Baxter-Magolda applies her insights to learning opportunities within and outside the classroom, indicating the central role which experiential learning occupies in her conception of education. Both Baxter-Magolda and Gilligan and her collaborators extend ideas about learning along the lines of Friere's *praxis* and Dewey's pragmatism and democratic education to transcend connections between location and learning. Learning is a process which occurs when people reflect on events, values, context and relationship—and articulate and conceptualize processes associated with particularities. In other words, as one reflects upon experience, one is able to extend the meaning of that experience in time so that one can use knowledge to transform future experiences toward the manifestation values (Dewey, 1916).

In feminist approaches claims to universal truth are avoided reflecting the constructivist commitment to remain conscious of context and specifics. Lyons, one of Gilligan's collaborators and a feminist teacher in her own right has written, "Any given dilemma is likely to emerge in its particularity because of who the teacher is . . . Standards held are not arbitrary, but honed out of the teacher's own perceptions of the context of the school in its community, the lives of students and their needs" (1994, p. 200). This aspect of learning has been described as "nested knowing, a characterization of the interdependence of students and teachers as knowers in learning . . . In learning teachers and students influence and are influenced by each other's ways of knowing: they are nested knowers" (Lyons, 1994, p. 209).

The need to remain conscious of context and specifics is a constant issue in student affairs and student development education. An advisor can teach students how to address conflicts within their organization or between organizations. There are many excellent texts available on conflict resolution and students can learn the principles and practices involved. They can learn the skills of non-judgmental communication, active listening, assertiveness and negotiation. However, the actual process of conflict resolution is affected by countless specifics—what cultures are represented in the conflict and what are their norms and typical behavior patterns in the situation? Anglo-Americans are often less emotionally expressive than Jewish, Italian or Greek Americans when discussing differences of opinion. Japanese (Americans or international students) are quieter still and have completely different ideas of how to communicate about conflicts, often using indirect methods which Anglo-Americans might consider manipulative or dishonest. A group's ability to handle a particular conflict is also affected by their past history of cooperation or competition, whether or not members of the different groups have friends in the other group, the groups' previous relationship with and trust of the advisor or mediator, the advisor's age, experience and skill, ethnicity, gender and even the part of the country where the advisor grew up or has lived. In addition, the specific situation on campus will affect the outcome. Are resources available to help both groups achieve their goals or is this a zero sum situation where the progress of one is achieved at the expense of the other? What is the public reputation of both groups? Is this a public or a private conflict? Will anybody outside either group care how the problem is resolved? One could go on describing context endlessly. Given the complexity of this situation, one which most people in student affairs face on a regular basis, is it surprising that when a member of the faculty asks a member of the student affairs staff why she can't get the students "under control", the student affairs staff member realizes that the faculty person isn't speaking the same language she speaks with students (Barr & Fried, 1981) and may not even be in the same intentional world.

The necessity for student affairs staff members to attend to context and be aware of specifics cannot be overstated. An error is perceiving or interpreting any small piece of information might lead to highly publicized or damaging results for the staff member, the students or the institution. One area of practice where this issue appears frequently is in addressing problems between "Black" and "White" students and making judgments about who the students are based on their appearance. Further investigation into the context and particulars might reveal that a problem has nothing to do with "race," but has a great deal to do with specific behavior, or that the "Black" students are actually Haitians, Jamaicans, Cape Verdeans and African Americans who aren't getting along among themselves and that the other students are tangential. The staff member's ability to address the issue or solve the problem may be related more to the trust which the students feel for him or her than any of the particulars of the conflict. Similar issues can appear in male/female conflicts. If an intervening staff member does not take time to discover the context in which the problem arose and the beliefs which the students hold about each other and the situation, the staff member may misunderstand what issues the students are concerned about and do more harm than good.

Feminist epistemology and pedagogy have reminded us that one teaches and learns in a complete human context which includes an awareness of the students' values and life experiences, of the teacher's values and life experience and of the situation in which they are interacting to advance learning and solve problems.

✳ ✳ ✳ ✳ ✳

Questions:

1) Do you think that academic learning is compatible or incompatible with caring about students?

2) Do you think that helping students learn how to treat each other with respect, manage conflicts and work together is teaching?

3) Do you think that objectivity is always better than subjectivity and that personal values ought to be kept out of work with students?

4) In thinking about empiricism, pragmatism and feminism, can you locate the boundaries of your own ideas about teaching and learning?

✳ ✳ ✳ ✳ ✳

Afrocentric Worldview and Student Development Education

> To the inhabitants of Space in General, this work is dedicated by a humble native of Flatland, In the hope that, even as he was initiated into the mysteries of Three Dimensions, having been previously conversant with Only Two, So the citizens of that celestial Region may aspire yet higher and higher to the secrets of Four, Five, or even Six Dimensions, Thereby contributing to the enlargement of the Imagination, and the possible development of that most rare and excellent gift of Modesty among the . . . Races of Solid Humanity.
>
> (From the dedication of *Flatland*, Abbott, 1984)

Feminist pedagogy can take us a long way from the empiricist, rational and objectivist world of traditional Western academic processes toward the complex world of subjective experience and learning from context. However, much feminist pedagogy is a product of Anglo-American scholars who have been trained in traditional Anglo-Eurocentric universities and remain constrained by one more border which has yet to be addressed. This is the border between the spiritual and material dimensions of human experience, a border which is almost impermeable in traditional western science.

In an Afrocentric worldview, "the nature of reality is believed to be at once spiritual and material" (Myers, 1987, p. 74). This worldview is also affirmed by Native Americans (Niehardt, 1961) and many Asians who support the Buddhist belief in "non-duality," or "mutual co-arising" or "interbeing" (Hanh, 1987) as well as Christian and Jewish mystics (Goldsmith, 1971) who believe in the Biblical guarantees that God provides for all His children. The Afrocentric belief system is far more typical of the human majority than is the Anglocentric, fragmented view articulated throughout this work (Ibrahim, 1991; Myers, Speight, Highlen, Cox, Reynolds, Adams & Hanley, 1991). Myers calls for the creation of an optimal conceptual system which is non-hierarchical, mutually respectful and acknowledges "the dynamic interplay between mystical intuition and scientific analysis" (1985, p. 32). Myers also mentions the interrelatedness of all phenomena which has also been described by Capra in *The Tao of Physics* (1975) and *The Turning Point* (1982), indicating that the worldview she describes, although unfamiliar and unbelievable to many people who see the world through the fragmented scientific lenses of empiricism, rationalism and objectivism, is quite believable from the perspective of quantum mechanics. Myers presents, "a paradigm that unifies the insights of modern physics and Eastern mysticism under the philosophical structure of traditional African philosophy" (1985, p. 32). Her perspective is built on two basic tenets: "(1) self-knowledge is the basis of all knowledge (epistemology); and (2) human and spiritual networks (ntuology) provide the process through which we will achieve our goals" (Myers, 1993, p. 3).

* * * * *

Exercise

Make a list of your objections to these ideas before you read the rest of this section. Then try to suspend your objections as you read the rest of this section. Your list will show you where your borders and boundaries are. Then you can decide who constructed them, whether or not you really believe they ought to be where they are and how you can transcend them if you wish.

* * * * *

The "deep structure" of Afrocentric culture affirms that reality is simultaneously spiritual and material and is known both through sensory and extra- (or non-) sensory perception (Myers, 1987, p. 74). Knowing involves the use of symbolic imagery and rhythm rather than logic and the organization of empirical data. Learning and knowing are holistic and intuitive rather than sequential, cumulative processes. The rhythm of the language in which one's knowledge is expressed is as important as its content. The individual self exists only in the context of the group and its environment.

> *I* am, because we are; and because we are, therefore, I am. *I* is the individual and the infinite whole. *We* is the individual and collective manifestation of all that is. *Self* includes all ancestors, the yet unborn, the entire community and all of nature. In my being is my worth, because I am not a separate finite, limited being, but an extension of—and one with all that is. (Myers, 1993, p. 20)

In contrast to the Western, scientific ways of knowing which rely on separation, observation, counting and measuring, Afrocentric ways of knowing involve immersion in situations, experiencing the dynamics of relationships between people and events, expressing one's understanding in metaphor, story or rhyme and assuming connection between oneself and that which one is learning. Within this worldview facts acquire their meaning only in context. Context includes not only present physical reality, but also the psychological realities of relationships, spiritual realities and the historical realities of the group, past, present and anticipated future. Knowledge is presumed to begin and end in experience. Knowledge is derived from perception and observation and is always subject to interpretation. Therefore, notions of distance and objectivity become self-deluding (Myers, 1984). Perceiving through an Afrocentric worldview, subject and object exist in relationship, observation is inseparable from interpretation and distance and "objectivity," distort understanding and mislead people.

The Afrocentric worldview presents an obvious and significant contrast to both Western ways of knowing (epistemology) and traditional ways of teaching and learning. Both subjectivity and spirituality have no place in the scientific assumptions of Western tradition. Both dimensions of knowing would be assumed to "lack rigor" from a Western scientific perspective because they are non-empirical, non-generalizable and can't necessarily be replicated on demand. Afrocentrism assumes a dynamic unity of all knowledge and experience while Western scientism assumes fragmentation and separation, the whole is exactly the sum of its parts. Perhaps the most significant issue here is that, while Afrocentric perspectives can acknowledge the validity and contributions of Eurocentric or scientific perspectives, the reverse is not true. Therefore, to repeat an earlier quote from Sancho Panza, "Whether the stone hits the pitcher or the pitcher hits the stone, its going to be bad for the pitcher." Myers refers to these two views as Eurolinear vs. Afrocircular. Both approaches have developed valuable ways of knowing but each has a different goal. Eurocentric science aims to predict and control while African and Asian inquiry aim to understand and unify (1984, p. 7). Each way of knowing has its uses. Given assumptions of complementarity, both ways can help students learn valuable lessons. Without such assumptions, they contradict each other. In our American universities, the Eurolinear approach dominates and controls, depriving the Afrocircular or Afrocentric approach of credibility. Is there a way to determine which approach to thinking about environmental degradation is more valuable? One way would involve a scientific approach, teaching people information about global warming, pollution from burning fossil fuels or carcinogens in landfills. Another way is a holistic approach in which students consider the Buddhist blessing before meals in which everyone looks at their food and thinks about the people who produced it, the place it came from, the sun, the rain, the wind, the earth, the sky, the hunger of others and the disposal of waste. Can either approach be complete without the other? The first approach provides information about the external, physical environment. The second approach places the person in the environment, the total physical/human context. Is either approach used singly as valuable and conducive to insight as both approaches used in complementary fashion?

※ ※ ※ ※ ※

Exercise
Review your list of objections to the Afrocentric perspective or worldview. Pay attention to your emotional responses as you think about this perspective. The stronger the resistance to an idea, the more rigid and impermeable the border. As Robert Frost wrote in "Mending Walls," "Before I built a wall, I'd want to know what I was walling in and walling out, And to whom I was like to give offense. Something there is that doesn't love a wall" (Frost, 1967, p. 48). You may also be wondering why more poetry is appearing in this section. Poetry is symbolic imagery. It is meant to be spoken aloud. It accesses the right side of your brain and provokes another way of knowing. Those who have been trained in empirical and scientific ways of knowing can easily suffer from atrophy of their creative processes. In worlds defined by empirical reality, creativity and vision are often put down with the expression "Get real." By this time, the reader should begin to wonder if reality is "out there", to be discovered, "in here", to be articulated, or "in process", to be developed continuously. Have you ever wondered if reality was a matter of opinion? Whose opinion?

※ ※ ※ ※ ※

Praxis, Pragmatism and Student Development Education

The cultural pedagogy or liberation education movement constitutes the final perspective in this review of teaching and learning and knowing. Although *Pedagogy of the Oppressed* (Friere,

1990) is the most widely known presentation of this perspective, the movement has a number of other spokespeople, most of whom have focused their attention on pedagogy and administration in elementary and secondary schools (Giroux, 1988a; Giroux, 1988b; Giroux, 1991; Giroux & McLaren, 1994; Heslep, 1989; Maxcy, 1994; Phelan & Davidson, 1993). Friere has created and explained the notion of critical consciousness or "conscienticazao" which he considers to be a primary goal of all education. "Conscienticazao" is the process of helping people see themselves in context and to read the messages which their environment sends them about who they are or ought to be and how they should interpret events. Critical consciousness helps people learn to read and label their world, describing and understanding events from their own perspective as shaped by race, class, gender, sexual orientation, religion and ethnic culture. Critical consciousness is developed through *praxis*, a process of action and reflection in which people engage in efforts to understand and transform their world to make it more just and to achieve greater self-direction and dignity. It is Freire's belief that all education is values education and that no education is value free. In this Friere and the critical pedagogues directly challenge the assumptions and methods of Western, scientific teaching and learning as well as the power structures of the institutions which are controlled by these assumptions and methods.

Friere and Dewey have much in common although they are separated by culture and era. Both men saw the need to educate people holistically, helping them to act on their world and transform it. Both men saw the power structures of their respective countries as dedicated to maintaining their own power while affirming other values in public. Friere began by developing a literacy program for Brazilian peasants which permitted the peasants to challenge the dominant and paternalistic land owners by challenging the interpretation of social values and events. Dewey wanted to help workers shape a democratic workplace in which the profits from their work were more equitably distributed and workplace decisions were made more democratically. Friere arose from an impoverished background, was educated in the European tradition and rose to become minister of education in his country. Dewey was the respectable son of a devoutly Christian entrepreneur. Although John Dewey lacked for little during his early life, he grew up in an industrializing city where living conditions were deteriorating and farmers were moving in from the country in search of a better life. Throughout his life, Dewey was concerned about the human problems of industrial democracy and the need to find means by which people could become active in understanding and solving those problems. Thus he spent his life writing about the means by which democracy could be supported, the educational methods appropriate to creation of democracy and the futility of war and other violent means for solving problems (Westbrook, 1991). Both men were driven by the need to help people learn to read their environments accurately, to develop communities, to act in concert with their fellow citizens and enhance their collective welfare and to establish justice and human dignity in their worlds. The teachings of both men had a great deal in common with the feminists and the Afrocentrists described above in their focus on context, position, relationships, understanding and transformation. In their approaches to education knowledge changes as context, conditions and participants change. In both Dewey's and Friere's approaches, teaching, learning and developing knowledge are part of an interactive process. All participants in the process must remain open to the probability that they will change their minds, feel deeply about their work and possibly shift power positions in relation to one another.

There is much to be learned from all these approaches if we wish to teach students how to learn from their environments, work together, solve problems, manage organizations and benefit from differences. If student affairs practice is grounded in pragmatist epistemology, then almost everything we do is educational in some sense, even if the education does not appear in the traditional teaching/learning framework which we have been taught to recognize. Therefore student development education can be seen as one facet of student affairs or student services administration, an educational consequence of a variety of activities, some of which appear to be teaching and learning and some of which appear to be managerial or administrative. Viewed through this lens, student affairs becomes a central part of the educational mission of colleges and universities, not simply a set of support services. The next questions are: Who's in charge of changing the lenses? Who decides which lens is appropriate or which picture needs to come into clearer focus?

The lens metaphor is a somewhat less threatening way to discuss power differentials in the university than direct discussion. Nevertheless, it is a discussion of power—who has it, who wants it and who benefits from using it. In the days when one lens

showed all, it may have been appropriate to view the educational activities of the university from a single epistemological perspective. If the goal of a college is to train a homogeneous
student body to become members of the learned professions, as
it was for Harvard, Yale and Princeton at their inception, then a
classical curriculum and a single teaching method could help
students and faculty achieve their educational goal efficiently
and effectively. In our times, however, goals for colleges and universities are far more complex and student bodies are far more
heterogeneous. Therefore, educational goals become operationalized in very complex ways, teaching methods become much
more diverse, curricula seem to multiply and divide endlessly
and student learning styles are similarly wide-ranging.

> Turning and turning in the widening gyre
> The falcon cannot hear the falconer;
> Things fall apart; the center cannot hold;
> Mere anarchy is loosed upon the world,
> The blood-dimmed tide is loosed, and everywhere
> The ceremony of innocence is drowned;
> The best lack all conviction, while the worst
> Are full of passionate intensity.
>
> *The Second Coming* (Yeats, 1933)

Symbolically, these words from Yeats describe the way many
people in higher education feel about what is happening to our
institutions, our students and ourselves. Yeats described his vision of a falcon circling far above the head of the falconer. Historically, the falcon would have been tethered or trained to circle
above the falconer's head, searching for prey and bringing it
back to its master. This is an excellent metaphor for the role
which education has played in training people to fit into the
system and for the role which rationalist, and empiricist epistemologies have played in controlling inquiry and the creation of
new knowledge and the teaching/learning processes. The falcon
circles in a circumscribed area whose boundaries are invisible.
The center holds. The falconer understands the process and controls it. Beginning in the 1960s anarchy was loosed upon the
world—internationally with the dissolution of the colonial em-
pires in Africa and Asia, domestically with assassination of John
Kennedy, Robert Kennedy, Martin Luther King and Malcolm X,
the upheavals in our universities and cities, the Vietnam war and
its domestic consequences, and the enactment of the legislation
which opened access to our universities for women, members of

historically underrepresented groups and returning Vietnam veterans. In the same era, women's studies and African American studies emerged, followed more recently by gender studies, gay and lesbian studies and a proliferation of the somewhat more traditional ethnic studies programs including the countries of Southeast Asia and Latin America. In sociology and anthropology, particularly, traditional methods of research began to be questioned because their Eurocentric borders and exploitative approaches to understanding group behavior had become more obvious (Diamond, 1974; Harrison, 1991). In the United States a new movement called community psychology arose which refused to see the individual as a completely autonomous unit and based its interventions on an "individual in context" approach where context was assumed to include elements of politics, economics, family and other relationships, geography, transportation, education, religion and so forth. This movement was self-consciously political and represented a drastic departure in analysis and intervention methods from the traditional Eurocentric, apolitical, individualized approaches (Bronfenbrenner, 1979; Levine & Perkins, 1987; Rappaport, 1977). For people who believe that reliable knowledge is discovered under controlled circumstances in laboratories and people who are searching for universal truths about anything, it certainly feels as if things are falling apart.

The second element of control which has disappeared and re-emerged in a different form is institutional control of and responsibility for student behavior. This has historically been the province of student affairs and remains so on most campuses. The problem is that many types of disruptive student behavior no longer fall within the rules. Administrators are having serious difficulty writing new rules to cover new situations. Many of these problems emerge from the diversity of the student body. Which rule covers the problem of a carpet in the hallway of the student union which gets soaked every Friday as Moslem students wash their feet in the lavatories and then walk barefoot down the hall to the meeting room where their Sabbath services are held? Who decides when a shouting match which erupts during a pick-up basketball game becomes a fight or a racial incident? When students, who come from countries where academic collaboration is normal, share answers during a test, is that cheating? It certainly is in American colleges. What is the college's responsibility to orient these students so that they don't break the American rules of academic honesty? How will the orientation staff know if they have communicated effectively with these students if the students come from a culture where asking questions is considered evidence of either rudeness or stupidity? The most intransigent of these problems currently seems to be in the area of hate speech/freedom of speech. When a student comes from a culture where "May a thousand camels defecate on your grave" is a typical insult, how does an administrator decide what to do with this student when he calls African American women water buffaloes?

The philosophical center of American higher education has been pulled apart by these developments. In the terminology of liberation education, the world has been decentered and it must be remapped. New maps must always identify context, relationships between groups in the context and cultural and power issues which are part of the context. These maps are multidimensional holograms and they can be reprogrammed at a moment's notice. There appears to be no foundational reference point from which to proceed in this decentered universe(ity). Universities and their contexts may be most accurately understood from the perspective of bootstrap theory, which sees the world as "a dynamic web of interrelated events. None of the properties of any part of this web is fundamental; they all follow from the properties of other parts and the overall consistency of their interrelations determines the structure of the entire web" (Capra, 1989, p. 51). This new map represents a constantly moving, incomprehensibly complex process in which the boundaries between teaching and learning, teaching and researching, teaching and managing are increasingly blurred into a process better described as a cycle of noticing, inquiring, acting and evaluating. All members of the university community may participate. "The elitism of intellectuals comes, not merely from our assumption that we already know the answers, but even more from our assumption that we already know the questions" (Grossberg, 1994, p. 20).

Liberation education or cultural pedagogy advocates a process by which power, role relationships and expertise are redefined as "[teaching] from where the student is at [sic] rather than where the teacher is at. This does not mean that the teacher denies his or her pedagogical intentions or specific expertise but merely that s/he respects the myriad expertise of the students that s/he does not share" (Grossberg, 1994, p. 20). Anybody might be a student and anybody might be a teacher at any given moment in addressing a particular problem. This is another way to describe the means by which effective student affairs staffs work with students.

Student affairs can learn a new language of border crossing from the proponents of cultural pedagogy—the language of teaching and learning in multiple contexts, using multiple modes which have often been called "teachable moments." In order to perform this function, however, the profession of student affairs must first re-define itself as a group of people who are truly educators, who help others learn from experience, often in situations where the designated experts are not the ones who know the most or have the most relevant information even though they may have the most power and where the students, why typically have the least power, may have the most reliable knowledge. Educators who operate from a pragmatist perspective manage the inquiry process and challenge people to generate theory from data rather than imposing "expert" or preconceived ideas and theories on data. They also focus on the process of discussion so that people who perceive themselves as having less power are not intimidated about stating their views. Student affairs professionals who act as cultural pedagogues ask questions and help people think about their assumptions and the implications of their ideas and perceptions before reaching for unexamined solutions. In one sense, seeing the profession of student affairs from an educational perspective is similar to re-engineering both our profession and our institutions because we are transforming our roles which, in turn, will transform the dynamics of our institutions. Our profession can take on the task of using the entire institution as an educational environment in which everybody can learn from everybody else as long as one group is willing to ask the hard questions (Crookston, 1973; Fried, 1993).

What are we attempting to accomplish here? Does this situation have any potential learning outcomes? Who decides which lens to use framing this situation? Who is most skilled at viewing the world through that lens? Who, in a given situation, is most able to help others see what she or he sees, to adjust the focus, to use wide angle or microscopic views? Would the use of multiple lenses or perspectives help in achieving an holistic understanding of the situation and its implications in many contexts? These are questions which relate to teaching, learning, managing, the flow of power and understanding around issues of common concern. While definition can lead to control of a situation, understanding can lead to fearlessness, cooperation, collaboration and evolving resolution. Some times it is necessary to define, limit, control and manage. Other times it is much more beneficial to understand and collaborate.

CONCLUSION

Community on campus has been a subject of great concern in this decade (Boyer, 1990). The concern seems to stem from the perception that things have fallen apart. Some observers blame students for their uncivil behavior and self-indulgent vocational-ism. Some blame faculty for their emphasis on research, con-sultation and personal aggrandizement. Some blame the larger society for the collapse of a value consensus, the disappearance of jobs, family dysfunction and so forth. In any given situation, student affairs often becomes the villain for failing to control "our" students. And of course, there are those who blame the formerly disenfranchised, the feminists, the students, professors and administrators of color, the cultural critics and pedagogues, for causing the problem by enforcing "political correctness" on all the people who disagree with them. What all the blamers have in common is their search for root causes which can be eliminated thus restoring our campuses to stability. Epistemolog-ically, we are still searching for rationalist principles which are true across time and context. Psychologically, we are searching for well-structured problems which can be thoroughly researched and solved (Kitchener & King, 1994). If William Perry were ob-serving this behavior, he might notice that we had reverted to the first three positions on his scale, somewhat revamped. If we can't find an Authority to tell us what to do, we would certainly like to be treated as if we are the Authority. But we aren't and neither is anybody else. It's just very hard to admit that we have all crossed a border together into a world in which process is content, where people want to belong, have influence and feel acknowledged, but in which nothing remains stable for very long. We are in many cases looking at our differences as if ac-knowledging them might provide us with some answers about how to manage teaching and learning. If we set up enough cul-tural studies programs, special program residence halls, cultur-ally oriented student groups, then people might feel comfortable and life can get "back to normal." The problem is that our dif-ferences, whether they be identified as race, ethnicity, gender or job title, cannot give us answers—they can only help us pose the questions which we can investigate together. As we go along, we must develop a common language to do common business.

* * * * *

We have arrived in a Brave New World where the major questions seem to be:

What do we need to know?
How can we learn it?
What difference does it make?
Is everybody on board who needs to be on board?
Do we all understand each other?

Can we get there from here or do we need to travel by way of some-where else? Wherever you go, there you are! Have you crossed any borders lately? Opened yourself to let people from other places into your awareness? What would it take to get ready to do this? What possible behaviors feel like risks? What languages must you learn? How will you know who you are?

all ignorance toboggans into know
and trudges up to ignorance again:
but winter's not forever, even snow
melts; and if spring should spoil the game, what then?
all history's a winter sport or three:
but were it five, i'd still insist that all
history is too small for even me;
for me and you, exceedingly too small.

Swoop(shrill collective myth) into thy grave
merely to toil the scale to shrillerness
per every madge and mabel dick and dave
—tomorrow is our permanent address

and there they'll scarcely find us(if they do,
we'll move away still further: into now

XXXIX, e. e. cummings

REFERENCES

Abbott, E. (1884) *Flatland: A romance of many dimensions.* London: See-ley and Co. Ltd. (Reissued by Dover Publications: New York, 1992).

Alcoff, L. & Potter, E. (Eds). (1993) *Feminist epistemologies.* New York: Routledge.

Bar On, B-A (1993) Marginality and epistemic privilege. In L. Alcoff & E. Potter. (Eds). *Feminist epistemologies.* New York: Routledge.

Barr, M. & Fried, J. (1981). Facts, feelings and academic credit. In J. Fried (Ed.). *Education for student development.* (pp. 87-102). *New Directions in Student Services. 15.* San Francisco: Jossey-Bass.

Baxter-Magolda, M. (1994) Gender and making meaning of experience. In J. Fried (Ed.). *Different voices: Gender and perspective in student affairs.* (p. 12-29). Washington, DC: National Association of Student Personnel Administrators.

Baxter-Magolda, M. (1992) *Knowing and reasoning in college.* San Francisco: Jossey-Bass.

Belenky, M., Clinchy, B., Goldberger, N. & Tarule, J. (1986) *Women's ways of knowing.* New York: Basic Books.

Boyer, E. (1990) *Campus life in search of community.* Princeton, NJ: The Carnegie Foundation for the Advancement of Teaching.

Bronfenbrenner, U. (1979) *The ecology of human development.* Cambridge, MA: Harvard University Press.

Brooks, J. & Brooks, M. (1993) *The case for constructivism classrooms.* Alexandria, VA: Association for Supervision and Curriculum Development.

Capra, F. (1989) *Uncommon wisdom: Conversations with remarkable people.* New York: Bantam Books.

Capra, F. (1982) *The turning point.* New York: Simon and Schuster.

Capra, F. (1975) *The Tao of physics.* Berkeley, CA: Shambala Press.

Chickering, A. (1969) *Education and identity.* San Francisco: Jossey-Bass.

Covey, S. (1989) *The seven habits of highly effective people.* New York: Simon and Schuster.

Crookston, B. (1976) Student personnel: All hail and farewell! in G. Saddlemire & A. Rentz (Eds.). (1986) *Student affairs: A profession's heritage.* (pp. 429-439). Alexandria, VA: American College Personnel Association.

Crookston, B. (1973) Education for human development. In C. Warnath (Ed.) *New Directions for College Counselors* (pp. 47-65). San Francisco: Jossey-Bass.

Dewey, J. (1960) *Theory of the moral life.* New York: Holt, Rinehart and Winston.

Dewey, J. (1916) *Democracy and education.* New York: The Macmillan Company.

Diamond, S. (1974) *In search of the primitive: A critique of civilization.* New Brunswick, NJ: Transaction Books.

Frankena, W. (1965) *Three historical philosophies of education.* Fairlawn, NJ: Scott, Foresman and Co.

Fried, J. (1993) Multiculturalism on campus: A milieu management approach. *Metropolitan Universities.* 4. (2). 32-43.

Friere, P. (1990) *Pedagogy of the oppressed.* New York: Continuum.

Friere, P. (1985) *Culture, power and liberation.* New York: Bergin and Garvey.

Frost, R. (1967) *Complete poems of Robert Frost.* New York: Holt, Rinehart and Winston.

Gilligan, C. (1982) *In a different voice.* Cambridge, MA: Harvard University Press.

Gilligan, C., Lyons, N., & Hanmer, T. (Eds.). (1990) *Making connections.* Cambridge, MA: Harvard University Press.

Gray, E. (1982) *Patriarchy as a conceptual trap.* Wellesley, MA: Round-Table Press.

Giroux, H. (Ed.) (1991) *Modernism, postmodernism and feminism.* Albany, NY: SUNY Press.

Giroux, H. (1988a) *Schooling and the struggle for public life.* Minneapolis, MN: University of Minnesota Press.

Giroux, H. (1988b) *Teachers as intellectuals.* MA: Bergin and Garvey.

Giroux, H. (1981) *Ideology, culture and the process of schooling.* Philadelphia, PA: Temple University Press.

Giroux, H. & McLaren, P. (Eds.). (1994) *Between borders.* New York: Routledge.

Goldsmith, J. (1971) *The mystical I.* San Francisco: HarperSanFrancisco.

Grossberg, L. (1994). Introduction: Bringin' it all back home. In H. Giroux & P. McLaren. (Eds.). *Between Borders.* (pp. 1-28). New York: Routledge.

Hanh, T. (1987) *Interbeing.* Berkeley, CA: Parallax Press.

Harding, S, (1993) Rethinking standpoint epistemology; What is "strong objectivity?". In L. Alcoff and E. Potter. (Eds.). *Feminist epistemologies* (pp. 49-82). New York: Routledge.

Harrison, F. (Ed.). (1991) *Decolonizing anthropology.* Washington, DC: Association of Black Anthropologists.

Heslep, R. (1989) *Education in democracy.* Ames, IA: Iowa State University Press.

Ibrahim, F. (1991) Contribution of cultural worldview to generic counseling and development. *Journal of Counseling and Development.* 70. 13-19.

James, W. (1910) *Pragmatism.* New York: Longmans, Green and Company.

Kitchener, K. & King, P. (1994) *Developing reflective judgment.* San Francisco: Jossey-Bass.

Kolb, D. (1984) *Experiential learning.* Englewood Cliffs, NJ: Prentice Hall.

Kuethe, J. (1968) *The teaching-learning process.* Glenview, IL: Scott Foresman.

Levine, M. & Perkins, D. (1987) *Principles of community psychology*. New York: Oxford University Press.

Lincoln, Y. & Guba, E. (1985) *Naturalistic inquiry*. Newbury Park, CA: Sage.

Lloyd-Jones, E. (1934) Personnel administration. In G. Saddlemire & A. Rentz (Eds.). (1986) *Student affairs: A profession's heritage*. (pp. 21-29). Alexandria, VA: American College Personnel Association.

Lloyd-Jones, E. (1940) *Social competence and college students*. (Series VI, No. 3) Washington, DC: American Council on Education.

Loxley, J. & Whiteley, J. (1986) *Character development in college students*. (Vol. 2) Schenectady, NY: Character Research Press and the American College Personnel Association.

Lyons, N. (1994). Dilemmas of knowing: Ethical and epistemological dimensions of teachers' work and development. In L. Stone (Ed.). *The education feminism reader*. (pp. 195-220). New York: Routledge.

Maxcy, S. (Ed.). (1994) *Postmodern school leadership*. Westport, CT: Praeger.

Moulton, J. (1983) A paradigm of philosophy: The adversary method. (pp. 149-164). In S. Harding & M. Hintikka (Eds.). *Discovering reality*. Boston: D. Reidel.

Myers, L. (1993) *Understanding an Afrocentric world view: Introduction to an optimal psychology*. (2nd ed), Dubuque, IA: Kendall Hunt Publishing Co.

Myers, L. (1987) The deep structure of culture: Relevance of traditional African culture in contemporary life. *Journal of Black Studies*. *18*. 72-85.

Myers, L. (1985) Transpersonal psychology: The role of the Afrocentric paradigm. *The Journal of Black Psychology*. *12*. 31-42.

Myers, L. (1984) The psychology of knowledge: The importance of worldview. *New England Journal of Black Studies*. *4*, 1-12.

Myers, L., Speight, S., Highlen, P., Cox, C., Reynolds, A., Adams, E., & Hanley, C. (1991) Identity development and worldview; Toward an optimal conceptualization. *Journal of Counseling and Development*. *70*. 54-63.

Niehardt, J. (1961) *Black Elk speaks*. Lincoln, NE: University of Nebraska Press.

Noddings, N. (1994) An ethic of caring and its implications for instructional arrangements. In L. Stone (Ed.). *The education feminism reader*. (pp. 171-183). New York: Routledge.

Noddings, N. (1984) *Caring: A feminine approach to caring and moral education*. Berkeley and Los Angeles: University of California Press.

Phelan, P. & Davidson, A. (Eds.). (1993) *Renegotiating cultural diversity in American schools*. New York: Teachers' College Press.

Rappaport, J. (1977) *Community psychology: Values, research and action*. New York: Holt, Rinehart and Winston.

Raymond, J. (1985) Women's studies: A knowledge of one's own. In. M. Culley & C. Portugues. (Eds.). *Gendered subjects: the dynamics of feminist teaching.* (pp. 49-63). Boston: Routledge and Kegan Paul.

Rich, A. (1979) Taking women students seriously. In A. Rich. *On lies, secrets and silence.* (pp. 237-246). New York: W. W. Norton.

Rogers, C. (1969a) *Freedom to learn.* Columbus, OH: Charles Merrill.

Rogers, C. (1969b) The interpersonal relationship in the facilitation of learning. In C. Rogers. *Freedom to learn.* (pp. 103-128). Columbus, OH: Charles Merrill.

Rogers, C. (1961) *On becoming a person.* Boston: Houghton-Mifflin.

Rogers, C. (1951) *Client centered therapy: It's current practice, implications and theory.* Boston: Houghton-Mifflin.

Russell, M. (1985). Black-eyed blues connections: Teaching black women. In M. Culley & C. Portugues (Eds). *Gendered subjects: The dynamics of feminist teaching.* (pp. 155-168). Boston: Routledge and Kegan Paul.

Scheffler, I. (1965) *Conditions of knowledge.* Chicago: Scott, Foresman.

Schetlin, E. (1968) Guidance and student personnel work as reflected by Esther Lloyd-Jones from 1929 to 1966. *Journal of the National Association of Women Deans and Counselors.* 31. (3) 97-102.

Schon, D. (1987) *Educating the reflective practitioner.* San Francisco: Jossey-Bass.

Scott, M. (1991) Naturalistic research: Applications for research and professional practice with college students. *Journal of College Student Development.* 32. 416-423.

Senge, P. (1990) *The fifth discipline.* New York: Doubleday.

Shweder, R. (1990). Cultural psychology: What is it? in J. Stigler, R. Shweder & G. Herdt. (Eds.). *Cultural psychology.* (pp. 1-46). New York: Columbia University Press.

Stetson, E. (1985) Pink elephants: confessions of a black feminist in an all-white, mostly male English department of a white university somewhere in God's country. In M. Culley & C. Porgues. (Eds.). *Gendered subjects: The dynamics of feminist teaching.* (pp. 127-130) Boston: Routledge and Kegan Paul.

Stevens W. (1964). Connoisseur of chaos. In *The collected poems of Wallace Stevens.* New York: Alfred A. Knopf.

Westbrook, R. (1991) *John Dewey and American democracy.* Ithaca, NY: Cornell University Press.

Yeats, W. B. (1933) *The collected poems of W. B. Yeats.* New York: The Macmillan Company.

Ziman, J. (1978) *Reliable knowledge.* London: Cambridge University Press.

6

Students of Color
and Student Culture

Dawn Person

INTRODUCTION

As an undergraduate African American, I attended a predominantly white college in the mid-1970s. Like many institutions, one goal of this college was to recruit and retain a more diverse student population. While many of us were recruited, far fewer were retained for a variety of reasons. Many of my peers experienced what they described as frustration and disappointment with their college experience. I returned to school for the sophomore year to find that over half of the Black students in my class had decided not to re-enroll for a second year. Many of my peers had threatened not to return. A significant number did not. These students "did not like it." They said that other Black students were not who they expected, and, "the college was just too white." Many of the students who left appeared to be as bright and capable as those who remained, but did not feel a part of the college community. During this time, at this college, there were two distinct communities; the Black students had their peer group, and the White students had several different peer groups and student networks.

What was really behind African American attrition? What prevented these students from feeling and becoming a part of the community? Why couldn't they find a way to cope and succeed academically and socially in this environment, particularly when some of them eventually graduated from other institutions? What made the difference? As a student affairs professional in later

137

years, I witnessed the same phenomenon. There seemed to be no clear reason why some African American students, and other students of color, did not "fit" with the institution, and other Black students. This was particularly puzzling at those institutions that provided support services and programs specifically designed to meet the needs of students of color.

An invisible network or system was in place that influenced the attitudes and behavior of many Black students. This network consisted primarily of Black students who formed a peer group, by choice or circumstance. This group worked toward the goals of academic success and creating a sense of community despite the obstacles. For some Black students, this peer group was a place of refuge and support, while for others it was a source of pain and rejection. Students in the latter group felt abandoned by the Black students and rejected by the White students and the institution.

This powerful network was a student culture. Student cultures serve as networks that pass on information, customs, traditions, and a way of life and survival on the college campus (Becker, Geer, Hughes, & Strauss, 1961; Horowitz, 1987; Kuh & Whitt, 1988; Leemon, 1972, 1977; Newcomb, 1962; Wallace, 1966). They often serve as places of refuge for members, helping to make sense of the web of systems on a college campus. From the classroom to athletic programs, to the student services offices, to the residence halls, student cultures serve as valuable learning vehicles connecting students to opportunities and resources.

This chapter explores the phenomenon of students of color and student cultures on predominantly white college campuses. In addition, the Black, Hispanic, Native American and Asian Pacific American students' experiences and the role of student cultures in their collegiate lives will be considered. Implications for student affairs, student recruitment and retention will conclude this section. A case will be presented for the paradigm shift necessary to include these students in the study of student cultures. Given this information, students of color will be better understood, served, and supported by student affairs professionals.

STUDENTS OF COLOR AND THE COLLEGE EXPERIENCE

The experiences of students of color at historically Black institutions or other institutions that primarily serve students of color varies significantly. For example, there are typically more students of color at historically Black, Hispanic or Tribal colleges, and the students are not treated as "minority" or "special population students." Because these colleges meet the vocational, cultural, psychological and personal needs of their specific constituents, the campuses honor the whole student (Fleming, 1984). The cultural self and the surrounding environment affirm the student in terms of his/her cultural heritage both in and out of the classroom. Student activities and programs encompass the diverse interests of the students. Students are encouraged to be involved with the mainstream of college life, and to be of service to the community. Their experiences are significantly different from those of their peers who attend predominantly white colleges (Fleming, 1984).

Enrollment by students of color at predominantly white institutions has increased over the past three decades. These students report different educational and cultural experiences from their peers who attend predominantly Black, Hispanic, or Tribal colleges. They report feeling less a part of the mainstream of campus life. They have few if any faculty of color as role models, and often believe they are a "second class citizen" (Fleming, 1984). Their experiences as people of color are neither affirmed in the classroom nor through on-going mainstream campus life activities and programs. Beyond the annual Black History Months, Cinco de Mayo celebrations, Pow Wows, and Asian Awareness Weeks, students of color typically have limited social and cultural programs for enrichment and renewal.

Peer groups often form in response to these conditions. Little is known about them, the ways they are formed and the conditions under which they support or detract from student success. To understand more about these peer groups, it is necessary to consider the experiences of students of color on predominantly white college campuses.

The term students of color encompass a vast array of individuals whose uniqueness and diversity sometimes get lost in such an umbrella term. For example, there are at least 530 Native American tribes in the U.S. which speak 149 different languages (Heinrich, Corbine & Thomas, 1990). While the term Hispanic is used to designate a particular group of people, Hispanics are multi-racial, multiregional and national, speak Spanish differently or not at all, and arrived in the U.S. at different times for different reasons. Similar examples of within group differences can be found in the African American community and the Asian Pacific American populations. These populations have continued to grow and diversify in this country, and higher education has experienced an increase in the visibility of and diversity within these populations. Enrollment of students of color has increased over the past three decades, yet these students remain underrepresented in the academy (Person, 1994; Simpson & Frost, 1993). In contrast, people of color will be one third of the U.S. population by the year 2000 (Hodgkinson, 1983; Levine, 1990; Simpson & Frost, 1993).

Many students of color enrolled at predominantly white institutions are first generation college students. These students typically come from homes where higher education is appreciated and supported (Leach, 1987). However, family members in these homes are often limited in their understanding of the college experience. Institutional rules, policies, federal and state regulations that govern financial aid, and social norms of the college environment are not as clear to these families as they are to nonfirst generation college students' families. Students from these households are expected to fit into unknown institutional and student cultural norms almost immediately.

Adversarial Relationships and Blocks to Achievement

Historically, students of color and predominantly white institutions have had an adversarial relationship (Wright, 1987). Blacks were not permitted to enroll in public white southern institutions until after World War I (Wright, 1987). When they did enroll at the end of the 1930s, it was mostly in segregated living and learning environments (Weinberg cited in Wright, 1987). Native Americans rarely participated in higher education. Lopez, Madrid-Barela, and Macias reported that Hispanics were as invisible as Native Americans until after the 1968 Civil Rights "La Raza" movement (as cited in Wright, 1987). Asian Americans immigrated to the U.S. as early as the 1800s, and did not have access to higher education. They too encountered racism and discrimination.

Many factors affect students' of color success in college (Pounds, 1987). These influences include social, economic, and political variables. The unique history of each group also affects their access, transition, acceptance, and persistence in the academy. Each group has had to struggle with differences within the group and the common experience of racial discrimination by the larger and more powerful majority. American colleges often exhibit institutional racism as a reflection of historically troubled race relations and ethnocentrism in the United States (Altbach, 1991; Fleming, 1984; Harper, 1975; Willie, 1972). In addition to racism, socioeconomic issues affect the recruitment and retention of students of color. Astin (1982) found a positive correlation between family income and student persistence. The lower the parental income, the less likely it is that the student would persist. Historically, many people of color, particularly women, have lived below the poverty line. The National Center for Educational Statistics in 1992 reported an increase in single parent households headed by women in the 1980s and 1990s (as cited in Elliott, 1994). Parental occupation also affects student persistence concerning career choice (Astin, 1982). Students of color whose parents have college degrees and well-paying occupations have strong role models and are more likely to persist. Unfortunately, parents of most students of color do not fit this description. The economic disparity between people of color and white people impacts on the likelihood for student persistence in college (Elliott, 1994)

Socioeconomic issues are not the only contributors to the disparity in educational attainment. Native Americans have the lowest graduation rate of all ethnic groups in higher education, and experience value conflicts between Native American culture and institutional culture and traditions (Steward, 1993). The financial burden of an education, combined with historical neglect and racism other issues that contribute to disparity in educational attainment.

Chan and Wang (1991) discussed the racial tensions on college campuses for Asian Pacific American students. They reported these incidents were quite similar to those experienced by Black students. Racism, both subtle and overt, has provoked increased hostility toward Asian Americans. Despite the myth of the model minority, there has been a backlash in our educational system, sparked by resentment of Asian Pacific Americans' educational achievements. Some institutions have imposed quotas on the number of Asian American students on their campuses (Chan & Wang, 1991).

Hispanic populations also have experienced the negative effects of racism in American higher education. Despite the tremendous diversity within this group, the term "Hispanic" has been used as a generic label. This group includes Mexican

American/Chicanos, Puerto Ricans, Cuban Americans who may
be of any race, or some combination (Quevedo-Garcia, 1987).
Hispanics are described as second class citizens in our society,
and as having experienced "academic colonialism" in higher education (De La Luz Reyes & Halcon, 1991; Olivas, 1986). Academic colonialism describes the marginalization of Hispanics in
higher education (Olivas, 1986). Because of linguistic, political
and cultural differences from the majority of Americans, Hispanic people have not had access to resources that would afford
them full access to the academic community. These resources
have been controlled by the dominant culture, with only limited
availability for the less dominant culture.

Typologies of Discrimination

De La Luz Reyes and Halcon (1991) described four categories
of discrimination that are related to academic colonialism and
affect Hispanics and other people of color. These categories include: a *type-casting* syndrome, tokenism, a *one-minority-per-pot*
syndrome, a *Brown-on-Brown research taboo*, and the *hairsplitting*
concept. Type-casting is similar to stereotyping, using gross generalizations to define an individual based on cultural or racial
background. Tokenism is the stigma placed on people of color
that suggests they are not qualified for their positions, and that
their presence is due to preferential treatment and substandard
evaluation criteria. One-minority-per-pot syndrome is reflected
throughout higher education where one often finds one faculty
member of color per department. The Brown-on-Brown research
taboo devalues research conducted by faculty of color on people
of color. Hairsplitting involves quibbling over non-essential issues, or engaging in petty behavior. These practices discourage
students of color and limit the number of faculty members and
administrators of color in higher education willing to serve as
role models. Inadvertent subjectivity and arbitrariness in making
decisions that serve the majority and exclude Hispanics and other people of color is often masked as concern. These practices
deter Hispanics and other people of color from full participation
and achievement in higher education, and affect their adjustment
and adaptation to the learning environment.

Jewelle Taylor Gibbs (1974) studied the adaptation patterns of
Black students at a predominantly white campus. She found that

Black students who experienced identity conflicts or stress related to cultural adaptation used four modes of adaptation to the dominant culture. Movement with the culture was labeled as *affirmation*, while movement toward the culture was defined as *assimilation*. Students who moved away from the culture were described as *withdrawn*, while those who moved against the culture experienced *separation*. The times of interaction and rate of interaction for the Black student with other Black students and with White students were determined by his/her coping mode. This mode was based on the background of the student (ethnic makeup of the neighborhood and school, and socio-economic level) and his/her response to the climate and conditions found in the college environment. In addition, many of these students did not find a sense of belonging within the traditional student culture; therefore, they created a student culture specific to their cultural, ethnic, and educational needs and values (Leemon, 1977).

The ability of students of color to achieve full participation and success in higher educational institutions depends on the level of comfort students find within the college environment. Students need friends, role models, professors and administrators to help in their transition to college and their academic success. The environment needs to be nurturing and supportive. Students should have opportunities to actively participate in campus life and experience academic success. They need to feel less alienation than reported in studies of Black student retention over the years (Fleming, 1984; Pounds, 1987). Given these realities, students of color often feel the need to support each other by forming both informal and formal networks of support (Pascarella, Terenzini, & Wolfe, 1991).

STUDENT CULTURES

Although students of color have attended institutions of higher education for several decades, their experiences and perspectives are not fully understood, particularly those perspectives shaped by student cultures (Kuh & Whitt, 1988; Person, 1990). Populations of color were not included in the traditional paradigm for studying student cultures until a shift occurred in the 1980s (Holland & Eisenhart, 1990; Person, 1990). This exclusion has limited knowledge and understanding of students of color and their peer group experiences.

Newcomb (1962) described peer group formation as an outcome of antecedent events. His model consists of four key components which influence peer group formation. The first component includes the background characteristics students bring with them to the college (e.g., family history, lifestyle, socioeconomic status, high school/educational background, level of exposure to subject matter in preparation for college). The second area involves encounters with an institutional mission shaped by its history and origins, and demonstrated through its traditions, policies, and cultures (faculty, student, administrative, alumni, etc.). The environment of the college, its layout, design, and architectural features either support or detract from student interaction. The third component comprises the challenge and support aspect of their peer group. Peer groups consist of people who are both different from and similar to them in terms of culture, academic preparation, social class, family backgrounds, and expectations of a college education. The final component entails interactions with the faculty, the curriculum and co-curricular activities and programs that help to mold and shape critical thinking skills, and belief systems. These four components affect students, their characteristics, and the way in which they grow, develop and change because of the total college experience.

Peer group formations are often called student cultures (Becker et al., 1961; Kuh & Whitt, 1988; Leemon, 1972; Newcomb, 1962; Wallace, 1966). They are changing phenomena with key components and characteristics, including shared goals, shared values, common conditions, and normative behaviors that are sanctioned by group members. Common language, customs, behaviors, and traditions are characteristics of a student culture. It should be noted that student cultures have the same characteristics as other cultures. They support group members and environmental factors that allow for the perpetuation of the culture and its values (Leemon, 1972; Moffat, 1987; Person, 1990). Members are supported or punished based on their behavior and the impact of that behavior on the group. If behavior supports the group, it is rewarded. If behavior detracts from the good of the group in favor of the individual or other cultures, the offender is punished (Wallace, 1966). Student cultures can be distinguished from one another based on these characteristics.

The lens traditionally used in viewing students of color in the context of student culture has been monocular. This viewpoint focused only on race and ignored other significant differences.

Additional differences such as class, gender, sexual orientation, abilities, and even regional/geographical differences have been less examined. It is necessary that a paradigm shift occur to include these other factors. To use race as the only lens for viewing and understanding culture distorts perception. Students are complex as are the cultural issues that create the context for their learning and worldview. Race is not the only, and is often not the most important factor. A Native American student brings not only her cultural self to the classroom, but her race, class, and gender self. She sits in the classroom listening, interpreting and clarifying her thoughts through all of these lenses. If a supportive and nurturing environment allows for the multiple dimensions of the student, then she will further develop the many aspects of herself. An African American student who is gay and learning disabled brings all that he is to the academic support center for assistance. Four offices which provide fragmented services cannot address his complex needs as effectively as a sensitive staff member who can perceive him in all his complexity and behave accordingly. Even in colleges with few Black students and other students of color, one will find significant diversity. Sometimes a group identified by race may in actuality have only that one factor in common. Language, customs, and traditional ways of life within the same racial group may be quite different. People labeled by these broad categories may define their common condition quite differently, and may also find the common condition to be artificially imposed by the environment.

Critical to understanding diverse student cultures is the notion of a shared common condition (Becker et al., 1961). The traditional paradigm for viewing student cultures has failed since it did not discuss the experiences and common conditions of students of color or their within group differences in history, identity, development and group evolution. The issues of race relations and group dynamics concerning majority versus minority status were not studied until recently. Moffat (1987) considered race as a factor in the study of general student culture, but did not discuss the role it played in the daily lives of Black, Hispanic or white students at Rutgers University.

STUDENTS OF COLOR AND STUDENT CULTURES

Since race and skin color have dominated the way in which Americans view each other, it comes as no surprise that race and skin color serve as a major instrument in the labeling of students and their cultures. Studies conducted at two liberal arts and engineering college campuses in Pennsylvania in the late eighties and early nineties revealed that even in situations where the Black student populations were small in comparison to the total student population, there were at least two fully functioning Black student cultures (Person, 1990).

Campus A is a residential undergraduate institution serving a total of 2,000 students and 161 faculty members. It has sixty Black students, one African American faculty member and five other Black faculty from African and Caribbean nations. Students are selected from a highly competitive applicant pool. The homogeneous student body is largely composed of second or third generation college students whose families have incomes of more than $50,000 a year. Of the 2,000 students, approximately 7% are considered ethnic minority (Black, Hispanic, or Asian American). The college has attempted to attract and retain Black students since the early 1970s. The number of Black students rarely rises above 60, despite the presence of admissions and financial aid programs to support them. Each spring prospective students of color spend a weekend at the college as guests of the college.

Campus B is quite similar to Campus A. It is primarily residential serving approximately 4,200 students including 115 Black students. The graduate student population is half the size of the undergraduate population. Two Black faculty members and three Black administrators work on campus. The applicant pool is competitive, and students are generally non-first generation. This institution became co-educational in the early 1970s and sought to diversify its student body. Campus B also holds a weekend program for students of color in the spring to convince them to attend the college and sponsors a six week residential summer program for students of color. This program provides students with the opportunity to begin their college education early with close supervision, guidance, and support.

Research conducted on both campuses suggests that Black students feel separate from much of the college community and unwelcome as full participants in the mainstream of college life. They believe in and value a sense of community among the Black students on campus. Current Black students encourage enrollment only for those prospective Black students they believe able to fit into the Black student culture. The recruitment activities are both formal and informal, using follow-up telephone conversations and personal contact between prospective and current students. These contacts are created by the Black student cultures of both schools and the administration at both institutions. The students work in concert with the Admissions Office to ensure some involvement in the perpetuation of the Black student culture. Prospective students who seemed less likely to "buy into" the common vision of a Black community and unity are not embraced by the student cultures.

Within these small numbers of students, there is a wide range of diversity. Diversity is most prominent in student discussions of their socioeconomic/class background and other cultural characteristics. Class and gender differences separate these students somewhat, but the major differences were in the amount of time students committed to the Black community. The rate and amount of interaction with and between students varied, but was central to the theme of perpetuating a Black student culture and Black community.

Black student cultures at both campuses were supported by the faculty and administration and functioned independently. In both cases, studies revealed that students had formed a peer group network as a place of refuge and support in response to a shared common experience and condition (Person, 1990). At Campus A, members of the student culture valued its members working to their full potential. This was an unspoken belief rarely discussed by group members. These students had difficulty creating a study test file for community use since they were concerned about revealing test scores to others whether they did well or not. Specific performance was not openly discussed by group members. Students did not want to feel they were in competition with other group members. The culture was supportive of academic programs sponsored by the administration, and encouraged students to use peer counseling and the Academic Deans' Offices for assistance. This student culture valued athletics, social and cultural activities that were Afrocentric in nature, and a sense of a unified Black community. The Black student culture valued the academic success of its members. While students reported their personal goals were primary, they continually mentioned the importance of group members succeeding. There was a strong sense of community and commitment to others.

The student culture punished those students who were less

involved with the Black community. Students who chose to participate in traditional White Greek fraternity life were rejected by the Black student culture, while those students who for financial reasons chose to participate in other mainstream programs (residence hall advisor, student athletes) were welcomed and included. All of these activities took students away from the Black student culture. The students who chose the White Greek system were doing so for social reasons rather than academic or financial reasons. Their involvement took them away from the Black student culture for a reason that was not valued by the culture.

The second institution, Campus B, was in many ways similar to the first. The Black student culture valued academics and placed a strong emphasis on group support and interaction. This institution sponsored a summer program for Black and Hispanic students that encouraged a sense of community and group study. The impact of the summer program was felt during the academic year even for students who were not summer program participants. While these students were generally less successful academically than the students in the previous school, they were more willing to discuss academic concerns within their peer group. This student culture valued the opportunity to assist group members with academic challenges, and to support the academic potential of its members. They valued the support services offered by the college, particularly those coordinated by other students (e.g., peer counseling and tutoring).

Like Campus A, these students valued a sense of a Black community, and spent time creating what they believed was missing in their immediate environment. Students dedicated tremendous energy and time to academic and cultural programs. Countless hours were spent on program design and implementation, from special events to daily informal social gatherings. These students valued a sense of spirituality within the student culture, and encouraged its members to grow and develop in a spiritual/religious context. This was shown through informal discussions about religion and many were members of the college gospel choir, and/or attended local church services in the surrounding community. Students discussed their desire for a stronger sense of unity between Black students and a need to work toward that goal. In an effort to achieve this sense of community, students often involved alumni of the college and local community members who served as role models to the students.

An important finding was the diversity within both small populations of students. At Campus A there were six clusters of students within the Black student culture. Students reported their interactions with each other using a sociometric system that identified daily interactions with Black students at the college, and were clustered by this data. Each cluster represented the students who identified each other as on-going participants in their social network. The clusters focused around the Black student union which was a connecting point that all students mentioned as symbolic of the Black community. These clusters were identified as the immediate network of interactions and supports gleaned from self-reported student data. Clusters included: student athletes affiliated with the Black student union, student athletes not affiliated, Black student union affiliates, independents associated with the Black student union, independents not associated with the Black student union, and a Caribbean student cluster with affiliates and non-affiliates to the Black student union. Each of these clusters interacted with each other, except the Caribbean cluster. The Caribbean cluster was directly tied to all of the other clusters, and had strong, but less visible influence on the total Black student culture.

Most of the college community viewed the Black students as a monocultural group. For years the diversity of this peer group and culture was not noticed or served, because it was not studied or understood. Race was used as the single identifying characteristic for the entire group. This narrow view shows institutional neglect and cultural racism in higher education. The range of students' needs within this group was not recognized or served because all Black students were viewed as essentially similar. As long as there were Black student unions, cultural activities, and a Dean responsible for minority students, the college staff believed it had fulfilled its obligations and met students' needs. The community only responded to and recognized the Black students affiliated with the Black Student Union. They served as the spokespeople for all Black students whether the discussion focused on a single program, Black History Month, or an academic issue. Members of the Black Student Union sat on all search committees where Black students were solicited, and they were frequently called upon to help the administration in decisions about Black students, policies and procedures. This often led to these select students feeling responsible for representing what they knew to be very diverse needs and interest. The students recognized their inability to achieve this task. However, they felt forced to be the spokespeople, since some representation was considered better than none at all. This situation often made students who were not asked to serve on committees feel more excluded, less a part of the college and of the Black student culture. This contributed to the marginalization of some Black students in terms of the Black student culture and the majority student cultures.

Preliminary results of a study currently underway at a predominantly Hispanic college in the southwest has shown similar diversity within student cultures presently on that campus (Mendez-Catlin, 1995). Echoes of this appeared in a focus group discussion with Native American students at a liberal arts college in the west (Person, 1994a). There students expressed frustration with administrators and faculty treating them all the same. Tribal differences in customs and language were often ignored, and these students found themselves misunderstood and categorized based on a generic understanding of Native American people by the dominant culture. The within group differences can serve as a strong educational force for student culture group members. The clusters described earlier supported students and served as an integral component of the Black student culture. Clusters could be differentiated from other student clusters and cultures on the college campus. Through the various cluster interactions, students learned from each other, and that while they were all Black, they shared different cultural orientations, values, and perspectives toward life. Again, this proves the power of the student culture as a learning tool.

SUMMARY AND CONCLUSION

Given the history and currently increased presence of students of color in American higher education, our ideas about student culture must go far beyond the traditional student cultures described by Horowitz (1987). It would be impossible for traditional student cultures to meet the needs of the "new" students. Non-dominant student cultures have served as a place of refuge from institutional and cultural racism. Students of color have, since the Civil Rights movement of the 1960s, insisted upon and demanded programs and services to meet their unique needs (Pounds, 1987). Student cultures are a significant part of the retention process for all students. The power of the peer group to educate and support is a dynamic phenomenon the student affairs profession must understand and work with, broadening the paradigm to include all student cultures found in American higher education. It is important that we in student affairs recognize how limited we are in our understanding of students of color and student cultures. The need to study and understand these phenomena is central to our ability to fully embrace diversity and to move beyond the traditional paradigm of student cultures as defined by and for White students.. The study of these dynamic student cultures on our campuses should be on-going. Information about an Asian-Pacific American student culture which is learned one semester, on one campus, cannot necessarily be used to make decisions over an extended period of time across campuses because student cultures change constantly due to the mobility and turnover of students in general.

Student cultures profoundly affect the experience of students of color. Their level of comfort and satisfaction with the college experience is directly affected by their peer group interactions. The student affairs profession will miss a critical link to all students' learning and our own professional development if we are incapable of studying, learning about, and working with student cultures. This is not information easily gleaned from daily observation or reading textbooks. Knowledge about student cultures must be incorporated into the new paradigms for teaching and learning that we create on college campuses. Through focus groups, interviews, surveys, and general discussions with students we can come to understand the influences and values of their student cultures and thus relate to their members more effectively.

There is one outcome we should consider as student affairs professionals. If we ask questions of students and through research methods probe into their lives and experiences, the process itself may raise students' expectations that the institution cares and will make changes to shift its cultural lens beyond race. Once expectations are raised, there will be no effective choice but to respond to the issues uncovered. In our strategic planning for the next decade we must include all that is part of the learning experience. Studies of the cultures in which students of color participate will provide data to address some important and as yet unanswered questions about student satisfaction, comfort, and retention in all groups.

REFERENCES

Altbach, P. & Lomotey, K. (1991). *The racial crisis in American higher education.* New York: State University of New York Press.

Astin, A. (1982). *Minorities in higher education,* San Francisco: Jossey-Bass.

Becker, H., Geer, B., Hughes, E., & Strauss, A. (1961). *Boys in White.* Chicago: The University of Chicago Press.

Chan, S. & Wang, L. (1991). Racism and the model minority: Asian-Americans in higher education. In P. Altbach & K. Lomotey (Eds.). *The racial crisis in American higher education* (pp. 43-67). New York: State University of New York Press.

De La Luz Reyes, M. & Halcon, J. (1991). Practices of the academy: Barriers to access for Chicano academics. In P. Altbach & K. Lomotey (Eds.). *The racial crisis in American higher education.* (pp. 167-186). New York: State University of New York Press.

Elliott, P. (1994). *The urban campus.* Phoenix: American Council on Education, Oryx Press.

Fleming, J. (1984). *Blacks in college: A comparative study of students success in Black and White Institutions.* San Francisco: Jossey-Bass.

Gibbs, J. T. (1974). Patterns of adaptation among Black students at a predominantly White university: Selected case studies. *The American Journal of Orthopsychiatry, 44,* 728-740.

Harper, F. D. (1975). *Black students: White campus.* Washington D.C.: APGA Press.

Heinrich, R. K., Corbine, J. L., & Thomas, K. R. (1990). Counseling Native Americans. *Journal of Counseling and Development, 69,* 128-133.

Hodgkinson, H. L. (1983). *Guess who's coming to college: Your students in 1990.* Washington D. C., State National Information Network.

Holland, D. & Eisenhart, M. (1990). *Educated in romance: Women, achievement and college culture.* Chicago: The University of Chicago Press.

Horowitz, H. (1987). *Campus life: Undergraduate cultures from the eighteenth century to the present.* New York: Alfred Knopf.

Kuh, G. D. & Whitt, J. (1988). *The invisible tapestry: Culture in American colleges and universities.* ASHE-ERIC Higher Education Report No. 1. Washington, D.C.

Leach, B. (1987). How to retain Black students on predominantly White campuses. *Black Issues in Higher Education, 4(7),* 36.

Leemon, T. A. (1977, March). *The student cultures: The challenge of privatism.* Keynote Address, American College Personnel Association, Denver, Colorado.

Leemon, T. A. (1972). *The rites of passage in a student culture.* New York: Teachers College Press.

Levine, A. (1990). *Shaping higher education's future.* San Francisco: Jossey-Bass

Mendez-Catlin, L. [Hispanic Student Culture]. Unpublished raw data.

Moffat, M. (1987). *Coming of age in New Jersey.* New Brunswick: Rutgers University Press.

Newcomb, T. (1962). *The American college.* New York: John Wiley and Sons.

Olivas, M. (1986). *Latino college students.* New York: Teacher College Press.

Pascarella, E. T., Terenzini, P. T. & Wolfe, L. (1991). *How college affects students.* San Francisco: Jossey-Bass.

Person, D. (1994a). [Student culture: Phase three]. Unpublished raw data.

Person, D. (1994b). Black and Hispanic women in higher education. In F. Rivera-Batiz (Ed.), *Reinventing urban education* (pp. 303-326). New York: IUME Press.

Person, D. (1989). The Black student culture of Lafayette College. *Dissertation Abstracts International,* (University Microfilms No. 9033891)

Pounds, A. (1987). Black students' needs on predominantly White campuses. In D. J. Wright (Ed.). *Responding to the needs of minority students* (pp. 23-38). San Francisco: Jossey-Bass.

Simpson, R. D. & Frost, S.H. (1993). *Inside college: Undergraduate education for the future* (pp. 39-66). New York: Insight Books/Plenum Press.

Steward, R. J. (1993). Two faces of academic success: Case studies of American Indians on a predominantly Anglo university campus. *Journal of College Student Development,* (34), 191-196.

Wallace, W. L. (1966). *Student culture: Social structure and continuity in a liberal arts college.* Chicago: Aldine Publishing.

Willie, C. & McCord, A. (1972). *Black students at White colleges.* New York: Praeger Publishers.

Wright, D. J. (1987). Minority students developmental beginnings. In D. J. Wright (Ed.). *Responding to the needs of minority students* (pp. 5-22). San Francisco: Jossey-Bass.

7

Multiculturalism in Counseling and Advising

Amy L. Reynolds

INTRODUCTION

Counseling and advising skills are core student affair competencies needed for roles which place student affairs practitioners in a helping capacity (Barr & Associates, 1993; Council for the Advancement of Standards [CAS], 1986; 1992; Delworth, Hansen, & Associates, 1989; Komives, 1990; Miller, Winston, & Associates, 1991). The acquisition of general counseling, advising, and helping skills is central to the ability of student affairs professionals to work effectively with students. Whether it be in a counseling or career center, a residence hall, an activities office, or an admissions office, all student affairs professionals must have important interpersonal, counseling, and advising skills including but not limited to: active listening, empathy, reflection, goal setting, paraphrasing, establishing rapport, group leadership, supervision, group process skills, assessment, nonverbal abilities, ethical sensitivity, confrontation, cross-cultural communication, and relationship-building.

These advising and counseling skills are necessary to building constructive and meaningful relationships with students. While not all student affairs professionals are counselors, many are given opportunities to counsel and work with students on a one-to-one basis. Counseling may not be a major component of their job description, yet often the circumstances of students' lives demand that student affairs professionals know how to respond to emotional and personal needs. Residence hall directors, financial aid counselors, student orientation staff, career counselors, and multicultural affairs staff may all need counseling skills. While the term advising is sometimes used interchangeably with the term counseling or may refer to a non-therapy oriented type of counseling or helping (i.e., offering advice), in a student affairs context, advising also means some specific roles and responsibilities. There are academic advisors who typically work one-on-one with students and student organization advisors who help student leaders develop the skills needed to lead their various groups or organizations, whether residence hall government, Greek organizations, or other student groups (e.g., Program Board, French Club). Other student affairs professionals also act as advisors to individual students or student groups.

Helping skills are also central in the efforts of student affairs professionals to reach out to and work effectively with students who have been historically under-represented or under-served in higher education (e.g., students of color, lesbian, gay, and bisexual students, students with disabilities, and white female students). It is often through the process of counseling and advising that student affairs practitioners have the opportunity to form meaningful relationships with students who are different from them, creating possibilities for growth and learning for all involved. Multicultural relationships are part of a learning process from which understanding and self-awareness can be developed. While working with and learning about people who are culturally different from us, we have the chance to learn about ourselves and to expand our world view. Multicultural counseling, advising, and communication skills create endless opportunities for student affairs practitioners to engage in and learn from multicultural dynamics and situations.

A growing number of student affairs professionals believe that "it is the collective responsibility of student affairs professionals to respond more effectively and knowledgeably to diverse student groups on college campuses" (McEwen & Roper, 1994, p. 49). The complex multicultural dynamics of many institutions demand that student affairs professionals be prepared to address multicultural issues as well as have the skills necessary to work effectively with culturally diverse populations and issues (Ebbers & Henry, 1990; Wright, 1987). Because of the discrepancy between professional training and demands of practice within student affairs, some authors have identified the need for specific multicultural skills (Ebbers & Henry, 1990; McEwen & Roper, 1994; Pope & Reynolds, 1994).

The purpose of this chapter is to examine the multicultural knowledge, awareness, and skills that student affairs professionals, in counseling and advising roles need to be effective and ethical in their practice. In order for student affairs practitioners to expand their competencies to work with students who are culturally different from them, counseling and advising skills must be redefined and reframed to include skills which are relevant and useful for working with individuals and groups who traditionally have been under-served and under-represented in higher education. The chapter offers information for conceptualizing, and ultimately developing, personal effectiveness in multicultural counseling and advising.

DEFINITIONS OF MULTICULTURAL COUNSELING

The notion of multicultural advising presented in this chapter is derived primarily from the counseling and psychology literature which has extensive scholarship in this area. These concepts and descriptions of multicultural counseling or helping can be generalized to add meaning to our understanding of student affairs advising.

As delineated by Ridley, Mendoza, & Kanitz (1994), there are various definitions of multicultural counseling. Some experts define multiculturalism exclusively around racial and ethnic issues and fear that broader definitions weaken the efforts to eradicate racism (Helms, 1994; Locke, 1990). Others adopt a broader definition which expands the definition of culture to include such areas as gender, socioeconomic status, sexual orientation, and national origin (Pedersen, 1988; Pope & Reynolds, 1990; Speight, Myers, Highlen, & Cox, 1991). These perspectives and definitions not only frame how multicultural counseling is viewed, they also determine what awareness, knowledge, and skills are seen as necessary for effective multicultural counseling and advising.

There are essentially two ways of viewing multicultural counseling: a) a culturally distinct perspective and b) a universal point of view. The culturally distinct view historically conceptualized the multicultural dyad as a helping relationship in which the counselor or advisor is typically Caucasian and the student is a person of color. Although many might agree that the assumption that the counselor or advisor is White is biased and inappropriate, most multicultural counseling training efforts have been targeted for Whites. As increasing numbers of people of color have entered the counseling and advising professions, it is important to assume that both the caregiver or client might be a member of any racial/ ethnic/cultural group rather than assuming that members of certain groups will be in specific roles. Counseling from the culturally distinct perspective requires knowledge of the culture and may involve indigenous practices and treatments. The culturally distinct counseling worldview primarily focuses on race and ethnicity and typically does not include other aspects of difference (e.g., religion, sexual orientation, gender).

The universal view of multiculturally counseling is defined as "any counseling relationship in which two or more of the participants differ in cultural background, values, and lifestyle" (Sue, Bernier, Durran, Feinberg, Pedersen, Smith & Vasquez-Nuttall, 1982, p. 47). From that point of view, the assumption is that all helping is multicultural because all humans differ in terms of cultural background, values, or experiences. A universal perspective often is based on the assumption of generic human dimensions and typically involves universal treatments and practices. A universal counseling point of view is more likely to incorporate a broader definition of cultural diversity (e.g., race, sexual orientation, gender, disability).

While there is no consensus as to which definition is preferable, it is important to acknowledge that these two perspectives create a false dichotomy. One does not have to consider *either* culturally specific *or* universal viewpoints; rather one can incorporate the strengths of both worldviews and definitions. When counselors or advisors are working with someone who is culturally different from them, they can look for commonalities as well as attend to culturally specific information that might be useful. Despite the pros and cons to both approaches, "'universal' and 'focused' multicultural approaches are not necessarily contradictory" (Sue, Arredondo, & McDavis, 1992, p. 478).

Redefinition of Multicultural Counseling

According to Speight et al. (1991), multicultural counseling must be redefined and "reconceptualized as fundamental counseling skills achieved through self-knowledge and a shift in worldview" (p. 29). In the past multicultural counseling skills were conceptualized as specialty skills that some professionals developed to work with specific populations. This distinction between "special" and "regular" counseling has been identified as being unresponsive to the needs of under-served groups (Speight et al., 1991). All counselors need basic awareness, knowledge, and skills that are relevant and helpful to the widest range of potential clients possible.

When counselors overemphasize learning cultural information about a specific group, they are more likely to apply that knowledge to the counseling process in a simplistic and reductionistic manner. This "cookbook approach" has been widely criticized because it does not allow for the possibility of individual differences within groups and does not encourage applying cultural understandings in a case by case manner (Ridley et al., 1994; Speight et al., 1991). While culture specific knowledge can be very informative and useful in understanding or explaining some group differences, it is important not to assume that every member of a particular cultural group is the same nor has had the same experiences.

Cultural knowledge and culturally specific techniques are not linked directly to effective therapy or positive outcomes (Sue & Zane, 1987). Contemporary multicultural counseling strategies based primarily in the culturally distinct model are too detached from the realities and complexities of multicultural counseling. It takes more than a little bit of cultural knowledge to be an effective multicultural counselor. Likewise, to ignore the significance of cultural knowledge for the pursuit of universal truths and similarities is to minimize the reality and experiences of many individuals, especially those who historically have been under-represented and under-served. According to Sue and Zane, "psychology must continually strive to devise new paradigms and practices" (p. 40) to better meet the needs of all clients. A growing number of psychologists are calling for a reformulation and redefinition of multicultural counseling that incorporates a more complex understanding of what is necessary to effectively work across cultures (Speight et al., 1991; Sue & Zane, 1987). This information must become infused into the conceptualization of multicultural counseling and advising in a college or university setting.

A unifying and holistic framework is needed to reconceptualize multicultural counseling outside of the culturally distinct/ universal dichotomy. Emphasizing cultural differences has oversimplified the differences that exist and caused many counselors and advisors to minimize the importance of individual differences and universal similarities. Focusing on similarities among people doesn't allow for the complexity of individual and cultural differences. Speight et al. (1991), in citing Kluckhorn and Murray's (1953) supposition that everyone is like all individuals, like some individuals and like no other individuals, emphasized the need to move away from either/or conceptualization. Speight et al. (1991), citing the Cox (1982) tripartite model of worldview, encouraged the exploration of the simultaneous influences of individual uniqueness, cultural specificity, and human universality. The "Cox model provides a coherent and practical conceptualization for understanding the complex blending of influences on individuals' worldviews" (Speight et al., 1991, p. 32). Moving away from a dichotomous world view to a cultural/individual/universal perspective allows us to embrace the true complexity of human beings.

Another important reconceptualization of the multicultural counseling process, by Sue and Zane (1987), suggests the use of counseling interventions which are more strongly connected to positive counseling outcomes, such as credibility and gift giving. According to Sue and Zane, counselor (and advisor) credibility is determined by the client's perception of the counselor (and advisor) as an effective and trustworthy helper. While some of this credibility may be based on cultural variables (e.g., the counselor's ability to know cultural specific information), much of it occurs when a counselor (or advisor) utilizes culturally consistent interventions and general helping skills. Sue and Zane believe that the role of cultural knowledge is to alert the helper to possible credibility problems. For example, if an academic advisor is working with a Latino student who is anxious about his academic performance, the advisor may need some cultural knowledge to work effectively with that student. If the advisor is unaware that in the Latino culture attending to relationships is often perceived as a precursor and important prerequisite to "getting down to business", then her/his efforts to begin their meetings by focusing immediately on tasks might cause the Latino client to view the advisor as insensitive. If the advisor is viewed in this way, s/he has lost credibility and effectiveness in the eyes of the student thus making it more difficult for them to work together.

Gift giving, a client's perception that something was received from the helping encounter, is another crucial aspect of building an effective multicultural counseling relationship. Most individuals need an almost immediate direct benefit from helping (e.g.,

anxiety reduction, goal setting, normalization, hope, skills acquisition, depression relief, and reassurance). Extending our previous example with the Latino student, while it is important for
the advisor to assess the student's issues and life situation, the
student also may need some symptom relief if he is going to experience their relationship as beneficial.

According to Sue and Zane (1987), the goal of multicultural
counseling is to minimize credibility problems and maximize gift
giving. This goal should not imply that interventions will or
should always match cultural expectations and norms. Effective
helping should provide opportunities for new learning which
may not always fit with one's cultural beliefs, expectations, or
accepted patterns of behavior. However, in order to develop
multicultural competence, counselors and advisors must learn to
detect culturally insensitive and inappropriate responses thus
incorporating a complex and dynamic understanding of multicultural counseling and advising.

MULTICULTURAL COUNSELING AND ADVISING COMPETENCIES IN A STUDENT AFFAIRS CONTEXT

Since counseling psychology and student affairs literature and
training programs have intersecting histories and overlapping
professional goals, using the counseling psychology literature as
a starting place is both a reasonable and appropriate choice (Forrest, 1989). Within the counseling psychology profession there
have been extensive efforts to explore and delineate the multicultural competencies necessary for effective clinical practice. The
counseling psychology literature provides useful models for addressing issues of multicultural competence, education, and
training (Copeland, 1982; LaFromboise & Foster, 1992; Margolis
& Rungta, 1986; McRae & Johnson, 1991; Midgette & Meggert,
1991; Ridley et al., 1994; Sue et al., 1992; Sue et al., 1982).

Multicultural competence is a necessary prerequisite to effective, affirming, and ethical work in student affairs. In order to
be multiculturally competent, student affairs practitioners need
to develop a substantial degree of awareness, knowledge, and
skills to work with the human diversity on campus. Multicultural counseling and advising competencies may be defined as the
awareness, knowledge, and skills necessary to work effectively
and ethically across cultural differences.

In order to be an effective and multiculturally sensitive counselor and advisor, the following competencies are necessary: a) an appreciation and knowledge of the history, current needs, strengths, and resources of communities and individuals which historically have been under-served and/or under-represented by the student affairs profession; b) an awareness of one's own biases and cultural assumptions; c) the ability to use that knowledge and awareness to make more culturally sensitive and appropriate interventions; d) content knowledge about culturally related terms and concepts such as world view, acculturation, and identity development; e) an accurate self-assessment of one's multicultural skills and comfort level; f) an awareness of the interpersonal process which occurs within a multicultural dyad; and g) an awareness of the cultural assumptions underlying the helping process.

Acquiring Knowledge and Understanding of Cultural Groups

It is vital that counselors and advisors have some content knowledge about the history, traditions, resources, and concerns of the various under-represented or under-served campus groups. That knowledge should include an awareness of the culture and experiences of those groups, including their experiences in higher education in general and on one's own campus. Without this important awareness and information, a counselor or advisor may make assumptions and lack empathy for the experiences and feelings of those individuals.

For example, if a Navajo student came to see her academic advisor about her grades which were substantially below what would have been expected considering her SAT scores, the advisor needs some understanding of American Indian culture, including the unique aspects of Navajo culture, to meet her needs effectively. Without such knowledge, the advisor might not consider the importance of family and culture and therefore, not assess how living over 500 miles from her family and living in the White world might be affecting her ability to perform to her best ability. If counselors or advisors lack the necessary information, they will not conceptualize students' presenting issues in a culturally affirming manner including not knowing what questions to ask in assessing the students' circumstances. Imagine an advisor working with a student government within a graduate residence hall in which the residents are predominantly international students. Each student has a different understanding and expectation of government based on her/his own cultural experiences and the realities of her/his country's government. If an advisor does not comprehend the complexity of those expectations and how they impact the students' interactions, s/he will have difficulty working with this group effectively.

Enhancing Self-Awareness

An awareness of one's own biases and assumptions is another necessary step to developing culturally sensitive counseling and advising skills. We are all shaped by our own cultural and individual experiences which include learning the various stereotypes that our society teaches about various oppressed groups. It is quite difficult to avoid exposure to the misinformation that is found in the media and popular culture and so the task must be to unlearn those stereotypes and biases. For example, because we live in a heterosexist society most individuals assume that people are heterosexual unless told otherwise. If a gay student talked about relationship difficulties with his counselor and the counselor assumed the student was referring to a heterosexual relationship and asked about his girlfriend, the gay student might decide not to return because of the counselor's insensitivity. Or if a career counselor is working with a female student who wants to major in engineering and the counselor attempts to steer her away from that field (even if it might be to "protect" her from the challenges of that male-dominated profession), that bias will have a negative effect on their working relationship as well as her/his ability to meet the student's needs.

Developing Culturally Responsive Interventions

Once counselors and advisors have gained the necessary knowledge of the various cultural groups and have developed adequate self-awareness, it is important that they learn how to use that information and awareness to make more culturally responsive interventions. Such skills would include knowing what questions to ask and being aware of when one's biases may be interfering with the counseling or advising process. If the advisor to the lesbian, gay, and bisexual (LGB) student union on campus is heterosexual and does not understand the unique aspects of LGB culture and relationships, s/he may have difficulty responding to their needs appropriately and ultimately not understand any difficulties in the advising relationship. Utilizing a previous example, instead of encouraging the Navajo student to emotionally separate from her family because that is what traditional Eurocentric developmental and counseling theories suggest, a culturally sensitive advisor would ask the student to talk about her family, her culture, and what they mean to her. A culturally responsive counselor would learn how to ask about clients' relationships in a gender neutral way until clients provide the gender specificity.

Increasing Knowledge About Cultural Concepts

Developing an understanding of significant cultural concepts is necessary in order to work effectively with students who are culturally different from one's self. Knowledge about concepts, such as acculturation and racial identity, is as important as understanding cultural-specific information. Imagine a Greek advisor who works with Black and White Greek organizations. Understanding racial identity development theory could be helpful in working with the Black students who pledge Black Greek organizations and other Black students who pledge White Greek organizations. If the advisor assumes that all of the Black students are the same without understanding that individuals have different meanings and significance attributed to their racial identity, s/he might not perceive any communication difficulties or tensions that could occur among the Black students in the different Greek organizations. If a Jewish man is advising a Jewish student group and becomes frustrated when their idea of being Jewish is different from his, he needs to understand the identity development literature and be open to exploring his own Jewish identity in order to be a competent group advisor.

Assessing Multicultural Skills and Comfort Level

In order to prevent cultural miscommunication, it is important that counselors and advisors learn how to assess their own multicultural skills and comfort level accurately. Rather than assuming they can work effectively with everyone, advisors and counselors should gather information on their effectiveness with various groups. While no one likes to believe s/he has biases or lacks skills to work with others, unless the questions are asked, the skills never will be developed or enhanced. This self-assessment might involve observing themselves in a variety of situations, asking others for feedback about their cross-cultural communication skills, and examining in what situations and with what groups they do not feel comfortable. This honest self-reflection and appraisal will allow counselors and advisors to seek out the training or supervision they need to become more culturally sensitive.

In order to assess their level of multicultural comfort, it may be helpful for counselors and advisors to consider the amount of contact they have with people who are culturally different from them. In other words, how diverse are the people in their life? For example, they might notice that most of their friends come from the same cultural group that they are and most of their activities are based in cultural frameworks similar to their own. (e.g., a White counselor having few friends who are people of color and who rarely attends cultural events that focus on appreciating communities of color or a heterosexual fraternity advisor who has never attended a gay, lesbian or bisexual event and assumes that all of his friends are heterosexual).

Developing an Awareness of the Dynamics of a Multicultural Relationship

Counselors and advisors need to acquire an awareness of the interpersonal process which occurs when working with someone who is culturally different from them. Cultural differences can have a profound effect on the communication and relationship development process. If counselors or advisors are unaware of how culture can impact communication then they are likely to make assumptions which will interfere with their ability to work with individuals who communicate differently.

For example, if an advisor for an international students group did not understand how students from some other countries might communicate differently (e.g., degree of eye contact, physical proximity), then s/he might act in ways that would make it difficult to develop effective relationships. Imagine an advisor who was affectionate and often hugged the students with whom she worked. If she did not understand how such physical contact was not always culturally appropriate behavior (e.g., in traditional Muslim cultures, unrelated women and men do not touch), her relationship with some international students could become strained.

Another illustration could involve an advisor to the Spring Fling Committee, a popular annual campus-wide programming event. The Committee traditionally has been predominantly

White; however, during the last year the students of color organized to increase their membership on the committee so their
voices would be heard and their programming interests and
needs would be met. During the planning meetings the tension
between some of the students of color and some White students
around entertainment choices was growing. Voices were raised
and anger expressed. If the advisor is unable to grasp the needs
of the various groups or understand how varying cross-cultural
communication styles, s/he may not be able to intervene and
interrupt the growing group conflict. S/he must have the content knowledge about cross-cultural communication as well as
some sensitivity to the nuances of group conflict.

Deconstructing the Cultural Assumptions
Underlying the Helping Process

The final area of multicultural competence needed by counselors and advisors is an awareness of the cultural assumptions
underlying the helping process. According to Katz (1985), the
values of counseling, as it is traditionally defined, are based on
White middle-class values. The ability to deconstruct these assumptions is paramount to understanding how to make counseling and advising more accessible and relevant to some people of
color and other individuals who may not subscribe to those values. For example, there is an underlying assumption that counseling interactions must occur in a private setting or office and
that a counselor cannot be a friend but instead should be a detached professional. That model of helping is very unfamiliar to
many people of color who are more comfortable asking for support and assistance from friends and family. For some individuals, from a cultural perspective, talking about their personal
problems with a complete stranger feels inappropriate, disloyal,
and uncomfortable. Advisors and counselors need to be able to
uncover the values underlying how they relate to and help others so that they can discover some of the more subtle and core
challenges to working with students who are culturally different
from them.

This process of deconstructing cultural assumptions in counseling and advising is similar to understanding the various epistemological assumptions underlying knowledge, learning, and
teaching which were explored earlier in this book. This aware-

ness of underlying meanings and assumptions is essential to uncovering the message and connotation of one's efforts and work with others who are culturally different or may operate according to different beliefs. Understanding diverse worldviews and presumptions is important because it creates increased opportunities for improved relationships and enhanced self-understanding.

The descriptions of these various multicultural competencies require some reconceptualizing of counseling and advising processes. In many ways the development of multicultural counseling and advising competence can be perceived as a new paradigm for working with students. Rather than responding to students as if they are all the same or in predetermined ways based on their cultural group membership, counselors and advisors must assess and understand how cultural differences affect each individual relationship. Instead of assuming that "generic" interpersonal and helping skills are enough to work with students, counselors and advisors need to clarify and deconstruct what is meant by "generic" and effective counseling skills. They must assess and enhance their helping skills so they are equipped to work with all students from a variety of cultures and experiences.

Developing multicultural counseling and advising competencies is an ongoing and developmental process. In order to work effectively across cultural differences, student affairs professionals must assess their strengths and weaknesses. Counselors and advisors can review these seven core multicultural competencies and appraise their own abilities and insights. Once they are aware of where they need to grow, they can create an individualized learning plan with the help of their friends, colleagues, and supervisors. Like any other competency or skill, developing multicultural sensitivity and skills requires intentional effort and practice. Developing critical consciousness or self-awareness through praxis (action and reflection) is necessary for counselors and advisors to change themselves and the world around them. Utilizing the counseling and advising multicultural competencies described in this chapter should offer most student affairs professionals a way to conceptualize and develop their own multicultural awareness, knowledge, and skills.

Cultivating multicultural competence should not be a goal in and of itself. It must be embraced as a process; of learning, growing, and understanding ourselves and others. Enhancing our ability to work with others who are culturally different from us encourages us to expand ourselves and our worldview. By changing ourselves and our relationships with others, we, as student affairs professionals, will enable ourselves to change higher education into a more culturally sensitive and inclusive environment.

SUMMARY

Advising and counseling skills are core competencies that all student affairs professionals need in order to work effectively with students who are culturally different from them. Multicultural relationships are part of an important learning process through which both students and student affairs practitioners can understand themselves and each other. While there are differing views about how to define and conceptualize multicultural counseling or advising, what is primary is the counselor and advisor's ability to develop a complex and multifaceted view of multicultural relationships and the skills and sensitivities necessary to facilitate growth. Incorporating a complex and dynamic understanding of multicultural counseling and advising is the first step to developing multicultural competence.

There are specific and concrete multicultural awarenesses, knowledge, and skills that are necessary to form meaningful and efficacious relationships with all students. Student affairs professionals must develop an understanding of these particular and fundamental insights and abilities. It is not enough to try to be more culturally sensitive, to read diverse literature, or to attend cultural events. Becoming multiculturally competent requires that student affairs practitioners create a new paradigm for working with students. Rather than responding to students who are different from them as if they represent something new to learn or instead of assuming that students who appear like them are actually similar to them, counselors and advisors, by incorporating the paradigm shift explored in this chapter, can begin to develop relationships with students that are based on an understanding and appreciation of how culture differences *and* similarities affect each individual relationship. Conceptualizing multicultural sensitivity in this way will help to remove the feelings of duty and guilt that many people who strive to build effective relationships with people who are culturally different experience. Instead, multicultural relationships are most exciting and fruitful if perceived as part of the overall landscape of the challenging and fascinating nature of human relationships.

REFERENCES

Barr, M., & Associates (1993). *The handbook of student affairs administration.* San Francisco: Jossey-Bass.

Copeland, E. J. (1982). Minority populations and traditional counseling programs: Some alternatives. *Counselor Education and Supervision, 21,* 187-193.

Council for the Advancement of Standards for Student Services/Development Programs [CAS] (1986). *Council for the Advancement of Standards: Standards and Guidelines for Student Services/Development Programs.* Washington, D.C.: Council for the Advancement of Standards for Student Services/Development Programs.

Delworth, U. & Hansen, G. (Eds.). (1989). *Student services: A handbook for the profession* (2nd ed.). San Francisco: Jossey-Bass.

Ebbers, L. H. & Henry, S. L. (1990). Cultural competence: A new challenge to student affairs professionals. *NASPA Journal, 27,* 319-323.

Forrest, L. (1989). Guiding, supporting, and advising students: The counselor role. In U. Delworth & G. R. Hansen (Eds.), *Student services: A handbook for the profession* (2nd ed.). (pp. 265-283). San Francisco: Jossey-Bass.

Helms, J. E. (1994). How multiculturalism obscures racial factors in the therapy process: Comment on Ridley et al. (1994), Sodowsky et al. (1994), Ottavi et al. (1994), & Thompson et al. (1994). *Journal of Counseling Psychology, 41,* 162-165.

Katz, J. H. (1985). The sociopolitical nature of counseling. *The Counseling Psychologist, 13,* 615-624.

Komives, S. R. (1990). Careers in postsecondary settings. In N. Garfield and B. Collison (Eds.). *Careers in counseling and human development.* Alexandria, VA: American Association for Counseling and Development.

LaFromboise, T. D. & Foster, S. L. (1992). Cross-cultural training: Scientist-practitioner models and methods. *The Counseling Psychologist, 20,* 472-489.

Locke, D.C. (1990). A not so provincial view of multicultural counseling. *Counselor Education and Supervision, 30,* 18-25.

Margolis, R. L. & Rungta, S. A. (1986). Training counselors for work with special populations: A second look. *Journal of Counseling and Development, 64,* 642-644.

McEwen, M. K., & Roper, L. D. (1994). Incorporating multiculturalism into stuent affairs preparation programs: Suggestions from the literature. *Journal of College Student Development, 35,* 46-53.

McRae, M. B. & Johnson, S. D. (1991). Toward training for competence in multicultural counselor education. *Journal of Counseling and Development, 70,* 131-141.

Midgette, T. E. & Meggert, S. S. (1991). Multicultural counseling instruction: A challenge for faculties in the 21st century. *Journal of Counseling and Development, 70,* 136-141.

Miller, T., Winston, R. & Associates (1991). *Administration and leadership in student affairs* (2nd ed.). Muncie, IN: Accelerated Development.

Pedersen, P. (1988). *A handbook for developing multicultural awareness.* Alexandria, VA: American Counseling Association.

Pope, R. L. (1993). An analysis of multiracial change efforts in student affairs. (Doctoral dissertation, University of Massachusetts at Amherst, 1992). *Dissertation Abstracts International, 53-10,* 3457A.

Pope, R. L. & Reynolds, A. L. (1990). *An annotated bibliography of multiracial resources for student affairs administrators.* Unpublished manuscript.

Pope, R. L. & Reynolds, A. L. (1994). *Student Affairs Core Competencies: Integrating Multicultural Awareness, Knowledge, and Skills.* Unpublished manuscript.

Ridley, C. R., Mendoza, D. W. & Kanitz, B. E. (1994). Multicultural training: Reexamination, operationalization, and integration. *The Counseling Psychologist, 22,* 227-289.

Speight, S. L, Myers, L. J., Cox, C. I. & Highlen, P. S. (1991). A redefinition of multicultural counseling. *Journal of Counseling and Development, 70,* 29-36.

Sue, D. W. & Sue, D. (1990). *Counseling the culturally different: Theory and practice.* New York: Wiley.

Sue, D. W., Arredondo, P. & McDavis, R. J. (1992). Multicultural counseling competencies and standards: A call to the profession. *Journal of Counseling and Development, 70,* 477-486.

Sue, D. W., Bernier, J. E., Durran, A., Feinberg, L., Pedersen, P., Smith, E. J., & Vasquez-Nuttall, E. (1982). Position paper: Cross-cultural counseling competencies. *Counseling Psychologist, 10,* 45-52.

Sue, S. & Zane, N. (1987) The role of culture and cultural techniques in psychotherapy: A reformulation. *American Psychologist. 42.* 37-45.

Wright, D. J. (Ed.). (1987). *Responding to the needs of today's minority students.* New Directions for Student Services (No. 38). San Francisco: Jossey-Bass.

8

Border Crossings in Higher Education: Faculty/Student Affairs Collaboration

Jane Fried

Borders and border crossings have provided one of the key metaphors for this book. The goal of this chapter is to examine a very important border more closely, the one which divides academic education from student development education. A brief description of the terrain which faculty members and student development staff occupy is followed by a discussion of the barriers to crossing. Examples of some very successful border crossings, situations in which academic faculty and student development educators have collaborated to develop a common language for teaching and learning are also described. These programs have evolved in response to the demands for new types of teaching and learning that are related to interdisciplinary studies, problem centered approaches and the development of core curricula for undergraduate students in complex universities where "the center" has apparently disappeared.

THE TERRAIN: INTENTIONAL WORLDS OF FACULTY AND STUDENT AFFAIRS

Earlier in this work, Shweder's notion of intentional worlds was introduced as a way to describe different sociocultural environments. These environments exist as a function of the ways their occupants create meaning, seize and use resources and attempt to influence events. These worlds are "real, factual and forceful but only as long as there exists a community of persons whose beliefs, desires, emotions, purposes and other mental representations are directed at it and thereby influenced by it" (Shweder, 1990, p. 2). Intentional worlds are similar to epistemological communities, "a group or community that constructs and shares knowledge and standards of evidence" (Nelson, 1993, p. 124). Epistemological communities are described in terms of interaction between people who know and that which is known. Nelson asserts that the category of epistemology "has no fixed or historical content . . . it is persons, embodied and situated in specific social and historical contexts, who 'know' both with their embodiment and their 'situations' relevant to their knowing" (Nelson, 1993, p. 121). Communities and environments alluded to here are more psychological than physical because they focus on the meanings which community members create about events and circumstances. Intentional worlds and epistemological communities consist of the daily circumstances in which occupants find themselves. These communities are multiple, contingent, dynamic, fuzzy, and overlapping (Nelson, 1993). Although there are physical elements to these environments such as office size, location and furnishings, availability of secretarial support and discretionary funds, accessibility to students and the availability of parking space near worksites, the major significance of these environments is in the meaning that members of the environment attribute to them. How a person thinks about his or her work, working conditions and status in the university has an enormous effect on the world they construct for themselves and how they function within it. "What we attribute to the world (verb) we subsequently take to be an attribute of the world (noun)" (Stein, 1987, p. 15).

Faculty cultures have been widely discussed and described. Although there is considerable diversity within faculty groups as identified by discipline, profession or campus allegiance, several common characteristics have been identified, "(a) the pursuit and dissemination of knowledge and the primary goal of higher education; (b) professional autonomy including the importance of academic freedom; and (c) collegiality expressed through self-governance" (Love, Kuh, MacKay & Hardy, 1993, p. 39). The creation and dissemination of knowledge, usually knowledge generated by research conducted according to scientific paradigms, is generally a singular pursuit requiring considerable autonomy for faculty members to control the time, circumstances and conditions of their work. Although many faculty work in teams, most of their intellectual work is solitary. Each is an expert in his or her field and expects to be accorded the respect given an expert (Whitt, 1988). Although faculty generally value self-governance, as indicated by their willingness to serve on institutional committees and disciplinary committees used to monitor quality of scholarship, informal descriptions of committee work almost always include references to interruption of scholarship, the main goal of the academic enterprise. The prototypical comment is, "I couldn't get any work done because I had to go to a committee meeting."

An additional characteristic of the faculty world is its order and predictability (Barr & Fried, 1981). Research tends to be conducted in laboratories under controlled conditions. Experiments are deduced from theoretical constructs and variables are manipulated one or a few at a time in order to achieve maximum credibility of results. When results don't conform to predictions there is generally enough time to think carefully about unanticipated results and then generate new hypotheses. There are few emergencies in the lab, and there are few immediate consequences to the work done there. Although the results of scientific research, particularly medical research are now widely and quickly reported, these reports are almost always accompanied by a statement warning the public that it will be several more years before they can be translated into specific applications, usually signifying a new treatment for one of the 20th century plagues. "Lorenzo's Oil," a recent film about a deadly neurological disease, displayed the tension between the slowness of scientific research, the time pressure of searches for cures and the emotional distress of those afflicted by both disease and impatience. Even faculty members who engage in much less controlled field research generally have extended time to contemplate the data they gather and decide when to release their results to the public. Faculty members tend to maintain control over their time, to identify inviolable time boundaries when they will be writing or in their labs. These commitments are both primary and sacred under ideal circumstances. Power to set standards, control the time and conditions of one's work, evaluate the work of others, have time to think about the long term implications of one's work and to be considered an expert have extremely strong shaping effects on one's world view and on the intentional world which one can create.

Members of student affairs staffs live in quite a different world. Work hours are established by institutional policy even though many staff members work nights and weekends in addition to their regularly assigned hours. Their work with students, as advisors, supports and counselors, follows the rhythm of student life. Student events and problems typically don't happen during business hours on residential campuses although they tend to do so on commuter campuses. The student affairs work world is generally not orderly. Although major programs and regular services are carried out in a fairly predictable fashion, a significant amount of responsibility involves unpredictable situations. Room selection, major concerts, career fairs and orientation all follow predictable schedules and are planned far in advance. Roommate conflicts, serious work problems within committees, conflicts between student groups, disciplinary problems and personal problems occur when they will and must be addressed as quickly as possible in order to prevent escalation and maintain student well-being.

Much student affairs work is guided by theory, but theory does not govern practice in the same way that it does in a lab. In thinking about educational and disciplinary situations, a student affairs specialist might consider the work of Baxter-Magolda (1993), Gilligan (1982), Kitchener & King (1994) or Perry (1970) and plan his or her intervention accordingly. As the intervention evolves, however, new issues may emerge which theorists have not addressed and the student affairs specialist must generally respond on the spot, using whatever knowledge or instinct is immediately available. Student affairs specialists learn to become "reflective practitioners," who use professional artistry (Schon, 1987) to achieve their goals. They create, transform and apply theory in brief time periods under dynamic conditions. They generally have espoused theories which they believe should guide practice and these theories may or may not conform to the theories-in-use which guide their practice in particular situations (Argyris & Schon, 1977).

The behavior of student affairs specialists has immediate consequences in the lives of the students with whom they work. "You can't change roommates until you discuss this problem with your current roommate," has an immediate impact on an unhappy student, the student's roommate and the other residents.

- "Your behavior was inappropriate and endangered others. Therefore you may not spend any time in the school cafeteria until the beginning of next term."

- "The money to support this project is only available if you co-sponsor with another student group."
- "Playing loud music at 2 AM in a residence hall is not a racial issue. It is a noise violation."
- "Nobody cares who you're having sex with, but they are offended that you are flaunting your sexual behavior in public."
- "Hazing is forbidden on this campus. Making your pledges walk around holding bricks, or wearing chains, is considered evidence of hazing and you may not do it."
- "Asking people if they have accepted Jesus as their personal savior does not fall within our definition of conducting research. You may not approach people in the student union and ask them these questions. Your behavior is considered harassment."
- "You may not register for this semester until you have made arrangements to pay your bills from the last year."

Any one of these statements, each of which might be made in the course of an ordinary day, could have immediate consequences for a small group of people or a large group, depending on the political climate of the campus.

Finally, student affairs staff members work in bureaucracies which tend to be organized hierarchically. They have supervisors, regular performance evaluations and limited rights to speak about controversial issues. They are expected to uphold institutional policy in public even when they disagree in private. Their professional obligations include being role models for students and they are therefore held to high standards of morality and ethics. There is little separation between work, personal values and public behavior. A graduate student in a student affairs preparation program was mugged in the red light district of a major city at 2 AM. He believed that what he did on his own time was his own business. Unless he learns to understand the obligations of this profession, he will not be able to succeed or even to hold a job for any length of time. A faculty member in a secular, urban institution would not have a comparable problem if he or she were involved in a similar incident. If such an incident got into the press, most colleagues would probably snicker or sympathize, but it is unlikely that the faculty member would be considered incompetent to perform his or her tasks. A physicist who drinks with underage students can still teach them physics. A hall director who does the same thing can no longer do his or her job effectively. Finally, most student affairs staff members work collaboratively to solve real world problems in real time with practical deadlines. Committee work is work, not an interruption of work. Students are the focus of most student affairs work. When we are talking to students we are working. Casual conversations are part of building trust and advising students. The human relations/problem solving environment is the student affairs work environment. It has few boundaries in space or time. When faced with a pressing student problem there is rarely a reason to refuse to respond within a very short period of time.

Work conditions for student affairs staff members are quite different than faculty conditions. We are involved in managing processes, solving problems and helping students. We have some evaluative responsibilities but most of our interactions are non-judgmental and attempt to help students make choices. Intrusion into our work space is generally permitted and often welcomed. Some decisions are made collaboratively. Some are imposed. Few are made in isolation. If the image of a faculty member at work is a solitary person looking through a microscope and recording observations, a student affairs staff member at work is in the middle of many other people, interacting constantly, leaving the group to implement some decision, reporting back to the group, evaluating collectively, moving on to the next problem and repeating the process. Student affairs people are embedded in a web of relationships through which their work is accomplished, often under restrictive conditions bordered by conflicting values, limited financial resources and conflicting student, staff and institutional needs. The problems we address are ill-constructed, ambiguous and generally have no right answers. We reveal what we know in action while faculty reveal what they know in reflection (Schon, 1987).

Barriers and Border Controls

Barriers to effective collaboration between members of the academic faculty and student affairs staffs are numerous, but not insurmountable. A distinction in terminology between boundaries and borders is helpful.

Boundaries are neutral lines between worlds, settings or contexts where sociocultural elements are equal and movement across is easy . . . Borders are lines that are not neutral, that separate worlds not perceived as equal . . . When borders are present, movement and adaptation are frequently difficult because knowledge and skills in one world are more highly valued and esteemed than those in another (Phelan, Davidson & Hanh, 1993, p. 53).

Throughout this book power differences between academic faculty members and student affairs staff, the hegemony of academic, scientific ways of knowing and the dominance of the primary mission of our institutions as creating and disseminating knowledge have been discussed. When one group has the power to define reliable knowledge within an hierarchical system of value, then all other types of knowledge automatically become less reliable and less valuable by comparison. Indeed, the educational mission and activities of the student affairs staff is not defined as education within the dominant epistemology. It is defined as management or housekeeping, or metaphorically, domestic responsibility. The gender metaphor is telling. As men lose status when they acquire female attributes or display stereotypically female behavior such as taking on child care responsibilities or showing their emotions in public (Kuk, 1994), academic faculty may also lose status when they take on housekeeping or nurturing responsibilities within the institution. Service does not contribute significantly to tenure or promotion in major research institutions which set national norms in the areas of tenure and promotion. In addition, many faculty members do not have high levels of the skills used in counseling, committee work and institutional service, not having been trained for them or experienced in using them. They become de-skilled when they cross this border. The same is true, somewhat reversed for student affairs specialists. They gain status by crossing the border into faculty terrain and teaching in a discipline. However, their student affairs skills are not valued in that setting, or even identified. They might become so preoccupied with student opinion and perceptions that they don't "cover the material" in a particular course, or maintain "high enough" academic standards by grading on the curve. They have to substitute a judgmental attitude for their typical non-judgmental approach. They have to discuss theoretical issues in the abstract without stopping to consider implications in the real world. Under the traditional conditions which govern classroom teaching, it's a bad fit and a hard crossing.

SUCCESSFUL BORDER CROSSINGS: PROCESS AND PROGRAMS

Despite the difficulty of crossing the borders from academic education to student development education, many successful crossings have been accomplished. These crossings occur in courses where different epistemologies or ways of knowing are permitted and valued, particularly where faculty members include experiential education in their pedagogy. Crossings also occur in faculty development workshops and in situations where co-curricular activities are coordinated with coursework. Crossings occur more or less naturally in courses where the subject matter requires self-disclosure and personal construction of meaning such as women's studies courses, African American studies courses and courses in a wide range of human services, counseling and the behavioral sciences (Butler & Walter, 1991; McLaren, 1994; Mohanty, 1994).

Process

Academic faculty members and student affairs specialists often work together on college committees and become acquainted through their common involvement with institutional or student problems. This type of interaction might occur in the parking committee, the senate, committees on academic honesty or student behavior, committees planning campus-wide events sports events or in the gym. Religious communities on campus are also a productive and neutral territory. These settings provide ideal opportunities for student affairs staff members to initiate discussions about education and professional areas of interest with academic colleagues. Unfortunately neither group seems to take advantage of these "meetings at the border" where areas of common interest occur. Initially neither may speak the other's language. Nonthreatening ways to initiate such conversations with faculty are quite similar to the ways in which student affairs staffs initiate conversations with students—by asking questions about the things the student cares about. With faculty colleagues such questions might include, "What is your area of study?" "What courses do you teach?" "In your experience have students changed much in the past few years?" "What's the most enjoyable part of teaching for you or the most frustrating part?" By initiating dialogue with faculty members about their common area of interest, students, most student affairs specialists can find common ground and find ways of contributing what they know about students to the conversation.

Both student affairs staff members and faculty members are strangers in each others' land. They don't speak each others' language, aren't familiar with the protocol in each territory and seem generally uncomfortable in each other's neighborhoods. Getting to know each other professionally can be considered a cross-cultural experience for each. Each group risks losing status by crossing the border. Depending on the direction of migration, each is in a position to host and acculturate the other. Student affairs staff members are used to orienting students and helping them learn to negotiate the new world of the college or university. We rarely think about using our orientation skills to help faculty members negotiate their discomfort in the world of student affairs and student life outside the classroom. Lamphere (1992) describes the process of structuring diversity as one in which the newcomer and the established resident learn to interact within the context of mediating institutions such as workplaces and schools. When newcomers and established residents develop trusting relationships in which each makes an effort to understand the worldview of the other, newcomers can be accommodated into existing structures with a minimum of conflict. The principles which Lamphere and colleagues discovered when describing population changes in urban neighborhoods around the United States can also apply to cross-cultural interactions between members of the faculty and student affairs specialists.

The bridge on which faculty and student affairs meet is group process. The action/reflection cycle called *praxis*. To this bridge the faculty brings its knowledge of the various academic disciplines and desirable learning outcomes. The student affairs staff brings its knowledge of interpersonal dynamics, communication processes, trust building in groups, managing conflicts in groups and helping students infer meaning from experience. Student affairs also brings an outsiders' awareness of the value system which governs the behavior and thought of the dominant group. Most successful members of marginalized groups in the United States, African Americans, Asian Americans, women, gays and lesbians, deaf people and all the others in the litany, are bicultural. They have learned how to function in the majority dominant culture as well as their own. Student affairs staffs have been marginalized in the academic culture to such a degree that we are not fully bicultural. We have observed the faculty culture as outsiders, but have not fully learned to understand its norms and values. Before we can successfully enter the culture, we must study it. We already know how to do this. We have simply not accomplished this task on many campuses.

Initiating conversations with faculty about student learning processes and group dynamics is generally a task that student affairs specialists must initiate. Faculty are frustrated with new student learning styles (Schroeder, 1993) and many are uncomfortable in teaching students from the many different cultures and age cohorts who have appeared in their classrooms in the past ten years. If faculty members are locked into traditional, two valued ideas about teaching and learning, their frustration with students becomes difficult to discuss because poor student performance has only two possible explanations. Either (a) the new students are less intelligent, lazier, poorly prepared or less motivated than earlier generations of students or (b) the faculty members have become poor teachers. Since (a) is far less embarrassing than (b), it is likely to become the explanation of choice. However, the possibility that (b) may be true, is a serious problem for many faculty. Finding ways to initiate difficult and awkward conversations in order to solve problems and improve situations is also a student affairs skill. Using it in a new venue is the only change. Many faculty members are surprisingly receptive to information about student learning styles, differing cultural norms about appropriate behavior in class and with professors, different international standards for writing, test taking, studying and so forth. All of this information can be construed as providing new theories with which to understand anomalous data, a perspective which is far more comfortable than either thinking that one has lost one's teaching skills or that all new students are incompetent. This is a situation in which dual valued logic is painful to those who use it and multiple ways of knowing, and constructivist understandings are much more helpful and productive in addressing the problem of student learning.

Opportunities for Collaboration

1. *Courses in which experiential education is used.* In any course which involves experiential education, *praxis* is part of the learning process. This particular approach is discussed more thoroughly elsewhere (Galligan, this volume). *Praxis* involves action and reflection. Students engage in activities specifically designed

to help them learn specific skills or familiarize them with new ideas. The need for experiential education and experiential training in teamwork and group dynamics has escalated in all the professions. Work situations have become less hierarchical and more dependent on the ability of professionals from a variety of disciplines to solve problems together (Drucker, 1993; Reich, 1992). The need to emphasize the learning component of experiential learning has increased accordingly. Learning isn't accomplished in experiential education until the students sit back, reflect and articulate what they have learned by discussing it with others or writing about it in a non-judgmental environment (Kolb, 1984). This process is used widely in leadership training, RA training and effective disciplinary interventions with students. It involves active listening, judicious use of questions designed to help students see connections between events and reactions and a whole range of other counseling skills. Most faculty members have not learned these skills. Most members of student affairs staffs have them. There may not be a bridge. Who will begin to build it?

2. *Courses in which the subject matter is controversial and personal.* These courses tend to fall in the humanities and social sciences and are heavily concentrated in areas where the curriculum has been changed to incorporate multicultural approaches and topics. In these settings the feminist slogan, "The personal is political" takes on new meaning. The line between information and personal meaning blurs and often disappears. Issues of pedagogy, personality, professionalism and power merge. Objectivity and all of the positivist virtues have limited value in these situations. What students learn about in these courses often upsets their sense of self, their understanding of their own individual and family history and brings insights in areas they are not used to thinking about in class. The intensity of student reaction is often upsetting and confusing to faculty members who aren't used to seeing such reactions and don't know how to respond in educationally effective ways. These courses are filled with powerful learning opportunities to increase multicultural understanding, but many faculty members don't know how to take advantage of them. Is there a bridge? Who will build it?

These projects involve both benefits and difficulties. A course called "Law, Culture and Difference" involved collaboration between this author and a law professor in the aspect of the course devoted to training peer discussion leaders. My contributions came from my experience in training RA's and student leaders in the areas of racism, oppression, homophobia, assertiveness, active listening and conflict resolution. Her expertise was in constitutional law, domestic violence and critical legal studies. Throughout the course the students and faculty struggled with our "isms," and our pain. The complications and confusions were many. The student facilitators were Anglo, Venezuelan, Philippine, Korean and African American. They were male and female, gay and straight, Jewish and Christian, ranging in age from twenty-two to mid-fifties. They reflected the composition of the law student body. The issues were real and controversial. Although we were less than successful in teaching all 250 law students how to engage constructively in cross-cultural debate, we created a powerful team of facilitators who were able to trust each other with their perceptions, their anger and their pain, to express themselves honestly and to understand each other as they worked on their differences. We learned a great deal about the difficulty of helping people learn these skills, our weaknesses and strengths in the situation and how to design more effective programs to teach these skills. The law students learned how their construction of categories, a skill which is essential in legal practice, shaped their perception of cultural and power differences. They also learned the limits of the law in effecting social change. We all learned that the problem of multicultural coexistence and understanding is confusing, ill-structured and does not lend itself to permanent solutions. Among other things, the law professor saw the issues which the law addressed being acted out before her eyes in the conflicts among the students who were the facilitators and first year students in the law school. No amount of non-experiential learning could have given any of us a comparable education. We built many bridges going in many different directions. Although I was a professor at the time, I could easily have done this work as part of my former role as a student development educator.

3. *Cooperative Education and Service Learning Programs.* These programs provide the most obvious opportunities for collaboration because of their experiential nature and the interdisciplinary perspective necessary to conduct them effectively. They are also often marginal in the academy, being neither academic nor student affairs responsibility exclusively. They almost demand team teaching in a seminar format. Service learning in particular assumes that students learn how to engage in the service activity, how to understand the needs of individuals and groups with

whom they work and how to place their particular efforts in wider social and historical context. This process is discussed extensively in the Galligan chapter. Walk across this bridge and watch for others who are making the journey with you.

4. *Coordinated programs.* These programs involve a different sort of collaboration. Student affairs co-curricular programs are coordinated with course requirements and professors often give students credit for participating in such programs and writing up their reactions to them. At the University of Hartford, the All University Curriculum has developed a number of coordinated program elements. All courses in the academic component of the program are defined by problems rather than disciplines and are interdisciplinary and team taught. A course might investigate natural healing remedies used in traditional societies, cultural and economic elements of international business, the social context of romanticism in art, literature and music, the history of agricultural technology, problems of adult life and so forth. All courses use active modes of learning and emphasize at least two skills from a list of "essential abilities, "including written communication, oral communication, critical thinking and problem solving, social interaction, values identification and responsibility for civic life. The target skills are listed on the course proposal when it is considered by the curriculum committee. The student affairs staff works with the AUC instructors in designing educational programs which are coordinated with topics covered in courses. One year a course in the American family required students to attend a discussion of male-female relationships among students conducted jointly by a member of the residence life staff and a course instructor. The students wrote a reaction paper which was submitted to the instructor for credit. The most obvious connecting categories in this program are social interaction, values identification and responsibility for civic life, but each set of essential abilities is potentially related to some activity which student affairs could supplement and reinforce through its educational, co-curricular programs. It is not necessary to have an AUC in place to engage in this type of coordination. The existence of professional relationships between faculty members and student affairs staff can lead to the development of coordinated programs relatively easily. The programs are often in place already. The biggest step is to bring them to the attention of the instructors and design methods for connecting in-class and out-of-class education. The bridges are in place. Walk across them.

5. *Faculty Development*. Another place where border crossing can occur is through faculty development activities conducted by student affairs staff members. This is a politically problematic area. While student affairs staff members are used to engaging in on-going training, faculty members often believe that they have already been trained in their disciplines and do not see the need for additional training, especially if it is provided by anybody outside their discipline or with less impressive credentials than their own. Faculty members often participate in faculty development activities which focus on improving student learning. Since others specialize in learning processes as their own academic specialty, there seems to be less resistance to this approach. Faculty development seminars often present information about student learning styles, student demographics and culture as they affect learning styles and cognitive development or the results of research about attitudes and opinions of students on a particular campus. Becoming involved in faculty development activities is often as simple as finding out what issues about students and campus life concern faculty and then identifying what student affairs knows about the issue and when and how to present the information to the faculty. These bridges from student affairs to faculty are designed campus by campus.

One particularly interesting faculty development activity emerged from collaboration between a student development specialist and an anthropologist. The two designed a content/process workshop for faculty, "Multicultural Perspectives in Curriculum Development and Teaching Strategies." The anthropologist presented information about the ways in which culture shapes perception and ideas about teaching and learning. Her presentation was academic and involved numerous research sources. The student affairs specialist gave a brief overview of the history of American higher education from the English collegiate model to the modern multiversity. Faculty participants engaged in a number of self-assessment activities which are typically used in student development diversity workshops and they discussed the results of their own self-assessment. The level of self-disclosure was unusual for a faculty seminar and permitted the group to develop a sense of trust which is also unusual in these types of events. Participants critiqued each other's syllabi from courses which they chose to present to the group and learned to identify cultural distortions and perspectives in each disciplinary area presented. Finally discussion leading methods which enhance collaborative learning and connected ways of knowing were modeled by the student affairs specialist. She had used many of these methods during the discussion and the summary of the process involved pointing out what had been done, how the participants reacted to these techniques and where they could learn to use them themselves. Content and process were merged in this workshop. The entire activity built on the strengths of the student affairs specialist and the anthropologist.

6. *Orientation Courses.* These programs began at the University of South Carolina under the leadership of John Gardener, They have now become instituted across the country as extended efforts to orient and retain students. Although they are generally under the direction of faculty members, the topics often include issues of adjustment to college which are student affairs specialties, such as male-female relationships, study skills, separating from parents, getting along with roommates, living in a culturally diverse community, managing conflicts, developing assertive communications skills and so forth. These courses are often jointly taught, with student affairs specialists being more expert in the subject matter than their faculty colleagues who have the formal power to teach and grant credit. This is an ideal opportunity for collaboration because many faculty who teach these courses feel an element of discomfort due to their lack of formal education and experience. Student affairs staff members generally know how to conduct these discussions but can't quite get comfortable with having the authority of a professor. Effective collaboration is a win/win situation and the students benefit.

ESSENTIAL ELEMENTS IN
SUCCESSFUL BORDER CROSSINGS

Border crossings are difficult to accomplish, but not impossible. A few essential elements for successful border crossings from student affairs to academic affairs are listed below:

1. Student affairs staff members must believe that our work is educational and be able to explain what we do and what and how students learn. We must be able to discuss theory as well as process, speaking the language of science, objectivism, empiricism and research in a format that academic faculty can understand. When student affairs staff members talk about student learning with faculty, they are involved in a border crossing and

a cross-cultural experience. This process should be approached as carefully as one might approach a student from another country to discuss a serious issue.

2. These conversations should be initiated as part of on-going professional relationships with faculty members who are open to the discussion. When entering another culture it is very important to have guides, friends and people who extend hospitality. Get to know faculty members on neutral turf if you can and seek out opportunities to do so. In the context of respectful and trusting relationships, these professors can be your guides.

3. Don't assume that student affairs understands a problem better than anybody else or that a student affairs approach is inevitably the most effective one. The development of programs should be integrated with the development of professional relationships. The process should begin as a discussion of joint concerns about student learning rather than a conversation which implies that one group has all the answers, or even knows which questions are the most important to address.

4. Be sensitive to power differences and your reactions to them. Although the academic faculty often has a great deal of power on campus, many professors believe themselves to be powerless and that the administration controls the campus. The important issue here is to understand how power is perceived in relationships between faculty members and student affairs staff members. Faculty are used to certain prerogatives and a sense of deference from junior colleagues and students. Faculty members may not know younger, less experienced student affairs staff members, or understand why you are approaching them to discuss student learning. They often don't understand what is involved with the various student affairs specialties and in some cases don't know they/we exist. When a student affairs staff member enters the intentional world of a faculty member, self-confidence, command of professional language and a sense of professional equity are often the first casualties. Gaining experience as an apprentice to a more seasoned student affairs professional helps in this process.

5. Don't personalize differences, delays or misunderstandings. Faculty operate on a totally different time frame than student affairs. They operate collegially when they are working outside the classroom or the lab and often need time to consult or think.

Their time frame is generally at least one semester, often an academic year. When delays in program development occur, try to understand which aspects of the culture are operating to provoke the delay, rather than thinking about who is trying to stop you.

6. Publicize your successes jointly with your collaborators, using language that makes sense to the groups you are addressing. Check the language of your public statements with your faculty colleagues before you say anything. The difference between training and development, for example, is significant.

7. Use the principles of TQM—share credit, praise achievements, work collaboratively and evaluate outcomes. Write thank you notes where appropriate, and particularly for non-tenured faculty members who can use them to enhance their tenure dossiers. Inform the student affairs staff of your work as well and extend opportunities for involvement to other interested people.

8. Remember that most of your student affairs skills for entering and understanding new cultures, orienting new people, managing discussions and planning activities are transferable if you learn how to translate them into the faculty culture on your campus.

9. Remember that you're not in college anymore. You are a member of the educational staff, as well as the administrative staff. Your work with students involves learning even when the teaching isn't obvious. Even your service and management work involves learning. Do not accept the dominant definitions of teaching and learning. Remember the philosophical roots of student affairs in the work of John Dewey, and experiential education.

10. The purpose of all colleges and universities is the creation, transmission and application of knowledge. Remember what part you play in all that and your world will change and open up. The two-way traffic on the bridge will increase to the benefit of all participants.

REFERENCES

Argyris, C. & Schon, D. (1977) *Theory in practice: Increasing professional effectiveness.* San Francisco: Jossey-Bass.

Barr, M. & Fried, J. (1981) Facts, feelings and academic credit. In J. Fried (Ed.). *Education for student development: New directions for student services. 15.* (pp. 87-102) San Francisco: Jossey-Bass.

Butler, J. & Walter, J. (Eds.). (1991) *Transforming the curriculum.* Albany, NY: SUNY Press.

Drucker, P. (1993) *Post-capitalist society.* New York: HarperCollins.

Hannaford, I. (1994) The idiocy of race. The *Wilson Quarterly. XVII.* (2) 8-45.

Kolb, D. (1984) *Experiential learning.* Englewood Cliffs, NJ: Prentice Hall.

Kuk, L. (1994) New approaches to management. In J. Fried (Ed.). *Different voices: Gender and perspective in student affairs administration.* (pp. 62-76) Washington, DC: National Association of Student Personnel Administrators.

Love, P., Kuh, G., MacKay, K. & Hardy, C. (1993) Side by side: Faculty and student affairs cultures. In G. Kuh (Ed). *Cultural perspectives in student affairs work.* (pp. 37-58) Washington, D.C.: American College Personnel Association.

Lamphere, L. (Ed.). (1992) *Structuring diversity.* Chicago: University of Chicago Press.

McLaren, P. (1994). Multiculturalism and post-modern critique: Toward a pedagogy of resistance and transformation. In H. Giroux & P. McLaren (Eds.). *Between borders.* (pp. 192-222) New York: Routledge.

Mohanty, C. (1994) On race and voice: Challenges for liberal education in the 90s. In H. Giroux & P. McLaren (Eds.). *Between borders.* (pp. 145-166) New York: Routledge.

Nelson, L. (1993) Epistemological communities. In L. Alcoff & E. Potter (Eds.). *Feminist epistemologies.* (pp. 121-160). New York: Routledge.

Phelan, P., Davidson, A. & Hanh, C. (1993) Students' multiple worlds: Navigating the borders of family, peer and school culture. In P. Phelan and A. Davidson (Eds.). *Renegotiating cultural diversity in American schools.* (pp. 52-88) New York: Teachers' College Press, Columbia University.

Reich, R. (1992) *The work of nations.* New York: Vintage Books.

Schon, D. (1987) *Educating the reflective practitioner.* San Francisco: Jossey-Bass.

Schroeder, C. (1993) New students-New learning styles. *Change. 25* (5) 21-26.

Shweder, R. (1990) Cultural psychology-what is it? in Stigler, J., Shweder, R. & Herdt, G. (Eds.). *Cultural psychology.* (pp. 1-46) New York: Columbia University Press.

Stein, H. (1987) *Developmental time, cultural space.* Normal, OK: University of Oklahoma Press.

Whitt, E. (1988) *Hit the ground running: Experiences of new faculty in the school of education at a research university.* Unpublished doctoral dissertation. Indiana University, Bloomington, IN.

9

Service Learning and Experiential Education

Ann M. Galligan

Stories are nails that I hammer into the wall. On those nails I can hang up the whole, usually highly abstract, conceptual stuff of a philosophy course. If there are no nails in the wall all the stuff falls down and will be forgotten. But if there are stories, illustrations, visualizations, there they will not be forgotten.

Loyola Center for Values and Service (1993).

Two main areas in which cognitive and affective education are combined with skill development are the fields of service learning and experiential education. This chapter illustrates the stories of four such programs in an effort to provide the "nails" for hanging the conceptual and theoretical framework of experiential learning theory. Seen in light of the paradigm shift explored throughout this book, they are model programs that transcend student affairs/ faculty boundaries as well as the boundaries between campus and community. They are interdisciplinary in nature and constructivist in approach. As such they provide a sense of direction for future faculty/student affairs collaboration.

Hegel (1807/1977) regarded education as a process of breaking through the familiar into the strange in order to see a world of possibility. Experiential education and service learning are environment-based models of education offering opportunities for students to move out of the familiar into the realm of the unknown, challenging them to go beyond academic learning as a means of acquiring knowledge and information. They also provide a means

189

of developing personal responsibility, active participation, personal commitment to a set of values, and a sense of self in the world. Learning by doing, or experiential learning, provides the opportunity to exercise, challenge, and extend the structures and capabilities of thought through the process of active engagement with the "real" world.

THEORIES OF EXPERIENTIAL EDUCATION

In this chapter, experiential learning refers to all forms of out-of-classroom learning, such as cooperative education, internships, apprenticeships, and leadership development. Service learning is one aspect of experiential education which adds the component of service (to community and others), community development and empowerment, as well as aspects of reciprocal learning between student and community.

Experiential learning is empowering. It allows students to capitalize on their practical strengths as they apply ideas and explore beliefs and perceptions about their world (Kolb, 1984). Learning is a social process that shapes the course of an individual's development through interaction with the environment and the cultural system—social knowledge (Kolb, 1985). The process of learning from experience provides the foundation for shaping and actualizing students' developmental potentials by presenting opportunities for growth through a process of integration and differentiation.

For such development to take place, challenges are needed to move the student beyond the status quo (Roark, 1989). The approach of "plus one" staging recognizes the student's current cognitive stage and addresses it at the next higher stage to encourage progression. Supports are required to sustain/uphold the student and to manage anxiety while the experience is assimilated. The role of the educator, in this case either the co-coordinator or the faculty member or student affairs professional facilitating the service learning experience, is to find challenges that are sufficient to require that the student moves to a new level, but not so intense or disturbing as to force the student to fall back on earlier primitive modes of adaptation which are doomed to fail (Sanford & Axelrod, 1964).

Common to all models of experiential learning is an educational strategy in which experience is central and development is promoted in all three learning domains: cognitive, affective, and behavioral. Experiential learning theory (Chickering & Reisser, 1993; Kolb, 1984) stresses the importance of experienced-based learning for critical thinking, value formation, self-awareness, adaptability, and perceptual and psychomotor skills (Cooperative Education Curriculum, 1994). Each of these models provides a means of explaining development as the individual moves from simplicity and absolutism to complexity and relativism, from concreteness to abstractness, and from external to internal regulation. While all learning, including classroom, involves a journey into "the strange," experiential learning is unique in that it seeks to educate the whole person, providing affective as well as cognitive challenges. Yet not all experiential education programs are alike. Many share similar conceptual frameworks that allow them to challenge students at different levels of experience, but programs may also vary greatly as a reflection of the uniqueness of the sponsoring institution. The remainder of this chapter provides a brief overview of a career-based cooperative education program in the arts at Northeastern University, and three service learning programs with varying emphases on community, justice, and faith at Bentley College, Stanford University, and Loyola College in Maryland. Each program description is followed by a description of the conceptual framework within which the program operates.

FOUR MODELS OF EXPERIENTIAL EDUCATION

Experiential education is best described as education from the inside out, engaging students as active agents in an interactive process with their environment in which they are challenged to make sense of their world while seen as an integral part of it. Service learning and experiential education are part of an evolving pedagogy that works to educate the whole person. They spring, in part, from the Deweyan tradition of pragmatic education which integrates education in democratic values with academic learning.

Education for a democratic citizenship involves human capacities relating to judgment, to choice, and, above all, to action. To be literate as a citizen requires more than knowledge and information; it includes the exercise of personal responsibility, active participation, and personal commitment to a set of values. Democratic literacy is a literacy of doing, not simply of knowing. Knowledge is a necessary, but not sufficient condition of democratic responsibility. (Morrill, 1982, p. 356)

Dewey's model of pragmatic education (1916) linked knowing and doing in a way that created a bridge between experience, critical thinking and participatory democracy. He saw a unity of work and thought that went beyond vocational education and simple skill development. Dewey called for a pragmatic, transformative model that saw the workplace as part of the educational setting rather than separate from it. In his scheme it was not enough to link academic study to work experience; it was also imperative to educate students in a way that equipped them with the tools to transform the workplace into an environment that fostered complete self-realization (Saltmarsh, 1993). In this sense, the workplace is not seen as the endpoint, but as a significant part of the educational process.

Program: Cooperative Education at Northeastern University

One of the oldest forms of workplace-based experiential education is cooperative education. Cooperative education, or co-op, is an educational strategy in which work experience is a structured part of the curriculum. Cooperative education was founded at the University of Cincinnati by Herbert Schneider. The co-op program was introduced at Northeastern in 1909 and has grown to encompass the entire undergraduate and graduate experience, including programs in engineering, law, nursing, business as well as the liberal arts. The program alternates periods of classroom study with planned, career-related work experience. With the co-op model, the workplace experience becomes an integral part of each student's total educational process (Cantwell, 1994).

The co-op program is directed by a central body of cooperative education faculty coordinators who guide students in the process of exploration and self-actualization. For example, the co-op coordinator for students in art, music and theater assists students through a three-step process of career exploration and workplace preparation such as resume writing and portfolio development, followed by a three-to-six month period of full-time, paid employment, and finally through a self-directed process of post-work reflection and analysis. While some of the main learning outcomes of the co-op process are skill acquisition and career development (Fletcher, 1989, 1991), students also learn a great deal about their cognitive and affective reactions as a result of their work experiences. In a business co-op, a student might review all the part time jobs he or she held during high school and learn to translate the skills developed on those jobs into a functional resume. Following the first co-op placement, the student would be asked to reflect, either verbally or in writing, on several of the following issues: What new skills did you learn? What skills transferred from previous jobs? What did you learn about communicating with your supervisor and your peers? What did you learn to do in searching for your next co-op? What did you learn to ask about or avoid, based on any discomfort you experienced in your first co-op? What surprised you the most about your co-op?

Theory: Developing Appropriate Challenges
    This sequence, described as "Co-op Flow," is based on the psychological flow theory of Mihaly Csikszentmihalyi (1990). Flow is a state of concentration that amounts to absorption in an activity (Csikszentmihalyi, 1990). The key to achieving the state of flow is in meeting an appropriate challenge. When the "co-op flow" occurs, students will feel as if all parts of the experience come together. If the level of challenge outweighs the level of skill, students feel anxious. If their skill level is low and yet the job is undemanding, they often become apathetic, or bored if their skill level high but the challenge too low. The workplace challenge should match the student's level of skill and cognitive development if true learning is to take place.
    For example, graphic design students typically begin the co-op cycle by working in a design firm or a desktop printing business. After moving through entry-level work at this co-op phase they go on to more advanced class work involving typography and computer graphics. Then are they ready for the challenge of the junior designer role. Placing a student in the role of a junior designer before the student has had the appropriate design theory or computer classes would be disastrous. It would be equally inappropriate to allow the student to spend more than one or two co-op terms in an entry level position. In both cases, co-op flow would not be achieved.

Developmental Underpinnings of Experiential Education
    Experiential learning is defined as a cycle of interaction between the individual and the environment (Piaget, 1978). Learning is the result of student openness to new experiences. Openness permits dynamic interaction as new information is assimilated and synthesized with existing knowledge. This leads to higher levels of cognitive functioning (Kolb, 1984) since increased cognitive capacity is required to process, redefine and understand experi-

ence in context. Higher levels of cognitive functioning permit recognition of increasing complexity which then makes students capable of differentiating among varying intellectual, attitudinal, or value positions—a precursor to perceiving choices and making commitments (Perry, 1970). Recognition of complexity requires the capacity to make distinctions among a set of rational principles of judgment and decision (Kohlberg, 1975).

Program: Service Learning at Bentley College

Dewey saw that cognitive development could not be separated from its experiential component. Through the co-op experience the student interacts with the work environment and both are changed by the interaction. With service learning models, both secular and religious, the location for learning shifts from the workplace to the community. While the educational process is similar, the learning outcomes are different. As Ernest Boyer (1994) recognizes, experiential education, particularly models of service learning, provides a unique form of reciprocal learning between the student and the community. The following section describes the process at Bentley College.

Bentley College, founded in 1917, has professional education in accounting and finance as its main focus. The college has been highly successful in integrating broad liberal arts and science programs within an increasingly diverse business curriculum. Since 1990, Bentley has established a service learning program that involves more than one quarter of its academic faculty and more than 1,500 students. The Bentley program offers approximately twenty courses per semester with service options, involving twelve departments which currently sponsor or recognize discipline-based service initiatives (Zlotkowski, 1993).

The Bentley Service Learning Project (BSLP) is coordinated by a central office which was created to identify needs, assemble resources, track individual efforts and maintain the coherence, direction, and vision of the program. While Northeastern has a centralized co-op model where a separate co-op faculty coordinates the program, Bentley offers a more decentralized model. The BSLP's role is to encourage the various departments to create their own service programs or "learning communities—courses from different departments linked by a common focus and a shared service assignment" (Zlotowski, 1993, p. 4). With the help of program of scholarships and grants, individual students also are encouraged to become "service entrepreneurs," (p. 6) fostering the creation of individual service projects as well as classroom or campus-sponsored efforts.

Each year Bentley publishes information packets for faculty and students describing possible service options. For example, a number of classes and individuals have collaborated on the Bentley-Project Place Partnership, the College's joint endeavor with a local urban multi-service agency. One class in managerial communications developed materials for Project Place's economic development program. They researched target audiences and designed informational materials. Another class developed public relations materials while a third class in business policy produced a financial and strategic analysis. Still other students receive grants to focused on individual Project Place projects.

In a sociology project at a shelter for the homeless, students were challenged to rethinking their assumptions on homelessness and the frequent failures of people in shelters to secure employment. Listening to the stories of the homeless men who had applied for work but who were passed over when potential employers returned calls and discovered that the men lived in a shelter or when their messages were misplaced or lost, students began to see the challenge of employment in a new light. By focusing on the problem as described by the men, rather than on preconceived believes about the causes of unemployment, students were able to offer a more emphatic and effective solution to the problem. With the help of their professor, they secured free voice mail services for the residents. Using a similar concept employed at other shelters around the United States, the professor approached New England Telephone with a request to pilot the program in the Quincy shelter. Each guest now receives a personal phone number and a recorded message that can be accessed from any phone. The men are no longer stigmatized by their residence or inconvenienced by the carelessness of other guests. Once the guest leaves the shelter, the message gives a forwarding number. The service gives the men a sense of individual control over the job-hunting process and restores their sense of personal dignity as well.

The College developed its program of service learning in response to a growing interest in both co-curricular service activities and individual student and faculty-driven efforts. This commitment to service learning evolved from a commitment to the ideals of service and justice and a pragmatic notion of the benefits of community involvement. Bentley College also recognized the growing trend toward global interdependence in business and saw service learning as an appropriate means of addressing educational concerns resulting from this trend.

Theory: Service as a Means of Shifting the Paradigm

It is easy for students to be absorbed in their own worlds and to ignore the demands and needs of those around them during the college experience. Through service programs such as Bentley's, students are able to enter into an experience in which a teachable moment may provide an opportunity to apply what is learned as well as develop a better understanding of and care for other human beings and become more aware of our global interdependency (Coles, 1990). Actively involving students in their community fosters a deeper understanding of the needs and realities of the larger world and is a fundamental step required in moving from egocentrism to global interdependence (Delve, Mintz & Stewart, 1990).

Interdependence is an important developmental task for students (Chickering & Reisser, 1993). Interaction with others, not just mere transaction, is needed in order to recognize such interdependence. In service learning students are asked to shift from a primary focus on self to an increased focus on others and in doing so, bridge the gap between learning and living by focusing on the living reality of the learning situation (Delve, Mintz & Stewart, 1990). Friere (1985) describes this process as problem-posing education which occurs in the realm of action and social change. The recognition of such interdependence, as illustrated by Bentley's service learning program and its successes, requires a paradigm shift on the part of both the student and the institution. Working with the community provides students with an opportunity for reciprocal learning. They are able to experience problems from a vantage point much closer to those who are afflicted by them than they would be able to do using other learning methods in which point of view is not explicitly acknowledged. Through such interaction, the student and the institution are moved into a living dynamic with those they seek to serve. The recognition of such interdependence, incorporated into Bentley's service learning program, leads to the paradigm shift.

Program: Public Service at Stanford University

The service learning model at Stanford University provides an excellent example of problem-posing education that operates through the development of heightening awareness on the part of students to the needs of others. It demonstrates how the process of reflection and action can go to an even deeper level by involving students in an analysis of social structure as they seek to find creative solutions to current social problems.

We know that where community exists it confers upon its members identity, a sense of belonging and a measure of security. It is in community that the attributes that distinguish humans as social creatures are nourished. Communities are the ground-level generators and preservers of values and ethical systems (Gardner, 1991).

Stanford University recently celebrated over a century of service with the expansion of its Haas Center for Public Service, a center of the student affairs division. At the heart of Stanford's program is the goal of community change. In the process of bringing about change, students learn to see the pluralistic aspects of society and learn to become more adaptable. They become aware that the traditional view of community as homogeneous and requiring a high level of conformity, no longer applies.

Established in 1985, the Haas Center for Public Service offers both undergraduate and graduate students a wide range of service options. The Center provides opportunities to become involved in hands-on projects and policy research. It also serves as a clearinghouse for community projects. Each year over 3,000 students participate in volunteer activities ranging from outreach to upward bound programs. A service component is in place in many classes as well. Stanford also offers a program in Washington, DC which offers seminars, tutorials, as well as internships through the guidance of on-site faculty and legislative experts. On the graduate level, Stanford medical students provide health services and preventive screening to elderly Chinese and Vietnamese through a social service organization in San Jose, California. They also run the Arbor Free Clinic for the low-income and homeless population of Palo Alto.

Theory: Development of Multicultural Awareness

Stanford University has a justice-based service model. The model contains ten components for the development of a sound and vital community: 1) wholeness which incorporates and promotes both diversity and healthy dissent with tolerance, accommodation, coalition-building and dispute resolution; 2) a reasonable base of shared values, i.e., justice, equality, freedom; 3) good internal communication required to combat we/they barriers; 4) caring, trust, team-work—spirit of mutuality and cooperation; 5) sharing of leadership tasks; 6) self-affirmation and morale building; 7) creating links beyond the community; 8) a sense of where it is going; 9) developing its young people; and 10) institutional arrangements for community maintenance. As these goals illustrate, a sense of community must be built from the ground up (Gardner, 1991).

> Men and women who have come to understand, in their own intimate settings the principles of wholeness incorporating diversity, the art of diminishing polarization, the meaning of teamwork and participation will be far better allies in the effort to build elements of community into the city, nation and the world. We should set about rebuilding community in any and every plausible setting (p. 12).

The service experience gives students a way of learning these principles directly in ways that could never be gleaned from a text or classroom discussion.

Development of Self and Group Identity through Service
The struggle to find self and group identity requires a process of evaluating personal beliefs in the context of both internal and surrounding cultures. Focusing on personal identity without acknowledging the many cultural influences within and around each person creates a fragmented and alienated sense of self. Ho's notion of "internalized culture" (1995, p. 5) creates a bridge concept, by describing the interaction between cultural elements which are derived from group experiences, shaping an individual's values and behavior and personality elements which are unique to each individual. In order to achieve awareness of multicultural influences in the environment and to act effectively within the environment, it is necessary to move from seeing oneself as a separate individual to seeing oneself as a member of many communities. This change requires a reevaluation of current values and theoretical perspectives.

The development of tolerance becomes more critical as cultural pluralism and encounters with people from different cultures and orientations increase (Thomas & Chickering, 1984). Anglo-American culture provides the standards and assumes that differences are deviant, abnormal or inferior and ought to be overcome or rejected (Manning & Coleman-Boatwright, 1991). When values are imposed, devalued individuals feel oppressed. This process often transforms the devalued person's consciousness into a sense of self-loathing or self-denigration (Freire, 1990).

What is required then is a change in focus from self to community so that the individual sees him or herself in community context. To be a part of the community is to give back to the community. In this way individuals are able to move toward a recognition of differences and move beyond self in order to incorporate the surrounding culture into the sense of identity. Mature identities must extend beyond an individualistic self to a generative caring for other groups and for the entire human species (Hoare, 1991). Movement toward inclusive identities results from the synthesis of experiential challenges and a change in perspective from monoculturalism to multiculturalism (Thomas & Chickering, 1984). Thus a multicultural organization can be "genuinely committed to diverse representation of its membership; . . . sensitive to maintaining an open, supportive and environment; [and] . . . working toward and purposefully including elements of diverse cultures in its ongoing operation" (p. 397).

> No matter the kind of service being rendered, the sponsorship, the age, the background of the person who is volunteering and the nature (location) of the work being done, the ultimate worth of the effort will depend a good deal on how a particular person manages to connect with those other beings in some way taught or healed or advised or assisted: the chemistry of giving as it works back and forth between individuals in one or another situation. (Coles, 1990, p. 64-65)

The Stanford model provides students with opportunities to make such connections through community problem-solving experiences as they move toward a recognition of differences and move beyond self in order to incorporate the surrounding culture into an expanded sense of identity.

Program: Loyola College in Maryland

The Stanford service learning model outlined above is often complemented by faith-development models and social-justice activities of campus ministries' staff (Swezey, 1990). Community service programs within the campus-based religious life offices such as the one at Loyola College of Maryland can encourage, support, and challenge students' spiritual development during their college experience.

Loyola College is a Jesuit institution living out its vision of encouraging the entire college community to be "men and women for others" through service and by providing an education that "attempts to transmit to students the inherited wisdom, the learning, and the values of the past and to develop them in an openness to truth, a sensitivity to principles and responsiveness to the needs of individuals and society" (Community Service Opportunities, 1993-1994, p. 1).

The Center for Values and Service acts as a clearinghouse for service opportunities and organizes social outreach and service programs on campus. It also promotes faith and justice education through reflection and lecture series and provides leadership for the integration of service with the academic curriculum. Finally it prepares students for service experiences by organizing orientation activities, having agency speakers and encouraging agency tours to enable persons to feel more comfortable before beginning service. The end goal is to foster leadership in the community. The purpose of the Center is also to implement the Jesuit vision of education.

> The service of faith through the promotion of justice . . . which is profoundly linked with our preferential option for the poor, (must) be operative in our lives and in our institutions. Jesuit education must be value oriented, anchored in the head, the heart, and the hand; in Jesuit education, reason should be shaped by compassion and put into action to the service of others (Community Service Opportunities, p. 1).

Students at Loyola have a number of service opportunities available to them. There are both one-time events such as day-long service projects and on-going community service placements in the areas of literacy, A.I.D.S., alcohol and drug prevention, crisis intervention, education, special needs and the environment. One distinctive feature of Loyola's program is its immersion experiences. These programs, such as Project Mexico, a ten-day experience living in the border communities near Tecate and Tijuana, offer students the opportunity to spend their January break working with local children. During the spring break, students are involved in similar projects in Appalachia and Mississippi. These projects give Loyola student volunteers "the opportunity to improve living and education conditions, learn about servant leadership, and gain a broader understanding and appreciation for people who may be different" (p. 8).

Theory: Faith Development

The faith-development model underlying this program was evolved by Parks (1986), Fowler (1987), and Westerhoff (1976), and regards faith as the manifestation of religious belief in action. Swezey (1990) concluded that community-service based models of faith development are compatible with other forms of service learning and have clear parallels with one another as well as similar, supporting developmental transitions and phases. Service learning within the context of faith can provide a viable avenue for students affairs professionals to respond to a wide array of student needs, offering a unique vehicle for values development and personal growth within the context of justice and care within a community setting. For this to occur, students must develop a caring sense of judgment, with responsibility both to others and to principles such as those developed through faith perspectives. The program philosophy asserts that integrating the complementary male and female orientations of justice and care will push society toward its full potential (Gilligan, 1982). Students experience new aspects of themselves as they work in different societies with people who have different values, beliefs and needs. Their ideas of culture and identity become more fluid, changing as their learning progresses. The service experience provides new opportunities for development as it is integrated into an individual's reality, often with the help of the campus ministry staff.

Culture, Individual and Community Identity

At the core of the Loyola program is the process of active and prayerful reflection on the service experience and its impact on the community. At the root of such reflection is the student's ability to explore both the way society is organized and the moral dimensions of that organization. The searching for solutions and transformations requires critical consciousness.

Students at Loyola are asked to do more than search for solutions to community problems. They are asked to engage in a process of contemplation that goes beyond service activity as a form of problem solving, moving beyond the search for solutions to the search for meaning. Two students could be involved in the same community service project, such as painting a wall, but the students might experience the project very differently. Thus the questions raised surrounding the experience often give it its texture and help to create its personal meaning for each student. It is for this reason that Jesuit education, as exemplified in the Loyola program, sees the role of education as helping the student to develop critical consciousness while recognizing the potential for change, both within the individual and in the surrounding social structures.

With the faith development model, the goal of the educational process is to develop each individual within the context of the human community, and with an awareness of the dialogue between faith and culture. In this sense, learning is both empathic and interactive. As Sweazy (1990) described one student's reflection on a service experience:

> I thought my experience of working with women and children would be different than it was. I found that everyone has the same needs and same desires in life. We may have different ways of living, yet the dignity of each person is important. My service experience has caused me to look at my directions and re-check my priorities . . . I have learned to listen . . . God speaks to me through others (p. 77).

Through the process of such reflections, students discover a sense of commonality and kinship with others that, in turn, informs and shapes their understanding of themselves and their world.

In this sense, the development of critical consciousness requires critical thinking and, in turn, critical thinking requires knowing. Knowing is a process which encompasses a social history and context and comes from the invention and re-invention of knowledge and experience. "Knowledge emerges through the restless, impatient, continuing, hopeful inquiry human beings pursue in the world, with the world, and with each other" (Freire, 1990, p. 53). This process is ever evolving based on the continual defining and redefining of the understanding of self in the context of ongoing experiences. As knowledge evolves, individuals redefine and restructure their own sense of identity. Students begin to realize that their ideas about who they are are shaped by their ideas about the external world. In this sense, identity is inseparable from the specific culture that shapes it. Personal identity and cultural identity are reciprocal, each impacting the other.

Identity both absorbs and reflects culture . . . a well-grounded psychosocial identity is necessary for the acceptance of persons who are culturally different and who may have different cultural realities, whether these realities are racially or ethnically based or group-ideology derived. (Hoare, 1991, p. 45)

Cultural identity reflects assumptions held about the world and perceptions of relationships to other people, nature, and time (Carter, 1990). Culture provides the context to answer personal identity questions. Thus an individual's reality is shaped by the culture or community in which the self is embedded (Hoare, 1991). When change occurs through the means of service programs such as Loyola's, it affects both the individual engaged in service as well as the community being served.

CONCLUSION

Education can be described as the means by which men and women deal critically with reality and discover how to participate in the transformation of their world. Authentic thinking, thinking that is concerned about human realities, does not take place in ivory tower isolation, but in communication between people (Freire, 1990, p. 58). Problem-posing education, such as that at Bentley, Stanford and Loyola, affirms men and women as beings in the process of becoming—as unfinished, uncompleted beings in and with a likewise unfinished reality. The unfinished nature of both human beings and external reality require education to be an ongoing activity (Friere, 1990). This type of liberating and liberal education consists of acts of cognition and transformation. It is a learning situation in which the knowers interact with what is known or what they are attempting to learn, in a process which involves teachers, students and the world around them. In this process, which Friere calls authentic reflection, people interact constantly with the world. External reality shapes human ideas and ideas transform reality.

In the field of experiential education, whether it is called co-operative education, internship, practicum, or service learning, experience is not marginalized. It is viewed as central to learning, the basis from which knowledge emerges. In all forms of experiential learning, affective and cognitive education are integrated. In Kolb's model (1984) concrete experiences such as the co-op work experience and the service models lead to reflective observations, abstract conceptualization, active experimentation, and more concrete experience in an endless cycle. For this reason experiential learning provides students with a learning model which enhances their intellectual development as it works to broaden their larger sense of multicultural awareness and communal identity. Service learning also provides a vehicle for the integration of curricular and co-curricular learning as a means of addressing student development (Stanton, 1991). Friere's concept of *praxis*, the action/reflection cycle which is endlessly repeated as people transform their world in the direction of greater justice and humanity (1990) is perhaps the most encompassing statement of this process. In *praxis* learning and action are completely embedded in the human experience. *Praxis*, which emerges from authentic, honest, mutually respectful dialogue, is the process by which people achieve significance and equality in the world. *Praxis* transforms education into meaningful learning which leads to meaningful action. Without *praxis*, learning can easily end when formal education stops.

Once a paradigm shift has occurred in one aspect of a student's education, the impact is felt in all modes of the learning experience, including, but not limited to, the classroom. "Crossing the border" into the field of cooperative education can have an effect on classroom teaching style. Two courses developed at Northeastern University illustrate this point. The courses are experiential in approach, interdisciplinary in nature and constructivist in outlook. The first, "Cultural Passages: Boston" asks students to explore the "language" in various art forms through a process of active participation and artistic creation with a variety of media. The second, "Mass Media, Crime, and Criminal Justice," asks students to explore the topic of the media's involvement in the criminal justice system from the vantage point of both their "backstage" co-op experience and as users and consumers of the media. The Rodney King case provided the basis for analyzing the issue of home videotape and it's impact on the criminal justice process since different audiences arrived at vastly different conclusions based on their perception and interpretation of the events captured by the camera (Galligan, 1994). Once the paradigm has shifted, an educational sea change occurs affecting all things in the educational ocean.

As experiential learning further moves the education of students into the community, new affective definitions of self and community will evolve. Part of the process of personal growth and self-definition is the acceptance of persons who are culturally different and who may have different cultural realities, whether these realities are racially or ethnically based or group-ideology derived (Hoare, 1991). Personal identity is based on answering questions such as Who am I? and What is my purpose? Cultural identity reflects assumptions held about the world and perceptions of relationships to other people, nature, and time (Carter, 1990).

In exploring these questions the individual looks to culture to provide the context for the answer. An individual's reality is shaped by the culture in which the self is embedded (Hoare, 1991). Experiential education calls both the academic faculty and student affairs professionals to search for ways to move the locus of such learning beyond the classroom into a more integrated relationship with both the college community and beyond.

REFERENCES

Boyer, E. (1994) Creating the new American college. *The Chronicle of Higher Education. 40 (27)*, p. A48.

Bridging the gap between town and gown. Palo Alto, CA: Stanford University conference materials, April 24, 1993.

Cantwell, L. et al. (1994). *Cooperative education curriculum.* Boston, MA: Northeastern University.

Carter, R. (1990). Cultural values difference between African Americans and White Americans. *Journal of College Student Development. 30.* 71-79.

Chickering, A. & Reisser, L. (1993). *Education and identity.* (2nd ed.) San Francisco: Jossey Bass.

Coles, R. (1993). *The Call of service: A witness to idealism.* New York: Houghton Mifflin.

Coles, R. (1990). *The spiritual life of children.* Boston: Houghton Mifflin.

Community service opportunities, 1993-94. (1993). Baltimore, MD: Center for Values and Service, Loyola College.

Csikszentmihalyi, M. (1990). *Flow: The psychology of optimal experience.* San Francisco: Harper & Row.

Delve, C. Mintz, S. & Stewart, G. (Eds.). (1990). Community service as values education. *New directions for student services. (50).* San Francisco: Jossey-Bass Publishers.

Dewey, J. (1916). *Democracy and education.* New York: Macmillan.

Fletcher, J. (1991). Field experience and cooperative education: Similarities and differences. *Journal of Cooperative Education. 27 (2).* 46-53.

Fletcher, J. (1989). Student Outcomes: What do we know and how do we know it? *Journal of Cooperative Education. 26 (1).*

Fowler, J. (1987). *Faith development and pastoral care.* Philadelphia: Fortress Press.

Friere, P. (1990). *Pedagogy of the oppressed.* New York: Continuum.

Friere, P. (1985). *The politics of education.* Westport, CT: Bergin and Garvey.

Galligan, A. (1994). Using courtroom television in the classroom: The 'Rodney King' case. *Journal of Criminal Justice Education. 5(2).*

Gardner, J. (1991). *A century of service: Celebrating our commitment.* Stanford Centennial Celebration. Palo Alto, CA: Stanford University.

Gilligan, C. (1982). *In a different voice.* Cambridge, MA: Harvard University Press.

Hegel, G. (1807/1977). *Phenomenology of spirit.* A. Miller, (Trans.) New York: Oxford University Press.

Ho, D. (1995). Internalized culture, culturocentrism and transcendence. *The Counseling Psychologist (23)* 1. 4-24.

Hoare, C. (1991). Psychological identity development and cultural others. *Journal of Counseling and Development. 70.* 45-53.

Kolb, D. (1985). *Learning style inventories.* Boston: McKerr.

Kolb, D. (1984). *Experiential learning: Experience as the source of learning and development.* Englewood Cliffs, NJ: Prentice Hall.

Kohlberg, L. (1975). The cognitive-development approach to moral education. *Phi Delta Kappan. 56.* 670-677.

Manning, K. & Coleman-Boatwright, P. (1991). Student affairs initiatives towards a multicultural university. *Journal of College-Student-Development. 32(4).* 367-74.

Morrill, R. (1982). Educating for democratic values. *Liberal Education. 68(4).* 355-356.

Parks, S. (1986). *The critical years: Young adults search for a faith to live by.* San Francisco: Harper & Row.

Perry, W. (1970). *Forms of intellectual and ethical development in the college years.* New York: Holt, Rinehart and Winston.

Piaget, J. (1978). *Behavior and Evolution.* New York: Pantheon Books.

Rodgers, R. (1989). Student Development. In U. Delworth & G. Hanson (Eds.). *Student services: A handbook for the profession.* (2nd ed.) San Francisco: Jossey-Bass.

Roark, M. (1989). Challenging and supporting college students. *NASPA Journal. 26(4).* 314-319.

Saltmarsh, J. (1993). John Dewey and the future of cooperative education. *Journal of Cooperative Education. 28(1).* 6-16.

Sanford, N. & Axelrod, J. (Eds.). (1964). *College and Character.* Berkeley, CA: Montaigne.

Schon, D. (1987). *Educating the reflective practitioner.* San Francisco: Jossey-Bass

Senge, P. (1990). *The fifth discipline.* New York: Doubleday.

Stanton, T. (1991). Liberal arts, experiential learning and public service: Necessary ingredients for socially responsible undergraduate education. *Journal of Cooperative Education. 27(2).* 55-68.

Swezey, E. (1990) Grounded in justice: Service learning from a faith perspective. In. C. Delve, S. Mintz & G. Stewart (Eds.). *Community service as values education: New directions for student services. 50.* San Francisco: Jossey-Bass. pp. 77-90.

Thomas, R. & Chickering, A. (1984). Education and identity revisited. *Journal of College Student Personnel. 25(5).* 392-99.

Westerhoff, J. (1976). *Will our children have faith?* New York: New Seabury Press.

Zlotkowski, E. (1993). *Service learning as campus culture.* Waltham, MA: Bentley College.

10

In Our Own Country: Student Affairs Preparation Programs

Jane Fried

An ounce of experience is better than a ton of theory because it is only in experience that any theory has vital and verifiable significance.

John Dewey, 1916, p. 169

Graduate preparation programs in student affairs are obvious places to begin the process of shifting paradigms and crossing borders. The borders which exist elsewhere in higher education between academic faculty and student affairs professionals barely exist in preparation programs. First, most part-time and full-time faculty members in these programs either are or have been practitioners in student affairs. These faculty members are bicultural in the sense that they have worked in two major segments of the university community. Second, many students in preparation programs are working concurrently in student affairs positions as graduate assistants, interns or professionals. Therefore, they can participate in the theory-to-practice dialogue required in constructivist and pragmatist pedagogy. Third, faculty members, as former or current student affairs professionals, have experience in designing constructivist learning experiences because that is the approach used in most student development education. Student development programs must be designed to meet the needs, interests and learning styles of the students who participate because attendance is voluntary and credit is rarely awarded. Therefore motivation must be intrinsic and the benefits of participation obvious to students. Finally, preparation programs are ideal places to begin because they are protected by the academic freedom of the classroom. Faculty members are free to challenge students' ideas and institutional practices as they present new or unorthodox perspectives on a wide range of issues. Administrators rarely have this type of intellectual freedom. Students, who are typically entry level practitioners, have even less freedom to challenge either ideas or practices in their capacity as employees. The classroom serves a very valuable function for everybody involved in the process. It becomes a testing ground for insights and new ideas, protected from political or practical consequences. Classroom discussions and other activities give participants time to think through the implications of a particular course of action or a particular set of ideas. They also provide the freedom to examine issues from a wide range of perspectives, giving the students the opportunity to learn about constructivist and pragmatist epistemology first-hand. Classes provide graduate students and faculty with the opportunity for joint inquiry, collaborative learning and gaining experience in the process of deconstructing and reconstructing the accepted categories of the profession.

MULTICULTURALISM IN PREPARATION PROGRAMS

During the past five years there has been a strong effort by graduate preparation programs to include education about cultural diversity in their curricula. A survey conducted in 1992 (Fried & Forrest), revealed that 100% of the responding programs had changed their curricula during the period to reflect multicultural content. More than 50% of all responding programs indicated that either one course was dedicated to multicultural issues, that parts of several courses were so dedicated or that multiculturalism was included in some form in all courses. Two programs reported efforts to infuse multicultural theory across all courses. Curricular infusion implies that the instructor is using standpoint epistemology as part of the pedagogical approach, identifying the cultural perspective or perspectives from which information has been organized, refusing to assume that there is a universal perspective. From a positivist perspective, all programs which responded to the survey made some effort to teach their students *about* multicultural issues.

Reported changes in pedagogy were not quite so dramatic. All programs used lecture/discussion methods of teaching and learning and all involved required reading. These were the dominant teaching methods in the majority of the programs. Films about non-dominant populations were used in 60% of the responding programs and simulations were used in 40%. A range of experiential and esthetics methods including use of literature, art, cultural/ethnic food, student panels, field trips, guest speakers, teleconferences, guest speakers and case studies was used in 35% of the programs. One program which uses the curricular infusion approach also reported the use of ethnographic research methods as a way to enhance student learning about culture and difference. Ethnographic research teaches students how to shift viewpoint while studying different cultures and reinforces the important of understanding standpoint as part of the process of constructing knowledge. All programs required completion of at least one practicum, but few of these practica were conducted on campuses with a "minority" population of more than 10%. Thirty per cent of the supervisors were members of non-dominant groups. Approximately 55% of the programs expected or encouraged students to participate in multicultural events on campus or in the surrounding community and almost all programs reported the presence of one or more ethnic studies programs on campus which might serve as providers of this type of programming. Some respondents were emphatic abut requiring student attendance at programs and involvement in cultural centers, while others failed to answer the questions indicating a range of attitudes among the preparation program faculty about the issue of multicultural education and pedagogical methodology as well.

Although there appears to be consensus regarding the importance of knowing about cultural difference, there seems to be much less understanding of methods which are effective in helping graduate students learn how to use what they know. Students in preparation programs report that they prefer to learn about cultural difference experientially rather than cognitively. McEwan and Roper suggest that students may not connect "formal teaching/learning with skill acquisition" and that many students "do not feel capable of designing programs sensitive to issues of race or of teaching others about issues of race" (1994, p. 85). It seems that faculty members in student affairs preparation programs generally use the same teaching methods as their colleagues in traditional disciplines, and that students do not find these methods helpful in teaching them how to address multicultural issues in professional settings. These methods are not particularly effective in helping people understand difference on an individual level. Preparation program faculty are less likely to use pragmatist or constructivist methods than methods based on positivist objectivism. Since 88.3% of students in preparation programs are white (McEwan & Roper, 1994), there is relatively little likelihood that the dominant cultural perspective will be challenged in class by peers. The majority of faculty in preparation programs are also white. Preliminary research with 250 faculty members in a large, midwestern university suggests that white male faculty members, in general, are uncomfortable with issues of racism and racial identity. They have difficulty understanding "the experience of discrimination and [demonstrate] a basic lack of insight as to how being ethnically different may have an impact on an individual's social predicament" (Pope-Davis & Ottavi, 1992, p. 393). The data on female faculty members is less clear but supports the general notion of discomfort in the area of empathizing with the situation of those who are members of non-dominant groups. Although these data pertain to a small group of faculty in one university, they point to the possibility of similar attitudes among preparation program faculty. Inability to empathize with the perspective of members of non-dominant groups is theoretically connected with difficulty in managing the teaching/learning process from a standpoint or constructivist frame of reference. The positivist objectivist tradition tends not to acknowledge the role of viewpoint in interpretation. If a professor is also uncomfortable with the perspectives of students from non-dominant groups, traditional approaches can interact with racism and discomfort to produce a rigid, monocultural environment in class. Racial, ethnic and other cultural implications of a particular standpoint are likely to go unnoticed in such relatively homogeneous settings.

LEARNING ABOUT MULTICULTURAL TRAINING FROM COUNSELING PSYCHOLOGY PROGRAMS

Counseling psychology programs considered most effective in training multiculturally competent practitioners report several common attributes: the presence of at least one faculty member who is committed to understanding the impact of culture in counseling, at least one required course in multicultural issues, an attempt to infuse cultural issues into all courses in the curriculum, visible presence of people from a range of cultural groups in the program and opportunities for students to practice in settings which expose them to people from a number of different cultural groups (Ponterotto & Casas, 1987). Preparation programs surveyed indicated that a number of these elements were present in many of the programs, but the creation of multicultural environments and teaching approaches cannot yet be considered widespread (Fried & Forrest, 1992). Effectiveness in teaching students about culture and in helping students develop multicultural competence requires a wide range of teaching and learning approaches in which pragmatism and constructivism are the thematic epistemologies (Ponterotto & Casas, 1987). The goal and outcome of these approaches is to help students understand the basic beliefs and practices of the cultures with which they come in contact. They must be able to observe cultural or intentional worlds from the borders of their own culture which provides a dual perspective, looking outward to other cultures and inward at the basic assumptions of their own. Borders are ideal vantage points form which to make comparisons and see differences. Students as practitioners-in-training must know about their culturally different students' belief systems and behavioral codes. They should also know how it feels to be immersed in other cultures and experience the intuitive discomfort of feeling different and trying to adapt. Ultimately, they must know cognitively, affectively and behaviorally how to empathize with members of other groups and how to engage in two way communication with them. They cannot see members of different cultural groups as cultural Others and also develop effective relationships with them. They must have the skill of listening non-judgmentally to culturally different interpretations about all kinds of data and events even when they don't agree with the interpretations in much the same way as effective counselors practice non-judgmental listening for the purposes of understanding what a client believes and establishing a trusting environment in which honest communication can continue.

This type of learning includes, but is not limited to positivist objectivist learning. It also involves learning from experience and learning how to reflect on experience. It involves cognition and behavior or skill development. Another parallel from counselor education is the notion of self-as-instrument in which the practitioner, at the moment when she or he needs to use knowledge, can only rely on the knowledge which has been integrated into the self. In the moment of authentic encounter between people, self is the only resource. Schon calls this type of knowledge "knowing in action . . . the sorts of knowhow we reveal in our intelligent action" (1987, p. 25). This formulation also brings to mind the Afrocentric perspective: all knowledge is self-knowledge because all of us are connected to each other , the world around us, our ancestors and our children (Myers, 1993). "I am because we are." All of these ways of knowing transcend the traditional epistemological distinction between subject and object. "Knowing in action", "All knowledge is self-knowledge" and "self-as-instrument" are all constructivist, pragmatist formulations in which self, situation and action are integrated for purposes of understanding and/or intervening.

NEW APPROACHES TO TEACHING AND LEARNING

The need to integrate theory and practice in preparation programs suggests increased use of three teaching/learning approaches which are not particularly well known in higher education. These approaches were developed by Kolb (1984), Schon (1987) and Friere (1990). Kolb's approach seems to be the most widely known in student affairs because it is also used as a guide to designing effective training programs (Pfeiffer, 1985). Kolb suggests that adult education should utilize a cyclic process which engages all learning styles at one or more points, making the learning both personal and powerful, cognitive and experiential. Students begin the cycle by participating in an experience designed to raise a particular issue or illustrate a specific point. This is typical of many training simulations. Participants are then given time and structure for personal reflection about the experience. Participants discuss their experience with at least one other person and look for patterns of behavior and events. Finally, they are asked to generalize or abstract principles from their experience and engage in further experiences to see whether or not these principles are accurate or true. Kolb's work is a direct outgrowth of Dewey's pragmatism and clearly follows Dewey's pattern of helping people use what they know to understand and interact with their environment in an on-going process. Kolb's methods can be used without providing direct experience if students have experience from outside class which bears on the subject the course covers and that experience can be discussed in class.

Kolb's learning style theory (1984) uses a four part grid. One axis draws a continuum from active experimentation to reflective observation. The second axis draws a continuum from concrete experience to abstract conceptualization. All students have a preferred style of apprehension, or acquiring information, and a preferred style of comprehension, or making sense of the information. Learning occurs along two axes: 1) the *abstract/concrete axis* in which people *prehend* or grasp experience. Prehension is divided into *apprehension*, "reliance on the felt qualities of immediate experience" (p. 41) and *comprehension*, "conceptual interpretation and symbolic representation" (p. 41); 2) the *active/reflective* axis, called *transformation*, which is divided into *intention*, "internal reflection" and *extension*, "active manipulation of the external world" (p. 41). "Knowledge results from the combination of grasping experience and transforming it" (p. 41).

> The central idea here is that learning and therefore knowing, required both a grasp or figurative representation of experience and some transformation of that representation. Either the figurative grasp or the operative transformation alone is not sufficient. The simple perception of experience is not sufficient for learning. Something must be done with it (p. 42).

In Kolb's approach learning must be approached holistically, integrating information, experience and the construction of meaning into the process. When students have learned something, in this schema, they have learned it cognitively, behaviorally and affectively. They can identify what they know, what it means to them, how they feel about the knowledge and how the knowledge might be used.

Educating the Reflective Practitioner is both the title of Donald Schon's book and a description of the process he presents (1987). Schon compares professional practice in the late 20th century to a "high, hard ground overlooking a swamp" (1987, p. 3). On the high hard ground are problems which are complex, but amenable to solutions which rely solely on technical knowledge and skills. In the swamp are confusing, messy problems which defy technical solutions and are not resolvable solely by examination of technical data or reference to widely accepted principles. Schon asserts that the most important problems which professionals face today are all in the swamp, in "indeterminate zones of practice [characterized by] uncertainty, uniqueness and value conflict" (p. 6). Problems which have simple, technical solutions are relatively less significant in the total scheme of things. For example, most universities now have data base management systems by which student billing is coordinated. Adding student damage charges to the billing process is a technical problem. Figuring out how to stop students from engaging in vandalism is a non-technical problem. Although recovering damage costs is very important, stopping vandalism and encouraging student responsibility or respect for property is generally considered far more important.

Schon points to the inadequacy of our epistemology of professional practice, one which is based in the scientific tradition described in this book. His suggestion is that professional education should help students realize the extent of their "knowing in action," that knowledge they have about how to work in their professional environment, even when they can't exactly explain what they are doing or why it works. When students' knowing in action is inadequate, or doesn't produce the results anticipated, they need to be coached in the processes of "reflection in action," the means by which people learn to use what they know to correct or improve their work when what they thought would work didn't.

> Reflection-in-action has a critical function, questioning the assumptions structure of knowing-in-action. We think critically about the thinking that got us into this fix or this opportunity; and we may, in the process, restructure strategies of action, understandings of phenomena or ways of framing problems. (Schon, 1987, p. 28)

Reflection leads to experimentation, establishing a cycle of observation, or construction of a problem, generation of ideas for addressing the problem, acting on the problem evaluating the results of the action, and, if the action was unsuccessful, rethinking the assumptions on which the action was based. When students are given a problem to solve, they may be able to do it in class, pooling the knowledge they have already developed. They may also go to the library, speak with people on other campuses, organize a survey of student opinion or a series of focus groups, or set up interviews with campus administrators to investigate the problem further so that they can address it more effectively.

The third type of knowing which Schon describes is "knowing in practice," which places one's knowledge of principles and problems typically included in one's professional expertise within an institutional setting such as a university, a hospital, a bank or other setting. This is also a constructivist or pragmatist process of teaching and learning because it focuses the student on the environment in which problems emerge and must be solved. Even if the students believe that they understand the problem, their effectiveness is minimized unless they acknowledge the impact of the institutional setting for the problem. Indeed, the setting may constitute the major part of the problem and cannot be discounted. Knowing in practice involves understanding organizational culture including all the aspects of tradition, professional practice, values and beliefs (Kuh, 1993). This may be the most difficult type of knowing to help graduate students with limited experience develop because of their tendency to focus on absolutes and dualistic ways to frame problems. However, knowing in practice is comparable to thinking through culture (Shweder, 1990) because it involves helping a person perceive a situation through the frame of reference of another person. This skill can be applied both the understanding cultural difference and understanding differences in perspective which develop because of different roles people play in an institution. Therefore, a skill which is learned in the process of understanding cultural difference can also be applied to analyzing organizational issues.

Schon describes the two most basic aspects of professional competence in the current era as "naming" and "framing" problems. Since the most important problems are messy or "ill defined" (Kitchener & King, 1994), there are multiple ways to construct, define or frame them and multiple ways to investigate them. A situation which appears to be a serious problem to one person may not be a problem to another or be a minor irritation to a third. A typical problem faced by counseling centers is that they are underutilized by members of non-dominant groups. What are the key elements of the problem: the students; unfamiliarity with the center, the services it provides and its general operating procedures? their lack of trust in or familiarity with the counselors? their belief that all problems should be solved within the family or the church? their fear of diagnosis or loss of self-respect? Deciding how to name and frame the problem is by far the most important part of solving it. If the problem is that students don't trust counselors, publicizing the location of the counseling center won't make it any more likely that students from the target groups use the services.

Another problem which has recently been widespread is low

occupancy levels in residence halls. Halls which are budgeted to maintain 95% occupancy may be only 65-75% full because of declining enrollment in the institution or changing demographic patterns among students. How the problem is framed determines how it will be addressed. If the halls must be full because they are relatively new and bonds are being paid off, mandatory residency requirements may be implemented. If the buildings are old and need to be rehabilitated, low occupancy presents an opportunity to consolidate space and rehabilitate buildings. If the college is planning to shift from a traditional residence program to a non-traditional night/weekend program, there may be other uses for the space which would, in a short period of time, enhance revenue. One Catholic women's college, when faced with this problem, redesigned several residence halls to create a life-care facility with increasing levels of care available as the occupants needed increasing support. The life-care facility was run in conjunction with undergraduate programs in nursing and geriatric social work and served as a location for practica and service learning projects for the undergraduate students. The naming and framing process shaped the solution.

From Schon's perspective, education of reflective practitioners should become a continuing practicum in which a significant portion of academic work is integrated with professional training, and the borders between classroom and work-sites are increasingly vague. The teaching style should resemble coaching rather than traditional teaching, and the emphasis should be on students solving problems with the advice and assistance of more experienced and well-informed professionals. Excellent professional practice is a form of artistry, according to Schon, whether the practice is in the profession being studied or in the teaching process itself. This artistry involves skill, knowledge, dialogue between student and teacher/coach and a high level of reflection in action, or self-correction. It requires a breakdown of the traditional hierarchy of knowledge assumed in the professions so that basic science, applied science and the "technical skills of day-to-day practice" (Schon, 1987, p. 9) interact in professional practice as problems are named, framed and resolved. Schon's notion of the reflective practitioner assumes that students are being trained to be their own best source of continuing education and that teachers continue to be excellent reflective practitioners as well.

TRANSFORMATION OF TEACHING AND LEARNING: CRITICAL/BORDER PEDAGOGY

The final teaching/learning approach to be described is the most radical and is likely to cause the most discomfort in any bureaucratic system. This approach is based on the writings of Paolo Friere (1985; 1973; 1970) Henry Giroux (1988; 1981), Ira Schor (1992) and many others. It has been described as liberation theology (Manning, 1992), critical pedagogy (Giroux & McLaren, 1994), pedagogy of the oppressed (Friere, 1970), border pedagogy (Aronowitz & Giroux, 1991) and empowering education (Shor, 1992). In this text, border pedagogy and critical pedagogy will be used interchangeably and are understood to encompass the meanings implied by the other terms as well. Shor frames the approach succinctly, "Education is politics" (1992, p. 11). Rooted in Friere's early work with illiterate Brazilian peasants, the goal of critical pedagogy is to teach people to read and transform their world. Initially reading meant literacy education. Literacy education, using Friere's methods, led immediately to reading the context in which one lived. The immediate consequence of teaching illiterate people to read is that they have access to a wide range of information and social criticism. They are no longer subject to the limited information given to them orally by the people in power. They develop the skill of describing and naming their own world. There is no way to separate effective literacy education from power. Literate people are powerful people who can challenge the dominant group because of their access to non-censored information. They can communicate broadly, name and frame issues, provide personal descriptions of their world which challenge the dominant descriptions and organize among themselves much more extensively than if they were limited to verbal communication. Knowledge is power. Literacy is a critical key to knowledge.

Critical pedagogy incorporates many of Schon's and Kolb's ideas about an action/reflection cycle, experiential learning and continuing self-education. However, it goes much further in that it examines borders between individuals and groups and asks what purposes the borders serve. Critical pedagogy assumes that context is critical to understanding and that knowledge, power, education and politics are inseparable. Critical pedagogy has incorporated John Dewey's idea of the problematic, an approach to discussing a situation or problem in which the problem is seen from multiple perspectives and two questions are asked: What are we discussing as part of this problem? What are we not discussing? For example, on many American campuses, students who violate the student conduct code are described as problems. Their behavior is problem behavior. If a problematic approach were used, other issues would be raised, e.g., For whom is this behavior a problem? Who is benefiting from this behavior? Why do we define this as a problem? Is there another way to frame the question? Would this situation be defined as a problem in another context? The problematic approach has been used in this book when discussing cultural "problems". For whom is the underutilization of the counseling center by "minority" students a problem? If there are other places in the environment where these students can get emotional support, then perhaps the underutilization is more of a problem for the staff of the center than for the students. Perhaps the type of counseling offered in the center is more of a problem for the students than their failure to utilize the services. African American students who congregate in campus cafeterias are sometimes defined as a problem called self-segregation. As a problematic, the framer of the question also has to ask, Why are all the Anglo students eating together? For whom is this a problem? Why are there so few African American (or Asian-American or Mexican) students on this campus that their association at lunch time is a matter for Anglo-Americans to notice? Is this an important problem, compared to the trash left on most of the tables at lunch time? What is being discussed in the description of this problem? What is not being discussed? Another issue which attracts notice is public displays of affection between gay and lesbian students. Why are public displays of affections between gay or lesbian students considered to be a problem when similar displays by heterosexual students generally go unnoticed?

Critical pedagogy tends to use Friere's basic principles (1970) to frame the way education is managed in and out of class: praxis, critical consciousness, dialogue and transformation of the world. Critical/border pedagogy also uses his notion of the contrast between banking education and problem posing education and discusses the educational process even as it explores social problems which occur outside class. These terms are often used in relation to one another, setting a total context in which people are empowered to reshape their world. The following definitions illustrate the integration of the ideas.

"Praxis" is a cycle of action and reflection in which people participate as they transform the world and establish a place of dignity for themselves within it. The goal of praxis is to humanize the world of those who participate in the dialogue. Humanizing involves restoring dignity to people who have been deprived of it by being deprived of the right to name and shape their world. They have been denied the right to trust their own interpretation of their experiences and their own judgment. Consequently they become dependent on the dominant group to provide information which they can trust and believe. In Friere's situation, this involved peasants many of whom believed that they were stupid and lazy, powerless to change the conditions of their lives or to exercise more power in their relationships with the padrones or landowners who owned the land they farmed. As Friere helped these people learn to read, he also helped them reshape their understanding of who they were and what they were capable of achieving. On an American campus praxis might occur among students when they begin to realize that high attrition rates among female engineering students or male nursing students are not related to intelligence but to other environmental factors which might be amenable to change.

"Dialogue" involves speaking the "true word," a word which names the experience of the speaker in authentic personal terms and does not support the mythologies created by the dominant group. Dialogues involve conversation among people who have similar experiences of the world and are oppressed by the dominating group that controls public opinion. An example of a mythology maintained about a non-dominant group in the United States is the notion that most people on welfare are African American single mothers with large numbers of children, also known as "welfare queens". The average welfare family consists of a mother with 1.9 children. Mothers are Black, (38.8%), White (38.1%) and Hispanic (17.4%). The average time on welfare is less than two years. Marriage, assistance from family and friends or increase in mother's income account for 62% of the movement from the welfare roles to self-supporting status (*New York Times*, 1992). Another myth is that all gay men molest little boys when the accurate information is that most children who are molested are girls and most molesters are heterosexual men. Dialogue among African American single mothers would focus on helping the women learn to appreciate their own strengths, to read the values of the dominant system and to transform their oppression into action to change the circumstances of their lives and increase their self-respect. Dialogue among gay men has been ongoing for at least the past 25 years as these men have deconstructed the demonized mythologies about themselves perpetrated by the dominant heterosexist culture. There are many psychological texts which describe this process, but one of the most touching is an autobiography, *Becoming a Man*, by Paul Monette (1992) which describes coming to terms with his gay identity and overcoming the self-loathing which crippled him for the first three decades of his life. The AIDS crisis has also transformed many gay men who learned to read government denial of the problem as an effort to deny their existence and let the epidemic run unchecked. Perceiving that government inaction was killing gay may by the thousands empowered the community to political action and a new reading of the dominant culture.

"Critical consciousness" and "transformation of the world" emerge from praxis and dialogue. When people seize the right to name their world and establish their place in it, they have begun to achieve critical consciousness, or conscientizacao. Critical consciousness is defined as "learning to perceive social, political and economic contradictions and to take action against the oppressive elements of reality" (Friere, 1990, p. 19). Critical consciousness leads to self-affirmation because it enhances the ability of the conscious person to trust his or her observations and inferences about the world. Friere considers education for critical consciousness synonymous with education as the practice of freedom (1973) because when one trusts one's observations and inferences, one is then free to act on them, to push the limits of what is possible, to hope for freedom from oppression and to believe in the ability of oneself and one's *compadres* or companions to achieve the goal through mutual action. Transformation of the world is the intended consequence of the combination of praxis, dialogue and critical consciousness.

Friere's description of traditional and empowering approaches to education explains how these ideas work in a classroom setting. His description of traditional education is called banking education, a metaphor which defines knowledge as quantifiable, factual information, transferred from teacher to student in much the same way as a person deposits money in a bank. Knowledge in the banking metaphor is static. "The teacher talks about reality as if it were motionless, static, compartmentalized and predictable" (Friere, 1970, p. 57). Through the use of narrative, the teacher describes reality for the students and expects the students to memorize the information without challenging it or expressing another perspective on it. The teacher delivers the official view of the dominant culture and class. The process involves, "a narrating Subject (the teacher) and patient listening Objects (the students). The contents, whether values or empirical dimensions of reality, tend in the process of being narrated to become lifeless and petrified" (Friere, 1970, p. 57). Friere and many others including John Dewey (1916) believe that a major goal of state supported education is to reproduce the values of the ruling class and to train people to support the economic system of the nation. Rather than teaching people to challenge and explore the implications of ideas, the system teaches people to accept the dominant view of reality and conform to the status quo. The question of the problematic arises immediately in the banking approach to education: What is being discussed and what is not being discussed? Who does the system serve? At whose expense is the system served?

Problem-posing education is Friere's contrasting approach. In problem-posing education, the goal is transformation and humanization of the world. Students and teachers collaborate to name and shape the relationship between people and their world through dialogue, praxis and transformation.

> The teacher is no longer merely the-one-who-teaches but one who is himself [sic] taught in dialogue with the students who in turn while being taught also teach. They become jointly responsible for a process in which all grow. In this process, arguments based on 'authority' are no longer valid; in order to function, authority must be *on the side of* freedom, not *against* it. Here no one teaches another nor is anyone self-taught. Men [sic] teach each other, mediated by the world, by the cognizable objects which in banking education, are 'owned' by the teacher. (Friere, 1970, p. 67)

The goal of problem posing education is to find the generative themes which are significant to both students and teacher, the issues which are indicative of injustice and the abuse of power in their world. Once these themes are identified, students and teachers investigate them, become better educated about them, propose methods of addressing them in the concrete world and begin the cycle of praxis and dialogue. In higher education today, one generative theme is the issue of incorporating diversity, or difference into the academy. Another way of naming this issue is to describe it as a problem of inviting non-dominant cultural groups to move from the margins of campus life to the center in both curriculum and governance. A third way to pose the problem is to look at the structure and content of academic life as an expression of Euro-American values and culture as ask if this structure, including both institutional governance and academic organization, continues to serve the United States or any particular campus well in an era of global interdependence. In a college student personnel/student affairs graduate program, the problem might be framed as: How can we make this program more reflective of cultural diversity by recruiting more students and faculty of color, lesbian and gay students, mid-life students or disabled students? It might also be framed as a question of epistemology and pedagogy. How can we redesign our teaching/learning methods and epistemological assumptions so that people who participate in this program learn to discuss standpoint and respect multiple perspectives?

Classroom Process: The Structure of Knowledge and Authority

Friere's problem posing education incorporates many of the elements described by Kolb and Schon, but his work goes significantly further. They intend to transform our ideas about teaching and learning, incorporating the role of reflection on experience as part of the learning process in the pragmatist tradition. Friere intends to do that and, in the process, help students and teachers join in the project of transforming the world, making it a more just, humane and equitable environment for all. All three approaches are constructivist in that they identify the role people play in constructing knowledge. Friere also incorporates standpoint epistemology because he demands that participants in the dialogue reveal their own vested interests and the way those interests shape their interpretations of events.

Incorporation of methods from any of these approaches radically transforms the learning process both in and out of the classroom. The focus shifts from teaching in the banking mode to learning. All these methods are based on an experience/reflection cycle, so that the split between theory and practice is overcome. However, the first two methods do not challenge the fundamental assumptions of power relations in the classroom. The teacher continues to be defined as the expert and arbiter while the students have less power and less expertise. The teacher determines what the students need to learn in order to be considered educated or competent and to evaluate their progress toward learning what they need to know. In critical/border pedagogy, both knowledge and authority shift frequently, depending on the expertise of the participants in the dialogue and the way in which problems, or generative themes are defined. The three approaches can be viewed on a continuum in terms of shaping knowledge and defining authority. In the Kolb approach, the teacher defines the activities or the ways in which extra-class experiences are discussed and the students participate in the teacher-defined experience. In the Schon approach, boundaries are somewhat more blurred because the teacher is also the trainer and supervisor and works with the student to address problems in context. The teacher, however, is still the source of authority and expertise. In the Friere approach, problems are jointly defined through dialogue. The purpose of the dialogue is mutual understanding and transformation of a situation toward greater justice. If those who are experiencing injustice or dehumanization or oppression happened to be called students, their expertise about how the problem is working in their lives, how it is inhibiting them from achieving their full potential, is likely to have greater value that the teacher's opinion about the situation. If a study group, or class, chooses to investigate a problem of injustice, the teacher alone is not necessarily the one best qualified to evaluate the results of the study or the intervention/praxis. Study, intervention and evaluation would be most effectively conducted by the entire group, students and teacher working together. The classroom itself might become the object of study and the teacher/student relationship, evaluation procedures and curricula become generative themes.

Friere reports that when he began using critical pedagogy, many were concerned about the welfare of his students. Members of the Brazilian government and education ministry believed that the peasants would feel as if their world were collapsing around them because the traditional authorities had withdrawn. Peasants were assumed to be terrified of freedom. Just the opposite occurred. Peasants reported a new sense of dignity and power. As illiterates the world appeared to them to be a given, a static place defined by others, in which their low status and

impotence was established. As they became literate, they reported a new sense of dignity, a new awareness of possibilities and
hope.

> I now realize I am a man, an educated man . . . We were blind,
> and now our eyes have been opened . . . Before this, words meant
> nothing to me; now they speak to me and I can make them speak
> . . . Now we will no longer be a dead weight . . . When this
> happens in the process of learning to read, men discover that
> they are creators of culture, and that all their work can be cre-
> ative . . . I work and working I transform the world. (Shaull,
> 1970, p. 14)

Is there anyone in the student affairs profession, whether a
faculty member in a preparation program or an administrator in
a division of student affairs, who would not enjoy hearing students say that they felt empowered, able to contribute to the
improvement of campus life, listened to and worth listening to?
People who feel respected and empowered direct their anger or
frustration to productive uses (May, 1972). They experience hope,
even in the absence of optimism (Coffin, 1993). People who feel
alienated and marginalized tend to express anger destructively
against others and themselves. Shaull's description of the effect
which Friere's approach has on peasants easily translates into a
discussion of alienation or mattering (Schlossberg, 1989) among
students and improving the level of student involvement on campus. The fears of the Brazilian establishment reflect a much
broader phenomenon—the universal fear of those in power about
what will happen if they relinquish power or share power. Friere warns that if the oppressed become the oppressors when they
become empowered, then nothing has changed or improved. The
goal of sharing power is to create justice, fairness, equity, respect, and in the case of this discussion, effective ways of helping students learn how to live in a multicultural world and work
as administrator/educators in student affairs. Student challenges
to authority will come to be seen as opportunities for learning
rather than threats to management systems, whether they are
systems of university governance or classroom process. Both
teachers and administrators become "joint learners" with students as they work to transform the institutions and the learning processes within them. This is a radical departure from
business as usual and represents an emotional, interpersonal and

administrative challenge to all of our institutions and preparation programs. In many ways, it represents another turn on the cycle which was so disruptive in the 1960s and 1970s and which caught so many colleges and universities unprepared.

APPLICATIONS OF THE NEW APPROACHES

Several student affairs preparation programs have begun to incorporate ideas from one or more of these approaches into the teaching/learning process. From her research on student learning Marcia Baxter-Magolda articulated three principles for transforming teaching: 1) Validating the student as knower; 2) Situating learning in the student's own experience and 3) Approaching learning as mutually constructing meaning (1992). Baxter-Magolda's work is complemented by Rogers' investigation of leadership (1992). Rogers describes emergent leadership in terms comparable to Schon's teacher/coach. An emergent leader helps people develop multiple frames or perspectives in order to manage complexity and contradiction. The emergent leader influences and shapes rather than controls and helps people make meaning out of situations rather than imposing rules on them for handling situations (1992).

Since teaching and leading have many areas of overlap in emerging organizational paradigms (Allen & Cherrey, 1994; Bensimon & Newman, 1993; Wheatley, 1992) the two sets of ideas have been combined to reshape the teaching/learning process for students in several courses at the Miami University of Ohio preparation program. Students are introduced to these learning principles at the beginning of their courses. The teachers and students discuss and agree upon learning behaviors, group norms and assessment methodologies. The students begin learning about student development by examining their own experiences as students and then designing methods by which they can learn more from current undergraduate students. Finally they shape the data they have gathered into patterns and compare their patterns to the most widely used theories of student development. Students struggle with the creation of meaning and become conscious of the process by which theory is constructed. They become agents of theory creation and realize that others are engaged in the same type of work. Theory becomes demystified and useful, a tool to be incorporated in understanding and shaping their work in student affairs. The process teaches them the skills of the reflective practitioner. It has clear parallels with the work of Schon, Kolb and Friere. It prepares graduate students to be both leaders in their profession and teacher/learners in their work with students. It demonstrates how people construct meaning and how learning can occur in any context whether or not it is described as an official learning experience. Finally, the process and the teacher/leaders demonstrate how borders are created and how they can be moved or crossed because students see border construction and movement occurring among them. Once students realize that people use "facts" to construct meaning, they can apply that insight in any situation where meaning is constructed differently by members of different groups. This includes student/teacher groups, groups with members from different ethnic or racial backgrounds, groups mixed by gender, sexual orientation or disability status and groups mixed by title, level of authority and power. Students have "true words" to describe the phenomena. They are empowered to transform the world.

Other preparation programs are incorporating learning methodologies that shift borders and encourage the action/reflection process. Journal writing is widely used as a vehicle to encourage reflection on experience. In the Florida State University preparation program, program director Barbara Mann uses anonymous summaries of journal entries to help students address generative themes which are common among them. An extremely powerful demonstration of this technique occurred when two lesbian students in the program began to struggle with the issue of "coming out" to their classmates. After obtaining consent from the two students to discuss their sexual orientation in class, Mann reminded all the students that a fundamental value of the student affairs profession is belief in the dignity and worth of every human being. She asked them to listen to the pain and struggle of the people who had written the journal entries. The other students were moved to tears as they listened to the words of their lesbian peers and colleagues. Over the next semester, the students continued to discuss the effect of homosexuality and homophobia on personal development, both from a theoretical perspective and from the perspective of their friends who had endured and were continuing to endure the process. The borders between people of different sexual orientations shifted as the students experienced not only what divided them, but what they had in common—the need to be seen as competent, to be accepted by colleagues and friends, to have satisfying intimate relationships and to live free from harassment and prejudice. It seems reasonable to assume that they became far more informed and critical readers of theories of homosexual identity formation as well a becoming more sensitive to the needs of gay and lesbian students with whom they might work. Finally, the students and Mann shaped their learning about homosexuality, gay/straight relationships and the personal and professional dimensions of the situation into several conference presentations so the circle of integrating theory and practice was complete (Barbara Mann, personal communication, 1994). The Florida State program also incorporates journal writing into all internships. Students are required to complete an in-depth analysis of their experience on each internship, comparing theory to practice in each site and discussing their personal and professional reactions to their internship experiences.

A third area of experimentation in boundary shifting occurs in discussion of the classroom process itself. Kathleen Manning, a professor in the preparation program at the University of Vermont, reports discussing the power relationships between students and teacher in her classes. Rather than assume that the "teacher dominant/student subordinate" model is a given, Manning calls attention to student attitudes toward her as authority figure, source of information and dispenser of meaning. When she feels that students are slipping unaware into the banking mode of teaching and learning, she points out the process and makes efforts to shift the boundaries of awareness and responsibility (personal communication, 1994). Jane Fried, program coordinator at Northeastern University carries on a similar process with particular attention to the construction of meaning by cultural group. In discussion of theories, programs and practices in student affairs, she asks students to analyze how the topic might be understood by a student of color from any one of several groups, by a gay or lesbian student, a disabled student or a student who is older than average. Role plays, research, films and guest speakers are used to enhance the students' cultural empathy with members of other groups. This approach is also used to help students understand how problems are named and framed differently by administrators and faculty members at different levels of power with different constituencies or in different areas of the institution. The goals of both these preparation program faculty members is to help students learn to shift perspective and understand how human beings construct meaning.

CONCLUSION

This chapter has shifted focus from teaching about multiculturalism to teaching about adopting multiple perspectives in the construction of meaning to helping students learn to shift their understandings of roles and perspectives, teaching and learning. All these shifts are intended to illustrate the processes by which meaning is constructed in various preparation programs and elsewhere on American campuses. Perspectives from which meaning is constructed are influenced by cultural experience, historical experience and personal experience. Effective educators and administrators in multicultural organizations must be able to shift roles, shift perspectives and examine issues from many perspectives before determining which perspective has the greatest relevance to the issue of concern. These educators must be comfortable with shifting borders and perspectives and they must have confidence in themselves as they understand and guide processes through which issues are addressed. One cannot learn these skills only by reading about them. Practice, praxis, action, reflection and respect are necessary to maintain both hope and dynamic equilibrium. A shift in one area of person's work world, intellectual world or personal life is likely to cause shifts in other areas as well. Within a universe of interrelationships and constant change, people must learn to maintain their balance and create a process by which to extend their understanding. What happens in class must extend to the boundaries of our common experience in higher education so that we can all continue to learn together.

REFERENCES

Allen, K. & Cherrey, C. (1994). Shifting paradigms and practices in student affairs. In J. Fried (Ed.). *Different voices: Gender and perspective in student affairs administration.* (pp. 1-11). *16.* Washington, D.C.: National Association of Student Personnel Administrators.

Aronowitz, S. & Giroux, H. (1991). *Postmodern education.* Minneapolis, MN: University of Minnesota Press.

Baxter-Magolda, M. (1992). *Knowing and reasoning in college: Gender related patterns in students' intellectual development.* San Francisco: Jossey-Bass.

Bensimon, E. & Neumann, A. (1993). *Redesigning collegiate leadership.* Baltimore, MD: Johns Hopkins University Press.

Coffin, W. (1993). Presentation to the Conference on Student Values, Tallahassee, FL.

Dewey, J. (1916). *Democracy and education.* New York: Macmillan.

Fried, J. & Forrest, C. (1992). Multicultural perspectives and practices in student affairs preparation programs. (unpublished manuscript).

Friere, P. (1990). *Pedagogy of the oppressed.* New York: Continuum.

Friere, P. (1985). *Culture, power and liberation.* New York: Bergin Garvey.

Friere, P. (1973). *Education for critical consciousness.* New York: Continuum.

Friere, P. (1970). *Pedagogy of the oppressed.* New York: Herder and Herder.

Giroux, H. (1988). *Schooling and the struggle for public life.* Minneapolis, MN: University of Minnesota Press.

Giroux, H. (1981). *Ideology, culture and the process of schooling.* Philadelphia, PA: Temple University Press.

Kitchener, K. & King, P. (1994). *Developing reflective judgment.* San Francisco: Jossey-Bass.

Kolb, D. (1984). *Experiential learning.* Englewood Cliffs, NJ: Prentice-Hall.

Kuh, G. (Ed.). (1993). *Cultural perspectives in student affairs work.* Washington, D.C.: American College Personnel Association.

Manning, K. (1994). Liberation theology and student affairs. *Journal of College Student Development.* 35. 94-97.

May, R. (1972). *Power and Innocence.* New York: W. W. Norton.

McEwan, M. & Roper, L. (1994). Interracial experiences, knowledge and skills of master's degree students in graduate programs in student affairs. *Journal of College Student Development. 35.* 81-87.

Monette, P. (1992). *Becoming a man.* New York: Harcourt, Brace, Jovanovich.

Myers, L. (1993). *Understanding an Afrocentric world view: Introduction to an optimal psychology.* (2nd ed.), Dubuque, IA: Kendall Hunt.

New York Times (June 19, 1994). Welfare as we've known it. Section E, p. 4.

Pfeiffer, J. (1985). *Reference guide to handbooks and annuals.* San Diego, CA: University Associates.

Ponterotto, J. & Casas, J. M. (1987). In search of multicultural competence within counselor education programs. *Journal of Counseling and Development. 65.* 430-434.

Pope-Davis, D. & Ottavi, T. (1992). The influence of white racial identity attitudes on racism among faculty members: A preliminary examination. *Journal of College Student Development. 33.* 389-394.

Rogers, C. (1961). *On becoming a person.* Cambridge, MA: Riverside Press.

Rogers, J. (1992). Leadership development for the 90s: Incorporating emergent paradigm perspectives. *NASPA Journal. 29.* 243-252.

Schlossberg, N. (1989). Marginality and mattering: Key issues in building community. In D. Roberts (Ed.). *New Directions for Student Services: Designing campus activities to foster a sense of community. 48.* (pp. 5-16) San Francisco: Jossey-Bass.

Schon, D. (1987). *Educating the reflective practitioner.* San Francisco: Jossey-Bass.

Shaull, R. (1970) Forward. In P. Friere *Pedagogy of the oppressed.* (pp. 9-15) New York: Herder and Herder.

Shor, I. (1992). *Empowering education.* Chicago, IL: University of Chicago Press.

Shweder, R. (1990). Cultural psychology: What is it? In J. Stigler, R. Shweder, & G. Herdt. (Eds.). *Cultural psychology.* (pp. 1-46) New York: Columbia University Press.

Wheatley, M. (1992). *Leadership and the new science.* San Francisco: Berrett-Koehler.

11

Multicultural Organizational Development: Implications and Applications for Student Affairs

Raechele L. Pope

INTRODUCTION

Paradigmatic shifts are essential for student affairs practitioners to create genuine and lasting multicultural campus environments. Kuh (1983) describes Kuhn's (1970) concept of a paradigm shift as a "radical change in the way in which the world is viewed" (Kuh, 1993, p. 1). Changing our world view is a necessary and first step to create new practices and strategies which will restructure and transform our campuses.

During at least the last three decades cultural diversity issues have been on the agendas of most colleges and universities. Campuses have responded to these issues in a variety of ways and the results have been, at best, uneven (Cheatham, 1991). In student affairs, attention to cultural diversity issues has prompted the initiation of various programmatic responses. Typically these responses have attempted to address cultural diversity or multicultural issues through the use of individual awareness or consciousness-raising activities (e.g., racial awareness workshops). Many of these interventions, however, are narrow in scope and overlook nonracial issues of cultural diversity such as gender, religion, or sexual orientation. Although these efforts are valuable, particularly on an individual basis, they have had little effect on the structure and day-to-day functioning of institutions (Jacoby, 1991).

A current trend on many campuses, in addition to cultural awareness programs, is to hire an individual whose primary responsibilities are to address the issues and needs of a specific group of students (e.g., students of color, lesbian, gay, and bisexual students, students with disabilities, etc.), including recruitment and retention efforts (Cheatham, 1991). Although these programs are necessary and serve an important educational function, they are not enough. According to Jacoby (1991), "institutional responses to the increased presence of different groups of students have generally been fragmented attempts to deal with immediate, specific problems rather than long-range and comprehensive" (p. 296). A sporadic and uncoordinated series of programs by dedicated and sincere individuals will not suffice or be effective over the long-term. Although such interventions may increase the numbers of students of color, they do not necessarily affect the level of racism, sexism, or other forms of oppression on campus in any positive, systematic fashion. At best, they serve to increase the numbers of a given social group (often students of color) on a particular campus, but do little to acknowledge the historical and current contributions, values, and interests of these groups (Manning & Coleman-Boatwright, 1991; Pope, Ecklund, Mueller, & Reynolds, 1990). Creating a multicultural campus clearly requires more than these sporadic efforts targeted primarily towards increasing numerical diversity. Instead, new strategies that alter our goals, expectations, perceptions, and practices are needed to transform and create multicultural campuses. In essence, a paradigm shift is necessary to create these multicultural environments.

This chapter focuses on interventions which will alter the fundamental structure of the student affairs division or campus culture. It provides a new paradigm with which new strategies and practices can be employed so that multicultural campus environments can be created. This chapter begins by visioning and defining what a multicultural student affairs divisions would entail. This is followed by an examination of a type of systematic planned change, multicultural organization development (MCOD), which is offered as a new paradigm for creating multicultural campuses. Finally, MCOD will be operationalized through the use of the Multicultural Intervention Matrix (MCIM) (Pope, 1993) including its applications and implications for practice, research, and policy development in student affairs.

CREATING MULTICULTURAL STUDENT AFFAIRS DIVISIONS

Recognizing that campuses can be different and that multiculturalism is possible—that campuses can become multicultural—

is a significant first step in the process of creating change. Further, organizations do not become multicultural overnight; it takes time (Katz, 1989). Creating multicultural environments and attaining a multicultural perspective is a process that requires expertise, focused reflection, commitment, specific competencies, and purposeful action (Pope & Reynolds, 1994). According to Katz (1989), in order to create change organizations must: (a) must first embrace a set of underlying beliefs and values that establish a foundation for their efforts; and (b) utilize some model or framework to conceptualize and guide these changes.

Underlying Beliefs

Multicultural organizations are built upon a foundation of essential values which include but are not limited to beliefs that: (a) It is possible to create multicultural organizations, (b) knowing the steps necessary to creating a multicultural organization helps people develop a plan for change, (c) change occurs through a cyclical process rather than in progressive linear steps; (d) people and systems will be upset as a result of this change and that this disruption is a natural and healthy part of the process; (f) individuals must be available to guide the change; and (g) the change must be systematically designed as an organizational and cultural change effort (Jackson & Hardiman, 1981; Katz, 1989).

Transforming these beliefs into action is difficult because the beliefs provide a sense of the process but not the actual end-product. Unless people are clear about what a multicultural campus will actually entail—what it will look like, and how it will function—successful creation of these environments is inconceivable and incomprehensible. An image of a multicultural environment is needed. In 1981 Jackson and Hardiman offered the following vision of a multicultural organization:

> A multicultural organization reflects the contribution and interests of diverse cultural and social groups in its mission, operations, and . . . service delivery; acts on a commitment to eradicate social oppression in all forms within the organization; includes the members of diverse cultural and social groups as full participants, especially in decisions that shape the organization; and follows through on broader external social responsibilities, including support of efforts to eliminate all forms of social oppression and to educate others in multicultural perspectives. (p. 1)

Incorporating this vision into the components of a multicultural student affairs division demands that the division dedicate significant attention, time, and other resources (e.g., monetary, human, etc.) to creating an openness to all diverse cultures and people, to distributing power and decision-making, and to eradicating social injustice. It means making a clear intentional commitment to change the structure and functioning of the division. This commitment would be evidenced, for example, through such conventions as an inclusive mission statement and anti-discrimination policy, extensive recruitment and retention efforts that support a multicultural vision, a multicultural curriculum, and programs and activities that create an awareness of and celebrates diverse cultures, values, and people. Further, Katz (1989) believes that a multicultural campus or student affairs division would foster the valuing of all people as adding to and strengthening the community. This belief would encourage community members to not only embrace their own cultural heritage but also to value and affirm the cultural identity of others. In addition, people of color and other underserved groups would be empowered to make their own unique contributions. The broadest and most inclusive definitions of effective management and leadership must be utilized to guard against cultural bias in our understanding of what constitutes a "good" manager or "successful" leader. For example, in the U.S., the dominant White culture values and rewards assertion and independence as effective leadership traits, while some other cultures reward and emphasize cooperation and consensus as the hallmarks of effective leadership. Neither approach is necessarily more effective. However, cultural bias or assumptions may encourage some supervisors to define the assertive approach as more valuable than the cooperative approach.

A Framework to Guide Change

Making intentional change to guide the transformation of campus environments and integrate the values and beliefs of multiculturalism is a complex undertaking. The existing planned change theories and social justice literature assert that long term change in institutions requires interventions that focus on the organization as a system (Cummings & Huse, 1989; Jackson & Holvino, 1988; Sargent, 1983). System-wide change strategies involve integrating equity and access issues into the strategic planning processes of student affairs divisions (Stewart, 1991). This integration would ensure that coordinated efforts to create multicultural environments permeate the campus.

Suggesting that student affairs utilize systemic change interventions is not new. Since at least the early seventies, student affairs scholars and practitioners have recommended the incorporation of systemic change interventions and, in particular, organization development techniques (Borland, 1980; Conyne, 1991). Organization development (OD) was suggested as a means for transforming the structure of student affairs divisions to infuse theories of student development into the mainstream of the profession (Borland, 1980). Similarly systemic change efforts can be utilized to infuse multicultural issues into the profession (Pope, 1993).

In addition to the lack of systemic change efforts oriented towards multicultural issues, student affairs staffs have not fully included the oppression or social justice agenda in their efforts to create multicultural campus environments. Many campuses have chosen to focus almost exclusively on cultural diversity or so called "civility" issues rather than the foundation issues of racism, sexism, heterosexism, or classism (Barr & Strong, 1989; Cheatham & Associates, 1991). Systemic approaches that address both the structure of the organization and the underlying social justice agenda are needed (Katz, 1989) if student affairs divisions are to integrate multicultural issues into campus organizations and programs. Multicultural organization development (MCOD) provides a framework for long-term multicultural systems change and addresses social justice issues (Driscoll, 1990; Jackson & Holvino, 1988). A brief review of organization development follows to provide a basis for contrast and an extended the exploration of MCOD.

Organizational Development in Student Affairs

The dynamic nature of OD precludes a single or unified definition with which all authors agree; rather, OD and related intervention strategies are regarded as evolving and changing (Conyne, 1991; Cummings & Huse, 1989). However, enough agreement does exist to suggest that OD is a process for beneficial systemic change (Conyne, 1991). Fundamentally, OD is concerned with planned, systemic change. OD is an approach to diagnosing and addressing organizational concerns which remains flexible and allows plans to be altered as new information is available (Cummings & Huse, 1989). Cummings and Huse (1989) noted that OD goes beyond merely activating a change program to a "longer term concern for stabilizing and institutionalizing change within the organization" (p. 2). An OD change strategy focuses attention and action on the core goals, values, and mission of the organization.

OD provides the necessary planned change strategies to institute long-term, systemic change. The OD perspective, however, remains embedded in the dominant culture and retains the organizational values, goals and practices which that culture produces. The founders of OD initially hoped that traditional OD change efforts would have an impact on social justice issues in organizations (Jackson & Holvino, 1988). They assumed that a new, more humane workplace would automatically be a socially just workplace. However, the humanization of the workplace is measurably different from the redistribution of resources and power that a social justice perspective necessitates (Driscoll, 1990; Holvino, 1988). Although OD is meant to examine and change existing suboptimal systems and structures, it is limited by its current practices and theories which are derived from the dominant culture. The most significant barrier to OD's attempts to transform organizational reality and culture lies in its ultimate acceptance of organizational culture in its current form (Driscoll, 1990). Over the past years, efforts to create more culturally diverse campuses have been proposed (e.g., Cheatham & Associates, 1992; Manning & Coleman-Boatwright, 1991; Wright, 1987) These attempts have lacked a framework for systemic change that would encourage creative experimentation with student affairs structures, processes, policies, and procedures.

MULTICULTURAL ORGANIZATION DEVELOPMENT: KEY CONCEPTS AND PRINCIPLES

The concept of MCOD as a method of planned change was developed in the early 1980s through the work of Jackson, Hardiman, and Holvino (Driscoll, 1990). Jackson et al., recognized the inherent limitations in OD and formulated a theory to respond more directly to issues of social diversity and social justice.

MCOD remains in the stage of knowledge production (B. W. Jackson, personal communication, March 28, 1990). An authoritative body of literature that describes, discusses, and debates its nature, function, and practices does not yet exist. MCOD has been defined as an "organizational transformation effort which has as its primary objective the creation of socially diverse and socially just organizations" (Driscoll, 1990, p. 129). An underlying goal of MCOD is the creation of efficient, effective, socially diverse, and socially just work environments. MCOD differs from OD in the fundamental belief that an organization cannot be effective and healthy *without* addressing issues of social justice (B. W. Jackson, personal communication [class lecture], Spring, 1990).

Much like OD, MCOD is a systemic, planned change effort that utilizes behavioral science knowledge and technologies for improving organizational effectiveness. MCOD incorporates and extends OD, challenges the status quo, and questions the underlying cultural assumptions and structures of organizations. Unlike OD, MCOD addresses the underlying racial, gender, disability, class, sexual orientation, and religious issues within an organization.

MCOD focuses on the major subsystems of an organization: mission and values, structure, technology, management practices, psycho-social dynamics, environmental interactions, and the "bottom-line" (the product or service an organization produces) (Morgan, 1986). The purpose of attending to the subsystems is to remove or reduce the harmful effects of monocultural processes or procedures in an organization which influence organizational effectiveness (Jackson & Holvino, 1988). According to Jackson and Holvino, "evidence is beginning to show that there is a direct relationship between the quantity and quality of the product or service an organization delivers and the ability of that organization to provide a just working environment for all its employees" (p. 14).

Although OD and MCOD theorists and practitioners utilize similar strategies and operate from similar epistemological and ontological assumptions about the nature of organizations and planned change, fundamental differences do exist. A primary difference involves the degree to which multicultural values and concepts influence or dictate the focus of the change effort. This difference also demonstrates a philosophical dissension in the level of significance that race/ethnicity, gender, and other social group memberships have on group interactions and group functioning.

MCOD: Implications for Student Affairs

The process of creating a multicultural campus or student affairs division is most likely to be successful when appropriate diagnoses and interventions are utilized (Katz, 1989). Models based on the principles of systemic planned change and MCOD can aid institutions in their efforts to create multicultural campuses. In order to understand the changes that are needed to create multicultural campus environments, extensive assessment and research are needed. The assessment and research processes must examine interactions between multicultural policies, procedures and potential interventions when institutions decide to undertake an MCOD effort.

Quite literally, the complexion of college and university campuses is changing. Current and projected demographic data suggest that within the next 10-15 years White male college students will be the numerical minority (Hodgkinson, 1986; Levine & Associates, 1989). Ebbers and Henry (1990) and others (cf., Barr & Strong, 1988; Katz, 1989; Manning & Coleman-Boatwright, 1991) have indicated that one of the most significant tasks facing higher education administrators is to develop and cultivate multiculturally sensitive environments. Campus environments must have students, faculty, and staff who not only tolerate, but also accept, appreciate, and celebrate cultural diversity. The institutional structures (policies, procedures, management practices, reward systems, etc.) must reflect this appreciation and celebration of cultural differences. Models sensitive to cultural diversity must focus on the institutional structures themselves and the overall campus culture (Barr & Strong, 1988; Pope, 1990; Stewart, 1991). The development of such models should be based in research that examines campus cultures and institutional structures that both create and hinder the infusion of multicultural values into higher education.

The models offered by Barr and Strong (1988), Manning and Coleman-Boatwright, and others (e.g., Stewart, 1991), have suggested utilizing interventions targeted at the structural level of the institution. However, the models do not focus on the variety of diagnostic and intervention typologies and models available in the planned change literature. MCOD fills in this gap by offering concrete behavioral science tools and techniques to institutionalize multicultural planned change efforts. MCOD offers a methodology which student affairs divisions can adapt to increasingly complex and uncertain cultural, economic, and political changes.

MCOD can assist student affairs staff in responding to these changes, and in many cases, can support the division's efforts to proactively influence the strategic direction of the institution. MCOD can be utilized to ensure a comprehensive and systemic incorporation of diverse people, cultures, values, and norms occurs on college and university campuses.

MCIM AND STUDENT AFFAIRS: OPERATIONALIZING MCOD

The Multicultural Change Intervention Matrix (MCIM) is a conceptual model which is based on the concepts of systemic planned change and MCOD. This 3 x 2 matrix has been developed as a schematic representation of MCOD principles as applied to student affairs and higher education. It provides a framework for codifying the range of activities that student affairs divisions currently use to address multicultural issues. One dimension of the MCIM identifies three targets of intervention: 1) individual— a student or staff member; 2) group—consisting of (a) either professional or paraprofessional staff or (b) student organization; and 3) institutional—in this example meaning the entire student affairs division. The second dimension of the MCIM classifies two levels of intervention: first- and second-order change.

Lyddon (1990) examined first- and second-order change which was initially differentiated by Watzlawick, Weakland, and Fisch (1974) in their discussion of family systems. Watzlawick, Weakland, and Fisch described first-order change as a change within the system that does not create change in the structure of the system. Second-order change is any change that fundamentally alters the structure of a system.

Lyddon offered a further explanation of first- and second-order change originally conceptualized by Watzlawick et al. (1974). This explanation uses fundamental mathematical concepts to distinguish between the two types of change. In arithmetic, a set of numbers may be combined in various ways using the same mathematical operation without changing the numbers or makeup of the set. For example, $(3+2)+6=11$ and $2+(3+6)=11$ are the same numbers added in different ways yet resulting in the same answer. Lyddon believes, in such a case, "a myriad of changes in the internal state of a group (that is, changes among its members) makes no difference in its definition as a group. This type of change maintains the coherence of a system and is referred to as first-order change" (p. 122). However, if the mathematical operation is changed from addition to multiplication such as (3x2)+6=12, then a different outcome results. According to Lyddon, this change depicts a transformation in the definition of the group and is second-order change. Second-order change then, is a paradigm shift. It is a radical transformation in the way in which the group is viewed and defined, a change in processes which transforms outcomes. In the domains of social science, for example, race has been used as an organizing construct to define groups for some purposes. Currently, race is considered by some scientists as "a myth, an outmoded way of classifying people" (Wheeler, 1995, p. A8). It is also considered outmoded by physical anthropologists, geneticists and hematologists. If the notion of dividing humanity into races disappears, new ways to organize a wide range of activities must emerge based, for example, on genetic characteristics, patterns of brain activity when decoding language or other, newly developed methods for describing group characteristics.

Another way of illustrating the radical transformation necessary for second-order change is through the use of one of the most familiar Gestalt psychology perception figures (Block & Yuker, 1987). The figure is perceived as either an old woman with a large nose or a young woman with fine features wearing a hat with a feather. To be able to see both images in the figure one must concentrate and make a conscious effort to view the figure differently from one's initial perception. This effort is sim-

TARGET OF CHANGE	TYPE OF CHANGE	
	1ST ORDER CHANGE	2ND ORDER CHANGE
Individual	A. Awareness	B. Paradigm Shift
Group	C. Membership	D. Restructuring
Institutional	E. Programmatic	F. Systemic

Figure 1. Multicultural Change Intervention Matrix (MCIM)

ilar to the paradigm shift needed to create second-order change in organizations, groups, or individuals.

As shown in Figure 1, the MCIM offers six different ways to conceptualize and structure multicultural change efforts. By increasing one's understanding of the range of targets and goals that may be used, the types of activities, strategies, and tools can be more easily expanded. Through exploration of the six cells of the MCIM, more multicultural [intervention] options can be considered.

Cell A change efforts (1st order change—individual) typically involve education at the awareness, knowledge, or skill level. This type of educational effort is often on content-focused such as information about various racial, religious, or other cultural groups. Possible examples include: cultural communication workshops, programs on the economic and social conditions of a particular cultural group, or an anti-racism presentation.

A Cell B change effort (2nd order change—individual) is education aimed at the cognitive restructuring level suggesting worldview or paradigm shifts. Such world view shifts require more intensive, interactive, or experiential emphasis in the program design. Often these interventions are more process oriented and challenge an individual's underlying assumptions. An example might include a prolonged and extensive consciousness raising workshop that is individually focused and experientially oriented (i.e., individual is challenged to examine belief/thought systems, and be introspective, and self-challenging).

A Cell C change effort (1st order change—group) is a change in the composition of a group in which members of under-represented groups are added, but there is no change in the goals or norms of the group. Cell C focuses on diversity in terms of numbers without examining the interpersonal and structural dynamics of a group. An example might be the traditional recruitment efforts that increase the number of people of color or white women on a staff without altering the environment or examining and modifying the unit or divisional mission.

Cell D change efforts (2nd order change—group) might involve total restructuring of a group with a new mission, goals, and members. This type of transformation examines group makeup, values, and goals prior to changing the group. Any new members must be involved this self examination and planning process. An example would be hosting a retreat for a specific unit or department to re-examine and reformulate its philosophy, values, and goals including the multicultural goals and objectives. Rather than adding a few multicultural goals, this approach demands a re-examination of the entire mission and purpose of the unit and allows multicultural issues to be integrated into the unit's central mission.

A Cell E change effort (1st order change—institution) might involve a programmatic intervention aimed at the institution or division which addresses multicultural issues but does not alter the underlying values and structure of the institution. Creating a new position within student affairs to direct a Cultural Center, or developing an on-going multicultural training program is an example of a change effort that may not alter the institutional dynamics, values, or priorities. Another example might be adding a multicultural section to a student affairs mission statement without changing the evaluation or budgetary criteria which typically will not create institutional or divisional change.

A Cell F change effort (2nd order change—institution) requires more direct examination of underlying institutional values, goals, and evaluation which then are linked to multicultural values and efforts. Examples might include requiring goal-directed multicultural initiatives within all student affairs units which directly link the outcome of those initiatives to budget allocations or basing hiring, salary, evaluation, and promotion decisions on individual multicultural competencies.

The six cells of the MCIM are separate and unique; however, their relationship with each other is fluid and dynamic. For example, awareness work is an important part of creating a paradigm shift within an individual. Or programmatic efforts may be a necessary precursor to the development of systemic change. The dotted lines between the various cells are meant to portray that interconnection and encourage the use of all six levels and targets of multicultural interventions. The relationships between the various cells have yet to be studied and research examining the philosophical assumptions of the MCIM must be undertaken. Since the MCIM is still a new model, there is much research to be completed. While the dualistic nature of our society might encourage readers to assume that second-order change is "better" than first-order change since it creates long-term and structural transformation, it is vital that all six types of interventions be seen as a valuable and necessary part of the multicultural change process.

MCIM Applications and Implications
in Student Affairs

A conceptual tool such as the MCIM has little value unless the model is applied to practice. Despite the newness of the MCIM, it has a variety of potential uses to assist practitioners and other interested individuals in their quest to create multicultural campuses. Three significant uses of the MCIM include: a) assessment, b) strategic planning, and c) curricular transformation.

Assessment

While the instrumentation for the MCIM is still in its early stages of development, the MCIM is well-suited for codifying and understanding the range of multicultural interventions implemented in student affairs and higher education (Pope, 1993). For example, Pope conducted a national study to identify, examine, and assess the number, level, and type of multiracial change interventions currently used on individual campuses. The MCIM provided the framework for discerning the type of interventions utilized nationally. Similarly, the MCIM can be used to assess the multicultural interventions employed on individual campuses, student affairs divisions, or single departments or units a campus. Because the MCIM is such a versatile model, it can be used effectively with quantitative, qualitative, and case-study research designs or assessment projects. The assessments can assist administrators and practitioners in setting goals and identifying the type and level of interventions required to ensure that a comprehensive incorporation of diverse cultures, values, norms, and ideas is developed.

Strategic Planning

The MCIM also has value in the area of strategic planning. Developing a strategic plan offers an institution vital evaluative information. It can answer the questions, "what it is doing, why it does so, who does it, and how well and how efficiently it is being done. Further, a [strategic] plan will help to determine if the institution is fulfilling its stated mission" (Ern, 1993, p. 442). Strategic planning is an essential tool in the creation of multicultural campuses. Campus leaders who strive to develop multicultural campuses and who include these goals in their institutional mission statements but do not include these issues in the strategic planning process are likely to be unsuccessful and ineffective in their efforts. In order to create multicultural campus environments, systemic and systematic change is needed. The MCIM can be used to conceptualize the multicultural change efforts currently being utilized, set goals and priorities, and to design future change efforts. For example, as one component of a strategic plan a student affairs division could: a) review its current goals and functional responsibilities; b) evaluate its internal and external responsibilities; c) create future-oriented goals; d) identify finance and resource needs; and e) integrate multicultural aspects into each of these four areas. The MCIM can be used to insure that these efforts are focused on second-order change and targeted at the divisional level. Strategic multicultural change at this level could directly link, for example, budget allocations, performance evaluations, and staffing decisions to current and longer-range goals and functional responsibilities.

Curricular Transformation

A third use of the MCIM is in the area of curricular transformation. The MCIM can be utilized as tool by those attempting to infuse multicultural issues into a specific academic program or department, a college division, or the entire academic unit of a campus. The MCIM not only can assist faculty in determining what types of outcomes they want for their individual courses or programs, but it may also offer a conceptual framework to assist faculty in deciding how to achieve their goals. For example, Reynolds (in press) proposed utilizing the MCIM as an alternative framework for conceptualizing multicultural teaching for use in counseling psychology training programs. According to Reynolds, "the MCIM can be used to design the goals and activities of an individual course or restructure an entire counseling curriculum" (p. 21). This model offers a useful framework which can be used to assess the type and level of multicultural education in the classroom.

SUMMARY

Despite nearly three decades of scrutiny, college and university campuses have failed to develop consistently successful responses to cultural diversity issues. Typically the responses have been a series of sporadic and uncoordinated interventions focused on resolving specific and immediate problems with little effort directed toward long-term organizational change. But it doesn't have to be that way. Campuses can become multicultural, but it will not happen immediately; it will take time, vision, focused reflection and purposeful action. Moreover, effective long-term multicultural change on campus requires that the interventions focus on the organization as a system. Further, to become multicultural, campuses will have to develop strategies that simultaneously integrate cultural diversity and social-justice issues into the strategic planning processes and other currently utilized organizational change strategies (e.g., TQM, Quality Assurance initiatives, etc.).

Multicultural Organization Development (MCOD) is an organizational change strategy with much promise in addressing multicultural issues on a structural and institutional level. The Multicultural Change Intervention Matrix (MCIM) is a conceptual model based on the concepts of systemic planned change theories, in general and MCOD specifically. Presented as a method of operationalizing MCOD, the MCIM has significant value for campus leaders particularly in the areas of assessment, strategic planning, and curricular transformation.

Thirty years is a long time to allocate time and resources for methods which have proven inconsistent and ineffective. The challenge to create multicultural campus environments is too important to the future of higher education and student affairs to leave to chance. What is needed is a paradigmatic shift so that campus leaders envision new practices and strategies that will restructure and transform our campuses.

REFERENCES

Barr, D. J. & Strong L. J. (1989). Embracing multiculturalism: The existing contradictions. *NASPA Journal, 26*, 85-90.

Block, J. & Yuker, H. (1987). *Can You Believe Your Eyes*. Hempstead, NY: Y & B Associates.

Borland, D. T. (1980). Organization development: A professional imperative. In D. G. Creamer (Ed.). *Student development in higher education: Theories, practices, and future directions* (pp. 205-227). Carbondale, IL.: American College Personnel Association.

Cheatham, H. E. (Ed.) & Associates. (1991). *Cultural pluralism on campus*. Washington, D.C.: American College Personnel Association.

Conyne, R. K. (1991). Organization development: A broad net intervention for student affairs. In T. Miller & R. Winston (Eds.). Administration and leadership in student affairs: Actualizing student development in higher education, (2nd ed.) (pp. 72-109). Muncie, IN.: Accelerated Development.

Cummings, T. G. & Huse, E. F. (1989). Organization development and change (4th ed.). St. Paul, MN: West.

Driscoll, A. (1990). Untitled comprehensive examination paper. Unpublished manuscript. Amherst, MA: University of Massachusetts.

Ebbers, L. H. & Henry, S. L. (1990). Cultural competence: A new challenge to student affairs professionals. NASPA Journal, 27, 319-323.

Ern, E. H. (1993). Managing resources strategically. In M. J. Barr (Ed.). The handbook of student affairs administration (pp. 439-454). San Francisco: Jossey-Bass.

Hodgkinson, H. (1986). The new demographic realities for education and work. Alden Seminar. Cambridge, MA: Harvard University.

Jackson, B. W. & Hardiman, R. (1981). Description of a multicultural organization: "A vision". Unpublished manuscript. Amherst, MA: University of Massachusetts.

Jackson, B. W. & Holvino, E. (1988). Developing multicultural organizations. Journal of Applied Behavioral Science and Religion, 9, 14-19.

Jacoby, B. A. (1991). Today's students: Diverse needs require comprehensive responses. In T. Miller & R. Winston (Eds.). Administration and leadership in student affairs: Actualizing student development in higher education (2nd ed.) (pp. 280-309). Muncie, IN: Accelerated Development.

Katz, J. (1989). The challenge of diversity. In C. Wollbright (Ed.). Valuing Diversity (pp. 1-22). Bloomington, IN: Association of College Unions-International.

Kuh, G. D. (Ed.). (1983). Understanding student affairs organizations. New Directions for Student Services (23). San Francisco: Jossey-Bass.

Levine, A. & Associates (1989). Shaping higher education's future: Demographic realities and opportunities, 1990-2000. San Francisco: Jossey-Bass.

Lyddon, W. J. (1990). First- and second-order change: Implications for rationalist and constructivist cognitive therapies. Journal of Counseling and Development, 69, 122-127.

Manning, K. & Coleman-Boatwright, P. (1991). Student affairs initiatives toward a multicultural university. Journal of College Student Development, 32, 367-374.

Pope, R. L. (1990). Creating multicultural campuses: An exploration of the literature. Unpublished comprehensive examination manuscript. Amherst, MA: University of Massachusetts.

Pope, R. L. (1993). An analysis of multiracial change efforts in student affairs. (Doctoral dissertation, Amherst, MA: University of

Massachusetts, 1992). *Dissertation Abstracts International, 53-10,* 3457A.

Pope, R. L., Ecklund, T. R., Mueller, J. A. & Reynolds, A. L. (1990, April). *Combating racism in higher education.* Paper presented at the American College Personnel Association Convention. St. Louis, MO.

Pope, R. L. & Reynolds, A. L. (1994). *Student affairs core competencies: Integrating multicultural awareness, knowledge, and skills.* Manuscript submitted for publication.

Reynolds, A. L. (in press). Challenges and strategies for teaching multicultural counseling courses. In J. G. Ponterotto, J. M. Casas, L. A. Suzuki, & C. M. Alexander (Eds.). *Handbook of multicultural counseling.* San Francisco: Sage.

Sargent, A. G. (1983). Affirmative action: A guide to systems change for managers. In R. A. Ritvo & A. Sargent (Eds.). *The NTL Managers' Handbook* (pp. 223-237). Arlington, VA: NTL Institute.

Stewart, J. B. (1991). Planning for cultural diversity: A case study. In H. C. Cheatham (Ed.). *Cultural pluralism on campus.* (pp. 161-181). Washington, D.C.: American College Personnel Association.

Wheeler, D. (February 17, 1995) A growing number of scientists reject the concept of race. *The Chronicle of Higher Education (XLI)* 23. pp. A8, A9, A1.

Wright, D. J. (Ed.). (1987). *Responding to the needs of today's minority students.* New Directions for Student Services (38). San Francisco: Jossey-Bass.

12

Conclusion: Evolving Paradigms and Possibilities

Jane Fried

During the early 1940s most male students were able to attend college only because they had been found physically unfit to serve in the armed forces. Burns B. Crookston was one such student. He played quarterback for his college football team despite the fact that he had serious vision problems, including the tendency to see multiple images. While carrying the ball toward the goal post in one game, he saw three defensive linemen in front of him. He knew that only one of them was real. He had to decide which was "really" there and which was an illusion so that he could set a course for the goal. He made a choice and ran using all the coping mechanisms he had developed for dealing with his disability. History does not record whether or not he made the right choice (Personal communication, 1973). Crookston's contributions to the world of higher education were not to be made on the football field, but in the evolving profession of student development education.

> The prologues are over. It is a question, now,
> Of final belief. So, say that the final belief
> Must be in a fiction. It is time to choose.
>
> *Asides on the Oboe* (Stevens, 1964)

Do we choose to believe in a fiction? A fiction is, after all, something which is made or created. Our construction of the student affairs/student development profession and the whole process of student learning a result of choices and beliefs. Student affairs, along with all of higher education in the United States, is now in the process of reinventing itself, reconstructing categories and reexamining values. We are trying to determine which obstacles are real and which are illusions, which choices lead toward our valued goals and which do not, what belief system will serve us well and what beliefs will interfere with our progress.

The process has radical and conservative elements to it. Radical means a change at the root, establishing a new foundation by changing fundamental assumptions. Student development education is rooted in a tradition of holistic education which emphasizes the integration of knowledge and values and combines character development with academic education. The roots of the modern student development movement lie in pragmatist approaches to education and the work of Esther Lloyd-Jones (1954). Radical has come to mean the provocation of upheaval. When calls for a return to holistic education appear as they did in the 1930s, the 1960s and in the current era, they signify the disintegration of one set of core beliefs about learning and a need for reintegration, or the creation of a new set of beliefs at another level of synthesis. Science and the elective system provoked the disintegration of the traditional curriculum, the trivium and the quadrivium. Calls for relevance in the 1960s upset the major/ minor system and provoked student interest in interdisciplinary, problem focused studies. Problem based learning, experiential learning, distance learning and credit for life learning have once again upset the classroom based approach to teaching, learning and evaluation. Global electronic communication has rendered the distinction between classrooms and other learning environments invalid and changed the ways teachers and students relate to each other. It has, in many cases, changed our concept of teacher and student from *people* with stable, defined roles to *functions* performed by numbers of people depending on context, area of expertise and need. These are indeed radical changes.

Truly radical changes must occur in organizational structures, ideas about teaching and learning, role definitions among professionals in higher education and even in the physical arrangements of our campuses. The essential values of the student affairs profession, rooted as they are in an holistic model of education, remain unchanged although these values are no longer always carried out in residential settings or face to face conversations. The context in which higher education is experienced has changed so dramatically that it has become quite difficult to remain aware of the continuity in values as the processes of teaching, learning and service delivery enter a state of permanent flux.

REINVENTING HIGHER EDUCATION AND STUDENT AFFAIRS

Two phrases which are significant for the evolution of student affairs have entered the higher education lexicon—the learning organization (Senge, 1990) and reengineering the organization (Hammer & Champy, 1993). The concepts described by these terms are radical. They ask basic questions which force a reexamination of root assumptions behind our organizational structures, processes and desired outcomes. In *The Learning Organization* we are asked to consider "the illusion of taking charge" (p. 20), "the delusion of learning from experience" (p. 23) and the danger of focusing on events rather than interactive processes. The learning organization is constantly attempting to extract knowledge and insight from its experiences and transform its knowledge into organizational, product and service improvements. We learned how to take charge from the painful experiences of the 1960s and 1970s in which students seized buildings, stopped classes and demanded relevance. We learned to develop contracts which protected our institutions against lawsuits and codes of conduct which kept student disruption to a minimum. Is our learning from experience now helping us or hurting us? What do we need to know now to improve our services and educational activities?

Reengineering higher education requires an emphasis on institutional integrity or interconnectedness of mission, leadership, process, outcomes and people (Hall, 1992). The reengineering processes require awareness of organizational mission throughout the system. Open communication among staff members, the development of integrated systems and procedures and creation of means by which teaching, learning and management can be delivered to students, their families and staff are basic to this approach. The organizational mission should rarely be obscured by territorial disputes or fragmented approaches. Both the learning organization and the process/concept of reengineering are distantly related to Chew's bootstrap theory described earlier. Both sets of ideas demand a reconstruction of the categories by which we describe and interpret our experiences. They accept the dynamism of the world environment and do not assume a return to stability. According to Senge, trying to get back to normal might be the most disastrous step an organization could take because previous ideas of normal are probably misleading for future contexts.

In order to "*really* reinvent" higher education (Drucker, 1995, p. 49) it has become necessary to give up the search for stable solutions and become more comfortable with the process of continuing dialogue and questioning. Higher education no longer presumes to transmit a body of eternal, unchanging knowledge from teachers and manuscripts to students. Higher education is now completely embedded in the larger world. The United States has become a leader in providing this resource to students from all over the world, particularly students who return to their home countries and take on leadership positions in government and other important social institutions. Researchers in American universities, in collaboration with colleagues from universities all over the world, provide continual technical support to individuals working in agriculture, the natural resources industries such as coal, oil and gas, banking and international economics, environmental management and myriad other areas of human concern. Universities have become producers of knowledge which can applied and tested in field settings very quickly. Even some academic journals are now being produced electronically to speed the dissemination of information, although the value of this type of rapid communication is also considered questionable because it diminishes time for reflection and validation of findings.

In order to provoke a shift from searching for answers to becoming comfortable with the process of asking questions, it is useful to reexamine Chew's bootstrap theory (Capra, 1988) in which no element of a system is considered fundamental and every process affects every other process. All aspects of a system are linked in dynamic interaction. The metaphors of derived from architecture such as creating a solid foundation or building a reliable structure, which have sustained administrative thinking for so long, may be effectively replaced or supplemented by metaphors from music or other dynamic processes. In music structure provides integrity to compositions, but the musical energy comes from the processes of moving between harmony and discord. Even the inner ear through which musical metaphors gain meaning must expand its imaginary repertoire, adding Indian ragas to the more familiar western harmonies. Ragas are improvised as they are played, the improvisation being based on musical principles which provide a great deal of freedom to the artist. Before it is actually performed, nobody can say for certain how a raga melody will emerge.

Traditional empiricist or objectivist thought is based on organizing data into mutually exclusive categories using principles of logic and reason. Since much academic training is based on this type of "either/or" thinking, it remains difficult for academicians, including student affairs professionals, scholars and administrators, to understand the value of "both/and" approaches. The willingness to consider "both/and" approaches can be profoundly disorienting because it assumes that the thinker is willing and able to keep his or her personal needs for certainty in abeyance when necessary. The transition to "both/and" thinking is manifest throughout this book by the author's inability and/or unwillingness to maintain student affairs in its separate administrative category and faculty in its teaching category. The focus has shifted from teaching and providing service to learning. When learning becomes the centerpiece, teaching and service must be reconfigured and reconstructed to support the achievement of the goal rather than becoming goals, or static structures, in themselves. This demand for flexibility is a challenge to all involved because it eliminates both job security and the security which derives from having a stable image of oneself as a professional.

In *Letters to a Young Poet* (Rilke, 1934/1954) Rilke told his protégé that he must give up searching for answers and learn to live the questions, knowing or hoping, that at some time in the future, he might live his way into finding the answers. All of us in higher education are involved in a period of enormous transition in which we must learn to live the questions we are asked to address because finding the means to understand and address them will shape the form in which our institutions and our profession survive. A basic issue we all face is how to shift from "either/or" to "both/and" thinking. How can we learn to become "reflective practitioners" (Schon, 1983) who can understand and analyze data, but also review and assess it from a values perspective? How can we learn that the bottom line, whose origins are so often taken for granted, is indeed constructed by combining values and data? How can we begin the arduous process of decentering ourselves (Giroux, 1993) and remapping the terrain to include multiple value systems brought to attention by competing concerns, populations and institutional priorities? How do we give voice to those whose voices have been considered disruptive so that the institution can rethink and reinvent itself to meet the needs of its emerging constituencies? What risks do we run in the process? What do those who have historically set the agenda, created the evaluation devices and decided what knowledge is credible, have to lose in this process? Is the loss to the dominant group worth the gain to the non-dominant groups and the larger global community in terms of enhancing learning? What strengths do individuals and professionals need to develop in order to set off on this journey whose destination is unclear?

Learning to live the questions is a radical act. It implies a willingness to move into uncharted territory in which all categories are called into question and all values must be evaluated. It involves risking the loss of status, control and certain knowledge in order to create the possibility of enhanced well-being, improved management and as yet unimagined approaches to problems which have not been addressed or solved under existing paradigms. Learning to live the questions involves a paradigm shift in which everybody goes back to "ground zero," (Burkan, 1990) and past knowledge may be of little help.

When new paradigms begin to replace the old, problems which were formerly insoluble can often be solved or may even disappear. For example, using the Newtonian paradigm to understand the behavior of matter and energy at subatomic levels frustrated and confused scientists in the early 20th century. If atoms were considered the fundamental building blocks of the universe, why were they not always visible when scientists looked for them in bubble chambers? The answer is that subatomic "matter" has a tendency to exist at certain times and places, but that the tendencies to exist can only be predicted in terms of probabilities, not certainties. The very act of looking, or attempting to measure mass and location, changes the atomic probabilities and processes. This is Heisenberg's Principle of Uncertainty (Capra, 1988). In addition, matter and energy exist in dynamic relationship to each other. Information is exchanged between atoms as energy in processes so subtle that they are impossible to perceive except in the aggregate. As a result of knowledge developed within the paradigm of quantum physics, the problem of finding the smallest, elemental building block of matter no longer exists. There do not appear to be any building blocks. In their place are processes, relationships, networks of interacting events which unfold in non-linear directions and have recently emerged in the literature as chaos theory (Gleick, 1987). Scientists objected to the new paradigm generated by quantum physicists (Kuhn, 1970). Having spent their entire careers attempting to answer questions within one paradigm, they did not willingly adopt a new paradigm which invalidated their questions and inquiry methods. Einstein expressed a fear that the ground had been pulled out from science, depriving it of all certainty. Heisenberg called the reaction of modern physicists violent and also stated that the foundations of physics had begun to move (Capra, 1988).

We are experiencing paradigm shifts with similar consequences in all areas of modern life, and particularly in student affairs in higher education. The call for emphasizing student learning and expanding our notions of learning to include the action/reflection cycle, praxis, experiential learning and the theory to practice to theory cycle is disruptive to business as usual. The need to incorporate a wide range of learning styles is also disruptive to people who assume that teaching means telling information. The demand that situated knowledge developed from a particular, explicit perspective, be respected is disruptive for people who believe that the most valid knowledge emerges from a universal everywhere/nowhere perspective (Code, 1993). The concept/process of considering the ways that differences in power affect individual and group ideas about legitimate knowledge is extremely disruptive to those who are used to dominating or defining any particular situation. The notion that academic faculty can attend effectively to some student development functions, either alone or in collaboration with student affairs staff members, is disruptive. Finally, considering student development education a valid component of the academic curriculum is disruptive because it calls into question almost all traditional ideas about teaching and learning within the objectivist, empiricist paradigms.

Paradigm shifts are personally and professionally disruptive because they mean that all bets are off. Those who were last may be first. Those who were highly skilled may become incompetent. Those whose skills were not obvious may become leaders. People may have to give up some of their cherished notions about students, learning, teaching and professional identity. But if the emphasis remains on student learning, preparing students to make contributions to the world and to live harmoniously with friends and family, all of the personal and organizational disruption and pain may well be worth it. Individuals must think and choose. People must talk and listen and strain to understand each other. Organizations must learn and reengineer.

> pity this busy monster, manunkind
>
> not. Progress is a comfortable disease:
> your victim (death and life safely beyond)
> plays with the bigness of his littleness
> -electrons deify one razorblade
> into a mountainrange; lenses extend
> unwish through curving wherewhen till unwish
> returns on itself.
> A world of made
> is not a world of born—pity poor flesh
> and trees, poor stars and stones, but never this
> fine specimen of hypermagical
> ultraomnipotence. We doctors know
> a hopeless case if—listen: there's a hell
> of a good universe next door; let's go
>
> e.e. cummings, *1x1, XIV*

REFERENCES

Capra, F. (1988). *Uncommon Wisdom*. New York: Bantam Books.

Code, L. (1993). Taking subjectivity into account. In L. Alcoff & E. Potter (Eds.). *Feminist epistemologies*. (pp. 15-48). New York: Routledge.

cummings, e. e. (1968). *Poems*. New York: Harcourt, Brace & World.

Drucker, P. (1995). Really reinventing government. *The Atlantic Monthly. (275)* 2, 49-61.

Giroux, H. (1993). *Living Dangerously*. New York: Peter Lang.

Gleick, J. (1987). *Chaos: Making a new science*. New York: Penguin Books.

Hammer, M. & Champy, J. (1993). *Reengineering the corporation*. New York: HarperBusiness.

Kuhn, T. (1970). *The structure of scientific revolution*. Chicago: University of Chicago Press.

Lloyd-Jones, E. & Smith, R. (1954). *Student personnel work as deeper teaching*. New York: Harper and Brothers.

Rilke, R. (1934/1954). *Letters to a Young Poet*. (M. D. Herter Norton, Trans.). New York: W. W. Norton.

Schon, D. (1983). *The reflective practitioner*. New York: Basic Books.

Senge, P. (1990). *The fifth discipline*. New York: Doubleday.

Stevens, W. (1964). *The collected poems of Wallace Stevens*. New York: Alfred Knopf.

About the Author

Jane Fried is an Assistant Professor at Northeastern University where she coordinates the master's degree program in College Student Development and Counseling. She received her BA in World Literature from Harpur College, SUNY in 1966, her MA in Student Personnel from Syracuse University in 1968 and her Ph.D. in Counseling Psychology and Human Development from the Union of Experimenting Colleges and Universities in 1977. She completed her doctoral coursework at the University of Connecticut where Burns B. Crookston was her advisor until his untimely death in 1975.

Dr. Fried has held many positions in ACPA including Member at Large of the Executive Council, member of the Executive Committee, Chair of the Standing Committee on Women, Chair of the Affirmative Action Committee, Chair of the Ethics Committee, Chair of the New Professionals Task Force, Directorate Member, Commissions I and XII and member of the Editorial Boards of the *Journal of College Student Development* and the Media Board. She is also a recipient of ACPA's Annuit Coeptis Award and past president of the Connecticut College Personnel Association.

Her previous publications include numerous columns in *Developments* on ethics, affirmative action and women's issues, as well as several articles on incorporating multiculturalism into teaching, training and organizational development. She is the author of a chapter on teaching in *Student Services: A Handbook for the Profession*, and the editor of two monographs, *Different Voices: Gender and Perspective in Student Affairs Administration* and *Education for Student Development*. Fried's previous professional positions include Director of Residential Life and Residence Education, University of Hartford and Coordinator of Staff Training, Student Development and Research, University of Connecticut. She is also a therapist and an organizational consultant.

About the
Contributors

Ann M. Galligan is Associate Professor and Cooperative Education Coordinator for the Arts at Northeastern University. She earned her bachelor's degree in English from Brown University, her master's degree in Communication and her doctorate in History of Education from Teachers College, Columbia University. She has written on experiential and multicultural education, helped to create a multicultural curriculum guide for dance presenters and written on Federal arts patronage.

Dawn Renee Person is an Assistant Professor of Higher Education at Teachers College, Columbia University in New York City where she is co-coordinator of the masters and doctoral programs in student personnel administration. She earned her bachelor's and master's degrees in special education from Slippery Rock University and her doctorate from Columbia University in student personnel administration. Her research and writing interests include recruitment and retention of students and faculty from historically underrepresented populations in higher education. She is currently Principal Investigator on a five-year study of persistence of Black and Hispanic students in Mathematics, Sciences and Engineering Technology. She is Co-chair of the ACPA Standing Committee on Women.

Raechele L. Pope is an Assistant Professor of Higher Education at Teachers' College, Columbia University in New York City. She earned her master's degree from Indiana University of Pennsylvania in student personnel and her doctorate in Organizational Development with a specialization in multicultural issues in higher education from the University of Massachusetts, Amherst. Her research and writing interests are in multicultural organizational development, multicultural competencies for student affairs administrators, psychosocial development of students of color and multicultural interventions in higher education. She is Chair of the ACPA Committee on Multicultural Affairs.

Amy L. Reynolds is an Assistant Professor of Counseling Psychology at Fordham University in New York City. She earned her master's degree in student personnel and her doctorate in counseling psychology from The Ohio State University. Her research and scholarly interests are in the areas of training and supervision of counselors and psychologists, multiculturalism, feminism and identity development, particularly among gay and lesbian people. She is Secretary of ACPA and has been Co-chair of the Standing Committee on Lesbian, Gay and Bisexual Concerns.

DATE DUE

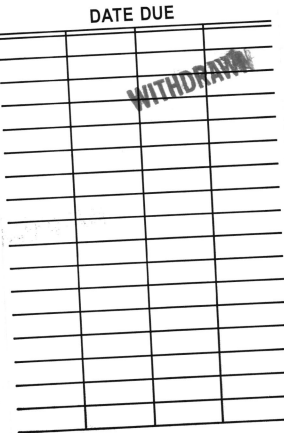

WITHDRAWN

DEMCO 38-296